American Regions Mathematics League Contests (ARML) Preparation

(Volume 1)

Yongcheng Chen
Sam Chen

http://www.mymathcounts.com/index.php

ACKNOWLEDGEMENTS

We would like to thank the following math contests for their mathematical ideas. Many problems in this book are inspired from these tests. We also cited some problems directly from these tests for the purpose of comparison with our own solutions.

The AMC 10/12. An examination in secondary school mathematics containing problems which can be understood and solved with precalculus concepts.

The AIME (American Invitational Mathematics Examination).

The ARML (American Regions Mathematics League). An annual high school mathematics competition held simultaneously at five locations in the United States.

ISBN-13: 978-1514765678
ISBN-10: 1514765675

Please contact mymathcounts@gmail.com for suggestions, corrections, or clarifications.

Table of Contents

This page is intentionally left blank.

BASIC KNOWLEDGE

Below is a list of useful equations to be aware of and know. They can all be derived through expanding or factoring.

Identity 1. $(x+y)^2 = x^2 + 2xy + y^2$ (1)

Proof:
$(x+y)^2 = (x+y)(x+y) = x^2 + yx + xy + y^2 = x^2 + 2xy + y^2$.

Note (1): Identity 1 can also be written as $x^2 + y^2 = (x+y)^2 - 2xy$.
(2): $x^2 + \frac{1}{x^2} = (x + \frac{1}{x})^2 - 2$.

Identity 2. $(x-y)^2 = x^2 - 2xy + y^2$ (2)

Proof:
$(x-y)^2 = (x-y)(x-y) = x^2 - xy - yx + y^2 = x^2 - 2xy + y^2$.

Note (1): Identity 2 can also be written as $x^2 + y^2 = (x-y)^2 + 2xy$
(2): $x^2 + \frac{1}{x^2} = (x - \frac{1}{x})^2 + 2$.

Identity 3. $(x+y)^2 = (x-y)^2 + 4xy$ (3)

Proof:
$(x+y)^2 = x^2 + 2xy + y^2 = x^2 - 2xy + 2xy + 2xy + y^2$
$= (x^2 - 2xy + y^2) + 4xy = (x-y)^2 + 4xy$.

Note (1): Identity 3 can also be written as $(x-y)^2 = (x+y)^2 - 4xy$ or $(x+y)^2 - (x-y)^2 = 4xy$.

(2): $(x+\frac{1}{x})^2=(x-\frac{1}{x})^2+4$.

Identity 4. $(x+y)^2+(x-y)^2=2(x^2+y^2)$ (4)

Proof:

(1) + (2): $(x+y)^2+(x-y)^2=2(x^2+y^2)$.

Identity 5. $(x+y+z)^2=x^2+y^2+z^2+2xy+2xz+2yz$ (5)

Proof:

$$x^2+y^2+z^2+2xy+2xz+2yz$$
$$=(x^2+2xy+y^2)+xz+yz+(z^2+xz+yz)$$
$$=(x+y)^2+z(x+y)+z(z+x+y)$$
$$=(x+y)(x+y+z)+z(z+x+y)$$
$$=(x+y+z)(z+x+y)=(x+y+z)^2.$$

Identity 6. $x^2+y^2+z^2-xy-yz-zx=\frac{1}{2}[(x-y)^2+(y-z)^2+(z-x)^2]$ (6)

Proof:

$$x^2+y^2+z^2-xy-xz-yz$$
$$=\frac{2}{2}(x^2+y^2+z^2-xy-xz-yz)$$
$$=\frac{1}{2}(2x^2+2y^2+2z^2-2xy-2xz-2yz)$$
$$=\frac{1}{2}(x^2+y^2+z^2+x^2+y^2+z^2-2xy-2xz-2yz)$$
$$=\frac{1}{2}[(x^2-2xy+y^2)+(y^2-2yz+z^2)+(z^2-2xz+x^2)]$$
$$=\frac{1}{2}[(x-y)^2+(y-z)^2+(z-x)^2].$$

Note (1): If $x^2+y^2+z^2-xy-xz-yz=0$, $x=y=z$.

(2): Identity 6 can also be writen as

$$x^2+y^2+z^2+xy+yz+zx=\frac{1}{2}[(x+y)^2+(y+z)^2+(z+x)^2].$$

Identity 7. $x^4+4y^4=(x^2+2xy+2y^2)(x^2-2xy+2y^2)$ (7)

Proof:

$x^4+4y^4=x^4+2\times 2x^2y^2+(2y^2)^2-4x^2y^2$

$=(x^2+2y^2)^2-4x^2y^2$

$=(x^2+2xy+2y^2)(x^2-2xy+2y^2)$.

Identity 8. $(a^2+b^2)(c^2+d^2)=(ac+bd)^2+(bc-ad)^2$ (8)

Proof:

$(a^2+b^2)(c^2+d^2)=(ac)^2+(bc)^2+(ad)^2+(bd)^2$

$=[(ac)^2+2(ac)(bd)+(bd)^2]+[(bc)^2-2(bc)(ad)+(ad)^2]$

$=(ac+bd)^2+(bc-ad)^2$

Note: Identity 8 can also be written as

$(a^2+b^2)(c^2+d^2)=(ac-bd)^2+(bc+ad)^2$.

Proof:

$(a^2+b^2)(c^2+d^2)=(ac)^2+(bc)^2+(ad)^2+(bd)^2$

$=[(ac)^2-2(ac)(bd)+(bd)^2]+[(bc)^2+2(bc)(ad)+(ad)^2]$

$=(ac-bd)^2+(bc+ad)^2$

EXAMPLES

Example 1. If $x = 2016(a - b)$, $y = 2016(b - c)$, and $z = 2016(c - a)$, compute the numerical value of $\dfrac{x^2 + y^2 + z^2}{xy + yz + zx}$, given that $xy + yz + xz \neq 0$.

Solution: –2.
Adding the equations produces $x + y + z = 0$. Squaring both sides gives $x^2 + y^2 + z^2 + 2(xy + xz + yz) = 0$, so the answer is –2.

Example 2. Compute: $201720162015^2 - 2 \times 201720162012^2 + 201720162011^2$.

Solution: 18.
Let 201720162012 be x.
Method 1:
$(x + 3)^2 - 2 \times x^2 + (x - 3)^2 = x^2 + 6x + 9 - 2x^2 + x^2 - 6x + 9 = 18.$
Method 2:
$(x + 3)^2 + (x - 3)^2 - 2 \times x^2 = 2(x^2 + 3^2) - 2 \times x^2 = 18.$

Example 3. Compute $\dfrac{20182016^2 + 20182018^2 - 2}{20182017^2}$.

Solution: 2.
Let 20162015 be n.
Method 1:

$$\frac{20182016^2 + 20182018^2 - 2}{20182017^2} = \frac{(n-1)^2 + (n+1)^2 - 2}{n^2}$$

$$= \frac{n^2 - 2n + 1 + n^2 + 2n + 1 - 2}{n^2} = \frac{2n^2}{n^2} = 2.$$

Method 2:

$$\frac{20182016^2 + 20182018^2 - 2}{20182017^2} = \frac{(n-1)^2 + (n+1)^2 - 2}{n^2}$$

$$= \frac{2(n^2 + 1^2) - 2}{n^2} = \frac{2n^2}{n^2} = 2.$$

Example 4. If $x = 2016(a - b) + 252$, $y = 2016(b - c) + 756$, and $z = 2016(c - a) + 1008$, compute the numerical value of $\sqrt{x^2 + y^2 + z^2}$, given that $xy + yz + xz = 0$.

Solution: 2016.
Adding the equations produces $x + y + z = 2016$. Squaring both sides gives $x^2 + y^2 + z^2 + 2(xy + xz + yz) = 2016^2$, so the answer is 2016.

Example 5. If $x = 2014a + 2015$, $y = 2014a + 2016$, and $z = 2014a + 2017$, what is the value of $x^2 + y^2 + z^2 - xy - yz - zx$?

Solution: 3.
$x - y = (2014a + 2015) - (2014a + 2016) = -1.$
$y - z = -1.$
$z - x = 2.$

$$x^2 + y^2 + z^2 - xy - yz - zx = \frac{1}{2}[(x - y)^2 + (y - z)^2 + (z - x)^2]$$

$$= \frac{1}{2}[(-1)^2 + (-1)^2 + (2^2)] = 3.$$

Example 6. Let x, y, and z be positive integers so that $x + y + z = 11$. Compute the smallest possible value of $x^2 + y^2 + z^2$.

Solution: 41.
Method 1:
The smallest possible value of $x^2 + y^2 + z^2$ is obtained when x, y, and z are as close as possible. So we set $x = y = 4$ and $z = 3$. The answer is $x^2 + y^2 + z^2 = 4^2 + 4^2 + 3^2 = 41$.

Method 2:

By Cauthy, $x^2+y^2+z^2 \ge \frac{(x+y+z)^2}{1+1+1} = \frac{11^2}{3} = 40.3$.
Since x, y, and z be positive integers, the smallest possible value is 41.
The equality occurs if and only if $x = y = 4$ and $z = 3$.

Example 7. Prove that the product of four consecutive positive integers plus one is a perfect square.

Proof:
Let the four consecutive positive integers be $(n-1)$, n, $(n+1)$, $(n+2)$.
$(n-1)\,n\,(n+1)(n+2) = [n \times (n+1)]\,[(n-1)(n+2)]$
$= (n^2+n)(n^2+n-2)+1 = (n^2+n)^2 - 2(n^2+n)+1$
$= (n^2+n-1)^2$

Example 8. Find $m^4 + \frac{1}{m^4}$ if $m + \frac{1}{m} = 4$.

Solution: 194.
Substituting m^2 for x and $\frac{1}{m^2}$ for y into $x^2+y^2=(x+y)^2-2xy$ gives us:

$$m^4+\frac{1}{m^4}=\left(m^2+\frac{1}{m^2}\right)^2-2=\left[\left(m+\frac{1}{m}\right)^2-2\right]^2-2=(16-2)^2-2=194.$$

Example 9. Find $m^8 + \frac{1}{m^8}$ if $m - \frac{1}{m} = 1$.

Solution: 47.
Substituting m^4 as x and $\frac{1}{m^4}$ as y into $x^2+y^2=(x+y)^2-2xy$ gives us:

$$m^4+\frac{1}{m^4}=\left(m^2+\frac{1}{m^2}\right)^2-2=\left[\left(m-\frac{1}{m}\right)^2+2\right]^2-2=9-2=7.$$

Substituting m^4 as x and $\frac{1}{m^4}$ as y into $x^2+y^2=(x+y)^2-2xy$ yields:

$m^8+\frac{1}{m^8}=\left(m^4+\frac{1}{m^4}\right)^2-2=49-2=47$.

Example 10. If $x=\frac{3+\sqrt{13}}{2}$, find the value of $x-\frac{1}{x}$.

Solution: 3.

Since $x=\frac{3+\sqrt{13}}{2}$ $\Rightarrow$ $2x-3=\sqrt{13}$

$\Rightarrow$ $4x^2-12x-4=0$ $\Rightarrow$ $x^2-3x-1=0$ (1)

Dividing both sides of (1) by x: $\Rightarrow$ $x-3-\frac{1}{x}=0$ $\Rightarrow$ $x-\frac{1}{x}=3$.

Example 11. Let r and s denote the two real roots of $x^2-\sqrt{7}x+1=0$. Then r^8+s^8 is an integer. Determine this integer.

Solution: 527.

$x^2-\sqrt{7}x+1=0$ $\Rightarrow$ $x+\frac{1}{x}=\sqrt{7}$ $\Rightarrow$ $(x+\frac{1}{x})^2=7$ $\Rightarrow$

$x^2+\frac{1}{x^2}=7-2=5$ $\Rightarrow$ $(x^2+\frac{1}{x^2})^2=25$ $\Rightarrow$ $x^4+\frac{1}{x^4}=23$

$\Rightarrow$ $(x^4+\frac{1}{x^4})^2=23^2$ $\Rightarrow$ $x^8+\frac{1}{x^8}=23^2-2=527$.

Example 12. Find $\frac{x-2xy-y}{2x+5xy-2y}$ if $\frac{1}{x}-\frac{1}{y}=3$.

Solution: 5.

Multiplying both sides of $\frac{1}{x}-\frac{1}{y}=3$ by xy gives us $x-y=-3xy$.

Hence $=\frac{(x-y)-2xy}{2(x-y)+5xy}=\frac{-3xy-2xy}{2(-3xy)+5xy}=\frac{-5xy}{-xy}=5$.

Example 13. (ARML 2007 T7). If $\frac{a-b}{c}=\frac{b+c}{a}=\frac{a-c}{b}$, compute all possible values of $\frac{a}{a+b+c}$.

Solution: $\frac{1}{2}$ and -1.

Metho 1 (official solution):

Let $k=\frac{a-b}{c}=\frac{b+c}{a}=\frac{a-c}{b}$. Then $a-b=kc$, $b+c=ka$, and $a-c=kb$.

Adding these three equations yields $2a=k(a+b+c)$, so $\frac{a}{a+b+c}=\frac{k}{2}$.

Since $b+c=ka$, then $a+b+c=a+ka=a(k+1)$. Thus, we also have $\frac{a}{a+b+c}=\frac{a}{a(k+1)}=\frac{1}{k+1}$ making $\frac{k}{2}=\frac{1}{k+1}$ $\Rightarrow k^2+k-2=0$ $\Rightarrow$ $k=-2$ or 1. Thus the possible values for $\frac{a}{a+b+c}$ are -1 and $\frac{1}{2}$.

For $a = 2$, $b = 1$, and $c = 1$, $\frac{a}{a+b+c}=\frac{1}{2}$.

For $a = -1$, $b = 1$, and $c = 1$, $\frac{a}{a+b+c}=-1$.

Method 2 (our solution):

By the propertional property, $\frac{a-b}{c}=\frac{b+c}{a}=\frac{a-c}{b}=\frac{a-b+b+c}{c+a}=\frac{a+c}{a+c}$

Case 1: If $a+c\neq 0$, we have $\frac{a-b}{c}=\frac{a+c}{a+c}=1$ $\Rightarrow$ $a-b=c$ $\Rightarrow$ $a=b+c$.

$$\frac{a}{a+b+c}=\frac{b+c}{b+c+b+c}=\frac{1}{2}.$$

Case 2: If $a + c = 0$, we have $a = -c$. So $\dfrac{a}{a+b+c} = \dfrac{a}{b}$.

From $\dfrac{a-b}{c} = \dfrac{a-c}{b}$, $\dfrac{a-b}{-a} = \dfrac{a+a}{b}$ $\Rightarrow$ $\dfrac{a-b}{-a} = \dfrac{2a}{b}$ $\Rightarrow b(a-b) = -a(2a)$

$\Rightarrow 2a^2 - ab - b^2 = 0 \Rightarrow (2a-b)(a+b) = 0$.

So we get $\dfrac{a}{a+b+c} = \dfrac{1}{2}$ or -1.

Thus the possible values for $\dfrac{a}{a+b+c}$ are -1 and $\dfrac{1}{2}$.

Example 14. If $x - y = a$, and $z - y = 10$, what is the smallest value of $x^2 + y^2 + z^2 - xy - yz - zx$?

Solution: 75.

We know that $x - y = a$, and $z - y = 10$. So $z - x = (z - y) - (x - y) = 10 - a$.

$x^2 + y^2 + z^2 - xy - yz - zx = \dfrac{1}{2}[(x-y)^2 + (y-z)^2 + (z-x)^2]$

$= \dfrac{1}{2}[a^2 + 10^2 + (10-a)^2] = a^2 - 10a + 100 = (a-5)^2 + 75$

When $a = 5$, the smallest value is 75.

Example 15. Find the value of a so that $a^2 - b^2 - c^2 + ab = 2019$ and $a^2 + 3b^2 + 3c^2 - 3ab - 2ac - 2bc = -2005$. a, b, and c be positive integers with $a \ge b \ge c$.

Solution: 254.

$a^2 - b^2 - c^2 + ab = 2019$ (1)

$a^2 + 3b^2 + 3c^2 - 3ab - 2ac - 2bc = -2005$ (2)

(1) + (2): $2a^2 + 2b^2 + 2c^2 - 2ab - 2bc - 2ac = 14$ (3)

(3) can be rearranged to: $(a^2 - 2ab + b^2) + (b^2 - 2bc + c^2) + (a^2 - 2ac + c^2) = 14$.

Or $(a-b)^2 + (b-c)^2 + (a-c)^2 = 14$.

There is one way to express 14 as the sum of three squares of positive integers: $14 = 3^2 + 2^2 + 1^2$.

We know that $a \ge b \ge c$.
Case 1: $a - c = 3$ and either $a - b = 2$ and $b - c = 1$.

Case 2: $a - b = 1$ and $b - c = 2$.

We get: $(a, b, c) = (c + 3, c + 1, c)$ or $(a, b, c,) = (c + 3, c + 2, c)$.

For the case 1,
$2019 = a^2 - c^2 + ab - b^2 = (a - c)(a + c) + (a - b)b = 3(2c + 3) + 2(c + 1)$ or
$8c + 11 = 2019 \qquad \Rightarrow \qquad c = 251$.

Solving we get $(a, b, c) = (254, 252, 251)$. The second case has no integer solution. Therefore $a = 254$.

Example 16. Calculate: $\dfrac{(7^4 + 64)(15^4 + 64)(23^4 + 64)(31^4 + 64)(39^4 + 64)}{(3^4 + 64)(11^4 + 64)(19^4 + 64)(27^4 + 64)(35^4 + 64)}$.

Solution: 337.
Method 1:
We know that $x^4 + 4y^4 = (x^2 - 2xy + 2y^2)(x^2 + 2xy + 2y^2)$.

$$n^4 + 4 \times 2^4 = (n^2 - 2(n) \times 2 + 2 \times 2^2)(n^2 + 2(n) \times 2 + 2 \times 2^2)$$
$$= (n^2 - 4n + 8)(n^2 + 4n + 8) = [(n - 4)n + 8][n(n + 4) + 8]$$
$$\frac{(7^4 + 64)(15^4 + 64)(23^4 + 64)(31^4 + 64)(39^4 + 64)}{(3^4 + 64)(11^4 + 64)(19^4 + 64)(27^4 + 64)(35^4 + 64)}$$
$$= \frac{(3 \times 7 + 8)(7 \times 11 + 8)(11 \times 15 + 8)(15 \times 19 + 8) + \cdots + (35 \times 39 + 8)(39 \times 43 + 8)}{(-1 \times 3 + 8)(3 \times 7 + 8)(7 \times 11 + 8)(11 \times 15 + 8) + \cdots + (31 \times 35 + 8)(35 \times 39 + 8)}$$
$$= \frac{39 \times 43 + 8}{-1 \times 3 + 8} = \frac{1658}{5} = 337$$

Method 2:

We know that $x^4+4y^4=(x^2-2xy+2y^2)(x^2+2xy+2y^2)$.

$n^4+4\times 2^4=(n^2-2(n)\times 2+2\times 2^2)(n^2+2(n)\times 2+2\times 2^2)$

$=(n^2-4n+8)(n^2+4n+8)=[(n-2)^2+4][(n+2)^2+4]$

$$\frac{(7^4+64)(15^4+64)(23^4+64)(31^4+64)(39^4+64)}{(3^4+64)(11^4+64)(19^4+64)(27^4+64)(35^4+64)}$$

$$=\frac{(5^2+4)(9^2+4)(13^2+4)(17^2+4)\cdots(37^2+4)(41^2+4)}{(1^2+4)(5^2+4)(9^2+4)(113^2+4)\cdots(33^2+4)(37^2+4)}$$

$$=\frac{41^2+4}{1^2+4}=\frac{1658}{5}=337.$$

Example 17. Compute: $\dfrac{(2^4+\frac{1}{4})(4^4+\frac{1}{4})(6^4+\frac{1}{4})(8^4+\frac{1}{4})(10^4+\frac{1}{4})}{(1^4+\frac{1}{4})(3^4+\frac{1}{4})(5^4+\frac{1}{4})(7^4+\frac{1}{4})(9^4+\frac{1}{4})}$

Solution: 221.

Method 1:

$$\frac{(2^4+\frac{1}{4})(4^4+\frac{1}{4})(6^4+\frac{1}{4})(8^4+\frac{1}{4})(10^4+\frac{1}{4})}{(1^4+\frac{1}{4})(3^4+\frac{1}{4})(5^4+\frac{1}{4})(7^4+\frac{1}{4})(9^4+\frac{1}{4})}=$$

$$\frac{(4^4+4)(8^4+4)(12^4+4)(16^4+4)(20^4+4)}{(2^4+4)(6^4+4)(10^4+4)(14^4+4)(18^4+4)}.$$

We know that

$n^4+4\times(1)^4=(n^2-2n+2)(n^2+2n+2)=[(n-1)^2+1)][(n+1)^2+1)]$.

So $\dfrac{(4^4+4)(8^4+4)(12^4+4)(16^4+4)(20^4+4)}{(2^4+4)(6^4+4)(10^4+4)(14^4+4)(18^4+4)}$

$$=\frac{(3^2+1)(5^2+1)(7^2+1)(9^2+1)\cdots(19^2+1)(21^2+1)}{(1^2+1)(3^2+1)(5^2+1)(7^2+1)\cdots(17^2+1)(19^2+1)}$$

$$=\frac{21^2+1}{1^2+1}=221.$$

Method 2:

$$n^4+4\times(\frac{1}{2})^4=[n^2-2(n)\times\frac{1}{2}+2\times(\frac{1}{2})^2)][n^2+2(n)\times\frac{1}{2}+2\times(\frac{1}{2})^2)]$$

$$=[(n-\frac{1}{2})^2+\frac{1}{4})][(n+\frac{1}{2})^2+\frac{1}{4})].$$

$$\frac{(2^4+\frac{1}{4})(4^4+\frac{1}{4})(6^4+\frac{1}{4})(8^4+\frac{1}{4})(10^4+\frac{1}{4})}{(1^4+\frac{1}{4})(3^4+\frac{1}{4})(5^4+\frac{1}{4})(7^4+\frac{1}{4})(9^4+\frac{1}{4})}=$$

$$\frac{[(2-\frac{1}{2})^2+\frac{1}{4})][(2+\frac{1}{2})^2+\frac{1}{4})]\cdots[(10-\frac{1}{2})^2+\frac{1}{4})][(10+\frac{1}{2})^2+\frac{1}{4})]}{[(1-\frac{1}{2})^2+\frac{1}{4})][(1+\frac{1}{2})^2+\frac{1}{4})]\cdots[(9-\frac{1}{2})^2+\frac{1}{4})][(9+\frac{1}{2})^2+\frac{1}{4})]}$$

$$=\frac{(10+\frac{1}{2})^2+\frac{1}{4}}{(1-\frac{1}{2})^2+\frac{1}{4})}=\frac{\frac{21^2+1}{4}}{\frac{2}{4}}=\frac{442}{2}=221.$$

Example 18. (2010 ARML) For digits A, B, and C, $(AB)^2 + (AC)^2 = 1313$. Compute $A + B + C$.

Solution: 13.
Rewrite $1313 = 13 \times 101 = (3^2 + 2^2)(10^2 + 1^2)$.
The two-square identity states:

$$(a^2+b^2)(c^2+d^2)=(ac+bd)^2+(bc-ad)^2$$

$$(a^2+b^2)(c^2+d^2)=(ac-bd)^2+(bc+ad)^2.$$

Therefore
$1313 = (30 + 2)^2 + (3 - 20)^2 = 32^2 + 17^2$ (ignored since the tens digits are different)
$1313 = (3 + 20)^2 + (30 - 2)^2 = 23^2 + 28^2$.
Hence $A = 2$, $B = 3$, $C = 8$, and $A + B + C = 13$.

PROBLEMS

Problem 1. If $x = 2017(a - b)$, $y = 2017(b - c)$, and $z = 2017(c - a)$, compute the numerical value of $\dfrac{xy + yz + zx}{x^2 + y^2 + z^2}$, given that $xy + yz + xz \neq 0$.

Problem 2. Compute $(2014 \times 2018)^2 - 2 \times 2016^2 - 2013 \times 2015 \times 2017 \times 2019$.

Problem 3. Compute $\dfrac{20162015^2}{20162014^2 + 20162016^2 - 2}$.

Problem 4. If $x = 2016(a - b) + 3$, $y = 2016(b - c) + 4$, and $z = 2016(c - a) + 5$, compute the numerical value of $x^2 + y^2 + z^2$, given that $xy + yz + xz = 36$.

Problem 5. If $x = 2014$, $y = 2015$, and $z = 2016$, what is the value of $x^2 + y^2 + z^2 - xy - yz - zx$?

Problem 6. Let x, y, and z be positive integers so that $x + y + z = 7$. Compute the greatest possible value of $x^2 + y^2 + z^2$.

Problem 7. Compute $m^4 + \dfrac{1}{m^4}$ if $m + \dfrac{1}{m} = 5$.

Problem 8. Find $m^8 + \dfrac{1}{m^8}$ if $m - \dfrac{1}{m} = 3$.

Problem 9. If $x = \dfrac{3 + \sqrt{13}}{2}$, find the value of $x^2 + \dfrac{1}{x^2}$.

Problem 10. Let r and s denote the two real roots of $x^2 - \sqrt{6}x + 1 = 0$. Then $r^8 + s^8$ is an integer. Determine this integer.

Problem 11. Find $\dfrac{4x^3+3x^2y-4y^3}{2x^3-2xy^2-2y^3}$ if $\dfrac{x}{y}=3$.

Problem 12. If $x=\dfrac{a}{b+c}=\dfrac{b}{c+a}=\dfrac{c}{a+b}$, find the value for x.

Problem 13. Find the value of $xy + yz + zx$ if $x + y + z = 0$ and $x^2 + y^2 + z^2 = 1$.

Problem 14. What is the smallest value of $x^2-6xy+10y^2-2y+2017$ if both x and y are real?

Problem 15. Calculate:

$$\frac{(7^4+324)(19^4+324)(31^4+324)(43^4+324)\cdots(103^4+324)}{(1^4+324)(13^4+324)(25^4+324)(37^4+324)\cdots(97^4+324)}.$$

Problem 16. Compute: $\dfrac{(5^4+\frac{1}{4})(7^4+\frac{1}{4})(9^4+\frac{1}{4})(11^4+\frac{1}{4})(13^4+\frac{1}{4})}{(4^4+\frac{1}{4})(6^4+\frac{1}{4})(8^4+\frac{1}{4})(10^4+\frac{1}{4})(12^4+\frac{1}{4})}$.

Problem 17. What is the smallest positive integer that can be expressed as the sum of two different non-zero-perfect squares in two different ways?

Problem 18. Find $m^4-\dfrac{1}{m^4}$ if $m-\dfrac{1}{m}=4$. Express your answer in the simplest radical form.

Problem 19. If $\dfrac{a+b}{a+c}=\dfrac{a-b}{a-c}$, where $a \neq \pm c$ and $a \neq 0$, $c \neq 0$, compute the numerical value of $\dfrac{10b^2+9bc+c^2}{2b^2+bc+2c^2}$.

Problem 20. How many positive integer values of $k \le 2000$ are there for which $x^4 + k$ can be factored into two distinct trinomial factors with integer coefficients?

Problem 21. Show that three real numbers, a, b, and c, not all the same, form an arithmetics sequence if $(a-c)^2 - 4(c-b)(b-a) = 0$.

SOLUTIONS

Problem 1. Solution: –1/2.
Adding the equations produces $x + y + z = 0$. Squaring both sides gives $x^2 + y^2 + z^2 + 2(xy + xz + yz) = 0$, so the answer is –1/2.

Problem 2. Solution: 7.
Let 2016 be x.

$$[(n-2)(n+2)]^2 - 2n^2 - (n-3)(n-1)(n+1)(n+3)$$
$$= (n^2-4)^2 - 2n^2 - (n^2-9)(n^2-1)$$
$$= n^4 - 8n^2 + 16 - 2n^2 - n^4 + 10n^2 - 9 = 7.$$

Problem 3. Solution: 1/2.
Let 20162015 be n.

$$\frac{20162015^2}{20162014^2 + 20162016^2 - 2} = \frac{n^2}{(n-1)^2 + (n+1)^2 - 2}$$
$$= \frac{n^2}{n^2 - 2n + 1 + n^2 + 2n + 1 - 2} = \frac{n^2}{2n^2} = \frac{1}{2}$$

Problem 4. Solution: 72.
Adding the equations produces $x + y + z = 12$. Squaring both sides gives $x^2 + y^2 + z^2 + 2(xy + xz + yz) = 12^2 = 144$, so the answer is $144 - 2 \times 36 = 72$.

Problem 5. Solution: 3.

$$x^2 + y^2 + z^2 - xy - yz - zx$$
$$= \frac{1}{2}(2x^2 + 2y^2 + 2z^2 - 2xy - 2yz - 2zx)$$
$$= \frac{1}{2}[(x^2 - 2xy + y^2) + (y^2 - 2yz + z^2) + (z^2 - 2zx + x^2)]$$
$$= \frac{1}{2}[(x-y)^2 + (y-z)^2 + (z-x)^2]$$
$$= \frac{1}{2}[(2004 - 2015)^2 + (2015 - 2016)^2 + (2016 - 2014)^2]$$

$= \frac{1}{2}[(-1)^2 + (-1)^2 + (2^2)] = 3.$

Problem 6. Solution: 27.

The greatest possible value of $x^2 + y^2 + z^2$ is obtained when x, y, and z are as far as possible. So we set $x = y = 1$ and $z = 5$. The answer is $x^2 + y^2 + z^2 = 1^2 + 1^2 + 5^2 = 27$.

Problem 7. Solution: 527.

Substituting m^2 for x and $\frac{1}{m^2}$ for y into $x^2 + y^2 = (x+y)^2 - 2xy$ gives us:

$$m^4 + \frac{1}{m^4} = \left(m^2 + \frac{1}{m^2}\right)^2 - 2 = \left[\left(m + \frac{1}{m}\right)^2 - 2\right]^2 - 2 = (25-2)^2 - 2 = 527.$$

Problem 8. Solution: 2207.

Substituting m^4 as x and $\frac{1}{m^4}$ as y into $x^2 + y^2 = (x+y)^2 - 2xy$ gives us:

$$m^4 + \frac{1}{m^4} = \left(m^2 + \frac{1}{m^2}\right)^2 - 2$$

Note that $x^2 + y^2 = (x-y)^2 + 2xy$,

$$m^4 + \frac{1}{m^4} = \left(m^2 + \frac{1}{m^2}\right)^2 - 2 = \left[\left(m - \frac{1}{m}\right)^2 - 2\right]^2 - 2 = 49 - 2 = 47.$$

Substituting m^4 as x and $\frac{1}{m^4}$ as y into $x^2 + y^2 = (x+y)^2 - 2xy$ yields:

$$m^8 + \frac{1}{m^8} = \left(m^4 + \frac{1}{m^4}\right)^2 - 2 = 47^2 - 2 = 2207.$$

Problem 9. Solution: 11.

Since $x = \dfrac{3+\sqrt{13}}{2}$ $\Rightarrow$ $2x - 3 = \sqrt{13}$ $\Rightarrow$ $4x^2 - 12x - 4 = 0$

$\Rightarrow$ $x^2 - 3x - 1 = 0$ (1)

Dividing both sides of (1) by x: $x - 3 - \dfrac{1}{x} = 0$ $\Rightarrow$ $x - \dfrac{1}{x} = 3$.

$$x^2 + \frac{1}{x^2} = x^2 - 2x\frac{1}{x} + \frac{1}{x^2} + 2 = (x - \frac{1}{x})^2 + 2 = 3^2 + 2 = 11$$

Problem 10. Solution: 194.

$x^2 - \sqrt{6}x + 1 = 0$ $\Rightarrow$ $x + \dfrac{1}{x} = \sqrt{6}$ $\Rightarrow$ $(x + \dfrac{1}{x})^2 = 6$ $\Rightarrow$

$x^2 + \dfrac{1}{x^2} = 6 - 2 = 4$ $\Rightarrow$ $(x^2 + \dfrac{1}{x^2})^2 = 4^2$ $\Rightarrow$ $x^4 + \dfrac{1}{x^4} = 16 - 2 = 14$

$\Rightarrow$ $(x^4 + \dfrac{1}{x^4})^2 = 14^2$ $\Rightarrow$ $x^8 + \dfrac{1}{x^8} = 14^2 - 2 = 194$.

Problem 11. Solution: $\dfrac{131}{46}$.

Since we are given that $\dfrac{x}{y} = 3$, we know that $x = 3y$. Substituting this into the given expression gives us:

$$\frac{4x^3 + 3x^2y - 4y^3}{2x^3 - 2xy^2 - 2y^3} = \frac{4\times(3y)^3 + 3\times(3y)^2 y - 4y^3}{2\times(3y)^3 - 2\times(3y)y^2 - 2y^3} = \frac{108y^3 + 27y^3 - 4y^3}{54y^3 - 6y^3 - 2y^3} = \frac{131}{46}.$$

Problem 12. Solution: $\dfrac{1}{2}$.

Case I. If $a + b + c = 0$

$b + c = -a$

$$x = \frac{a}{b+c} = \frac{a}{-a} = -1$$

Case II. If $a + b + c \neq 0$

$$x=\frac{a}{b+c}=\frac{b}{c+a}=\frac{c}{a+b}=\frac{a+b+c}{b+c+c+a+a+b}=\frac{a+b+c}{2(a+b+c)}=\frac{1}{2}$$

Problem 13. Solution: $-\frac{1}{2}$.

We know that $(x+y+z)^2=x^2+y^2+z^2+2xy+2xz+2yz$.
We are given that $x+y+z=0$ and $x^2+y^2+z^2=1$, so

$$0=1+2(xy+yz+zx) \quad \Rightarrow \quad xy+yz+zx=-\frac{1}{2}.$$

Problem 14. Solution: 2016.

$$x^2-6xy+10y^2-2y+2017=(x^2-6xy+9y^2)+(y^2-2y+1)+2016$$
$$=(x-3y)^2+(y-1)^2+2016.$$

Since both x and y are real

$(x-3y)^2 \ge 0$

$(y-1)^2 \ge 0$

When $x-3y=0$ and $y-1=0$, i,e, $y=1$, and $x=3y=3$,
$x^2-6xy+10y^2-2y+2017$ has the smallest value 2016.

Problem 15. Solution: 865.

We know that $x^4+4y^4=(x^2-2xy+2y^2)(x^2+2xy+2y^2)$.

$$n^4+4\times 3^4=(n^2-2\times n\times 3+2\times 3^2)(n^2+2\times n\times 3+2\times 3^2)$$
$$=(n^2+6n+18)(n^2-6n+18)=[(n-6)n+18][n(n+6)+18]$$

$$\frac{(7^4+324)(19^4+324)(31^4+324)(43^4+324)\cdots(103^4+324)}{(1^4+324)(13^4+324)(25^4+324)(37^4+324)\cdots(97^4+324)}$$

$=$

$$\frac{(1\times 7+18)(7\times 13+18)(13\times 19+18)(19\times 25+18)\cdots(97\times 103+18)(103\times 109+18)}{(-5\times 1+18)(1\times 7+18)(7\times 13+18)(13\times 19+18)\cdots(91\times 97+18)(97\times 103+18)}$$

$$=\frac{103\times 109+18}{-5\times 1+18}=\frac{11245}{13}=865.$$

Problem 16. Solution: 73.

$$n^4+4\times(\frac{1}{2})^4=[n^2-2(n)\times\frac{1}{2}+2\times(\frac{1}{2})^2)][n^2+2(n)\times\frac{1}{2}+2\times(\frac{1}{2})^2)]$$

$$=[(n-\frac{1}{2})^2+\frac{1}{4})][(n+\frac{1}{2})^2+\frac{1}{4})].$$

$$\frac{(5^4+\frac{1}{4})(7^4+\frac{1}{4})(9^4+\frac{1}{4})(11^4+\frac{1}{4})(13^4+\frac{1}{4})}{(4^4+\frac{1}{4})(6^4+\frac{1}{4})(8^4+\frac{1}{4})(10^4+\frac{1}{4})(12^4+\frac{1}{4})}$$

$$=\frac{[(5-\frac{1}{2})^2+\frac{1}{4})][(5+\frac{1}{2})^2+\frac{1}{4})]\cdots[(13-\frac{1}{2})^2+\frac{1}{4})][(13+\frac{1}{2})^2+\frac{1}{4})]}{[(4-\frac{1}{2})^2+\frac{1}{4})][(4+\frac{1}{2})^2+\frac{1}{4})]\cdots[(12-\frac{1}{2})^2+\frac{1}{4})][(12+\frac{1}{2})^2+\frac{1}{4})]}$$

$$=\frac{(13+\frac{1}{2})^2+\frac{1}{4}}{(2-\frac{1}{2})^2+\frac{1}{4}}=\frac{\frac{27^2+1}{4}}{\frac{5}{2}}=\frac{730}{10}=73.$$

Problem 17. Solution: 65.

We know that

$(a^2+b^2)(c^2+d^2)=(ac-bd)^2+(bc+ad)^2$

$(a^2+b^2)(c^2+d^2)=(ac+bd)^2+(bc-ad)^2$

We need to choose the smallest possible values for a, b, c, and d with $ac\neq bd$; $bc\neq ad$.

First we try $a=1$, $b=1$, $c=2$, $d=3$.

$(a^2+b^2)(c^2+d^2)=(1+1)(4+9)=26$.

$26=(2-3)^2+(3+2)^2=1^2+5^2$

$26=(2+3)^2+(3-2)^2=5^2+1^2$.

We do not have two different non-zero-perfect squares.

We then try $a=1$, $b=2$, $c=2$, $d=2$.

$(a^2+b^2)(c^2+d^2)=(1+4)(4+4)=40$.
$40=(2-4)^2+(4+2)^2=2^2+6^2$
$40=(2+4)^2+(4-2)^2=6^2+2^2$.

We do not have two different non-zero-perfect squares.

Next we choose $a = 1$, $b = 2$, $c = 1$, $d = 3$.
$(a^2+b^2)(c^2+d^2)=(1+4)(1+9)=50$.
$50=(1-6)^2+(2+3)^2=5^2+5^2$ (not the sum of two different non-zero-perfect squares).
$50=(1+6)^2+(2-3)^2=7^2+1^2$

Next we assign $a = 1$, $b = 2$, $c = 2$, $d = 3$.
$(a^2+b^2)(c^2+d^2)=(1+4)(4+9)=65$.
$65=(2-6)^2+(4+3)^2=4^2+7^2$.
$65=(2+6)^2+(4-3)^2=8^2+1^2$.
So the smallest integer is 65.

Problem 18. Solution: $144\sqrt{5}$.

Squaring both sides of $m-\frac{1}{m}=4$: $(m-\frac{1}{m})^2=16 \Rightarrow \left(m^2+\frac{1}{m^2}\right)=18$.

We also have $\left(m^2+\frac{1}{m^2}\right)=18 \Rightarrow m^2+\frac{1}{m^2}+2=18+2 \Rightarrow$

$m^2+\frac{1}{m^2}+2m\times\frac{1}{m}=20 \Rightarrow (m+\frac{1}{m})^2=20 \Rightarrow (m+\frac{1}{m})=2\sqrt{5}$.

$m^4-\frac{1}{m^4}=\left(m^2-\frac{1}{m^2}\right)\left(m^2+\frac{1}{m^2}\right)=18\left(m^2-\frac{1}{m^2}\right)=18(m-\frac{1}{m})(m+\frac{1}{m})$

$=18\times4\times2\sqrt{5}=144\sqrt{5}$.

Problem 19. Solution: $\frac{9}{5}$.

$$\frac{a+b}{a+c}=\frac{a-b}{a-c}=\frac{a+b+a-b}{a+c+a-c}=\frac{2a}{2a}=1.$$

So $\frac{a+b}{a+c}=1 \Rightarrow \quad a+b=a+c \Rightarrow \quad b=c$.

$$\frac{20b^2+bc+6c^2}{5b^2+2bc+8c^2}=\frac{27}{15}=\frac{9}{5}.$$

Problem 20. Solution: 4.

By Identity 7: $x^4+4y^4=(x^2+2xy+2y^2)(x^2-2xy+2y^2)$, we have $x^4+k=x^2+4y^4$.

So $y=\sqrt[4]{\frac{k}{4}}$ and $y^2=\sqrt{\frac{k}{4}}=\frac{\sqrt{k}}{2}$.

$$x^4+k=(x^2+2x\times\sqrt[4]{\frac{k}{4}}+2\frac{\sqrt{k}}{2})(x^2-2x\times\sqrt[4]{\frac{k}{4}}+2\frac{\sqrt{k}}{2})$$

$$=(x^2+2x\times\sqrt[4]{\frac{k}{4}}+\sqrt{k})(x^2-2x\times\sqrt[4]{\frac{k}{4}}+\sqrt{k})$$

Both $\sqrt[4]{\frac{k}{4}}$ and $\sqrt{k}$ must be positive integers.

Since $k \le 2000$, and $256 = 4^4 < \frac{k}{4} < 4^5 = 1024$, $4 = \sqrt[4]{4^4} < \sqrt[4]{\frac{k}{4}} < \sqrt[4]{4^5} \sim 5$.

Therefore we get 4 values of k for which $x^4 + k$ can be factored into two distinct trinomial factors with integer coefficients (4, 64, 324, 1024).

Problem 21. Solution:

$(a-c)^2-4(c-b)(b-a)=0 \Rightarrow \quad a^2-2ac+c^2-4bc+4ac-4ab+4b^2=0$

$\Rightarrow \quad (a^2+2ac+c^2)-4b(a+c)+4b^2=0$

$\Rightarrow \quad (a+c)^2-2(a+c)\cdot 2b+(2b)^2=0$

$\Rightarrow \quad (a+c-2b)^2=0 \quad \Rightarrow \quad a+c-2b=0 \Rightarrow \quad b=\frac{a+c}{2}$.

BASIC KNOWLEDGE

In this lecture, we introduce nine very important algebraic identities that are very useful in calculating values for expressions, factoring, solving equations and system of equations, and proving proofs.

Identity 1. $x^3 + y^3 = (x + y)(x^2 - xy + y^2)$ (1)

Proof:
$(x + y)(x^2 - xy + y^2) = x^3 - x^2y + xy^2 + yx^2 - xy^2 + y^3 = x^3 + y^3$.

Note:
(1) Identity 1 can also be written as
$$x^3 + y^3 = (x + y)[(x + y)^2 - 3xy]. \quad (1.1)$$
(2) Let $y = 1/x$, Identity 1.1 becomes: $x^3 + \frac{1}{x^3} = (x + \frac{1}{x})[(x + \frac{1}{x})^2 - 3]$ (1.2)

Identity 2. $x^3 - y^3 = (x - y)(x^2 + xy + y^2)$ (2)

Proof:
Let $y = -y$ in (1):
$x^3 - y^3 = (x - y)(x^2 + xy + y^2)$.
Or $(x - y)(x^2 + xy + y^2) = x^3 + x^2y + xy^2 - yx^2 - xy^2 - y^3 = x^3 - y^3$.

Identity 3. $(x + y)^3 = x^3 + 3x^2y + 3xy^2 + y^3 = x^3 + y^3 + 3xy(x + y)$ (3)

Proof:
$(x + y)^3 = (x + y)(x + y)^2 = (x + y)(x^2 + 2xy + y^2)$
$= x^3 + 2x^2y + xy^2 + yx^2 + 2xy^2 + y^3 = x^3 + y^3 + 3xy(x + y)$.

Notes:
(1) Identity 3 can also be written as $x^3 + y^3 = (x + y)^3 - 3xy(x + y)$ (3.1).
(2) $(x + y + z)^3 = x^3 + y^3 + z^3 + 3(x + y)(y + z)(z + x)$ (3.2)

Identity 4. $(x-y)^3 = x^3 - 3x^2y + 3xy^2 - y^3 = x^3 - y^3 - 3xy(x-y)$ (4)

Proof:
Let $y = -y$ in (3): $(x-y)^3 = x^3 - 3x^2y + 3xy^2 - y^3 = x^3 - y^3 - 3xy(x-y)$.

Notes:
(1) Identity 4 can also be written as $x^3 - y^3 = (x-y)^3 + 3xy(x-y)$ (4.1)
(2) Adding Identities (3) and (4): $(x+y)^3 + (x-y)^3 = 2x^3 + 6xy^2$ (4.2)

Identity 5. $a^3 + b^3 + c^3 - 3abc = (a+b+c)(a^2 + b^2 + c^2 - ab - bc - ca)$ (5)

Proof:
Method 1:
$$a^3+b^3+c^3-3abc = a^3+b^3+3ab(a+b)+c^3-3ab(a+b)-3abc$$
$$=(a+b)^3-3ab(a+b)+c^3-3abc$$
$$=[(a+b)^3+c^3]-3ab(a+b+c)$$
$$=(a+b+c)[(a+b)^2-(a+b)c+c^2]-3ab(a+b+c)$$
$$=(a+b+c)(a^2+b^2+c^2-bc-ca-ab).$$

Method 2:
$$(a+b+c)(a^2+b^2+c^2-bc-ca-ab)$$
$$=[(a+b)+c][(a^2-ab+b^2)-c(a+b)+c^2]$$
$$=(a+b)(a^2-ab+b^2)-c(a+b)^2+(a+b)c^2 + c(a^2-ab+b^2)-c^2(a+b)+c^3]$$
$$=a^3+b^3-c(a+b)^2+c^2(a+b)+c(a^2-ab+b^2)-c^2(a+b)+c^3$$
$$=a^3+b^3+c^3-3abc$$
Note:

Since $(a^2+b^2+c^2-bc-ca-ab) = \frac{1}{2}[(a-b)^2+(b-c)^2+(c-a)^2]$, Identity 5 can also be written as:

$$a^3+b^3+c^3-3abc = \frac{1}{2}(a+b+c)\left[(a-b)^2+(b-c)^2+(c-a)^2\right] \quad (5.1)$$

Identity 6. If $a + b + c = 0$, then $a^3 + b^3 + c^3 = 3abc$ (6)

Proof:

Method 1:

Substituting $a + b + c = 0$ into Identity 5:

$$a^3 + b^3 + c^3 - 3abc = \frac{1}{2}(a+b+c)[(a-b)^2 + (b-c)^2 + (c-a)^2]$$

$$= \frac{1}{2}(0)[(a-b)^2 + (b-c)^2 + (c-a)^2] = 0.$$

Thus $a^3 + b^3 + c^3 = 3abc$.

Method 2:

Since $a + b + c = 0$, we can write $c = -(a + b)$.

Substituting in $-(a + b)$ for c into the equation $a^3 + b^3 + c^3 = 3abc$ we have:

$a^3 + b^3 + c^3 = a^3 + b^3 - (a + b)^3 = a^3 + b^3 - a^3 - 3a^2b - 3ab^2 - b^3$

$= -3ab(a + b) = -3ab \cdot (-c) = 3abc$.

Notes:

(1) If $a^3 + b^3 + c^3 = 3abc$, then $a + b + c = 0$, or $[(a-b)^2 + (b-c)^2 + (c-a)^2] = 0$ (6.1)

Proof:

From Identity 5, we have

$$a^3 + b^3 + c^3 - 3abc = \frac{1}{2}(a+b+c)[(a-b)^2 + (b-c)^2 + (c-a)^2].$$

Since $a^3 + b^3 + c^3 - 3abc = 0$, the above identity becomes:

$(a+b+c)[(a-b)^2 + (b-c)^2 + (c-a)^2] = 0$.

So we have either $a+b+c=0$ or $[(a-b)^2 + (b-c)^2 + (c-a)^2] = 0$.

(2) If $a^3 + b^3 + c^3 = 3abc$, where a, b, and c are real numbers not all the same, then $a + b + c = 0$.

Proof:

From Identity 5, we have

$$a^3+b^3+c^3-3abc=\frac{1}{2}(a+b+c)\left[(a-b)^2+(b-c)^2+(c-a)^2\right].$$

Since $a^3 + b^3 + c^3 - 3abc = 0$, the above identity becomes:

$$(a+b+c)\left[(a-b)^2+(b-c)^2+(c-a)^2\right]=0.$$

We know that *a, b*, and *c* are real numbers not all the same. So

$$\left[(a-b)^2+(b-c)^2+(c-a)^2\right]>0.$$

Thus $a + b + c = 0$.

Identity 7. $a^3 + b^3 + c^3 + d^3 - 3abc - 3abd - 3acd - 3bcd$
$= (a + b + c + d)(a^2 + b^2 + c^2 + d^2 - ab - ac - ad - bc - bd - cd)$ (7)

Proof:

$(a + b + c + d)(a^2 + b^2 + c^2 + d^2 - ab - ac - ad - bc - bd - cd)$
$= [\,(a + b + c) + d)][(a^2 + b^2 + c^2 - ab - ac - bc) - ad - bd - cd + d^2)$
$= [\,(a + b + c) + d)][(a^2 + b^2 + c^2 - ab - ac - bc) - (a + b + c)d + d^2)]$
$= a^3 + b^3 + c^3 - 3abc - (a + b + c)^2 d - d^2 (a + b + c) + d(a^2 + b^2 + c^2 - ab - ac - bc) - d^2 (a + b + c) + d^3]$

$= a^3 + b^3 + c^3 + d^3 - 3abc - d(a^2 + b^2 + c^2 + 2ab + 2ac + 2bc - a^2 - b^2 - c^2 + ab + ac + bc)$
$= a^3 + b^3 + c^3 + d^3 - 3abc - 3abd - 3acd - 3bcd$

Identity 8. If $a + b + c + d = 0$, *a, b, c, d* are real numbers, then $a^3 + b^3 + c^3 + d^3 = 3(abc + abd + acd + 3bcd)$ (8)

Proof:

Method 1:

In Identity 7, let $a + b + c + d = 0$.

We have $a^3 + b^3 + c^3 + d^3 - 3abc - 3abd - 3acd - 3bcd = 0$ $\Rightarrow$
$a^3 + b^3 + c^3 + d^3 = 3(abc + abd + acd + 3bcd)$.

Method 2:

We write $a + b + c + d = 0$ as $a + b = -(c + d)$.

Cubic both sides: $a^3 + 3a^2b + 3ab^2 + b^2 = -c^3 - 3c^2d - 3cd^2 - d^3$

So $a^3 + b^2 + c^3 + d^3 = -3(a^2b + ab^2 + c^2d + cd^2)$
$= -3[(ab(a + b) + cd\,(c + d))$
$= -3[(-ab\,(c + d) - cd\,(a + b)]$
$= 3(abc + abd + acd + 3bcd)$.

Note: Identity 8 can also be written as If $a + b + c + d = 0$, then
$a^3 + b^3 + c^3 + d^3 = 3(a + d)(b + d)(c + d)$ (8.1)

Proof:
We write $a + b + c + d = 0$ as $a + b + c = -d$.
Cubing both sides: $(a + b + c)^3 = -d^3$
We know by (3.2) that $(a + b + c)^3 = a^3 + b^3 + c^3 = 3(a + b)(b + c)(c + a)$.
That is $-d^3 = a^3 + b^3 + c^3 = 3(a + b)(b + c)(c + a) \Rightarrow$
$a^3 + b^3 + c^3 + d^3 = 3(a + b)(b + c)(c + a)$

Example 1. (1990 ARML) Compute $\dfrac{(1990)^3-(1\,000)^3-(990)^3}{(1990)(1000)(990)}$.

Solution: 3.

Method 1 (official solution)

$$\frac{(a+b)^3-a^3-b^3}{(a+b)(a)(b)}=\frac{3a^2b+3ab^2}{(a+b)(a)(b)}=\frac{3ab(a+b)}{(a+b)(a)(b)}=3$$

Method 2 (our solution)

Let $a = 1990$, $b = -1000$, and $c = -990$.

Since $a+b+c=1990+(-1\,000)+(-990)=0$, $a^3+b^3+c^3=3abc$.

$$1990^3+(-1\,000)^3+(-990)^3=3\cdot(1990)\cdot(-1\,000)\cdot(-990)$$

$$\frac{(1990)^3-(1\,000)^3-(990)^3}{(1990)(1000)(990)}=\frac{3\cdot(1990)\cdot(-1000)\cdot(-990)}{(1990)(1000)(990)}=3.$$

Example 2. (1992 NYML) Compute the largest prime factor of $3^{12}+2^{12}-2\cdot 6^6$. [Reminder: Calculators may *not* be used.)

Solution: 19.

Method 1 (official solution):

This is $(3^6-2^6)^2=[(3^3-2^3)(3^3+2^3)]^2=[35\times 19]^2$. Thus the answer is 19.

Method 2 (our solution):

This is $(3^6-2^6)^2=(9^3-4^3)^2=[(9-4)(9^2+9\times 4+4^2)]^2=[5\times(81+36+16)]^2$ $=[5\times 133]^2=[5\times 7\times 19]^2$. Thus the answer is 19.

Example 3. (1992 NYML) The number $(9^6 + 1)$ is the product of three primes. Compute the largest of these primes.

Solution: 6,481.

Method 1 (official solution):
Using the fact that $x^3 + 1 = (x + 1)(x^2 - x + 1)$,we have $9^6 + 1 = (9^2)^3 + 1 = (9^2 + 1)(9^4 - 9^2 + 1) = 82\cdot 6481 = 2\cdot 41 \cdot 6481$. From the given information, it must be true that 6,481 is a prime, and that must be the correct answer.

Method 2 (our solution):
$x^3 + y^3 = (x + y)[(x + y)^2 - 3xy]$
$9^6 + 1 = 3^{12} + 1 = (3^4)^3 + 1 = (3^4 + 1)[(3^4 + 1)^2 - 3 \times 3^4] = 82\cdot [(82)^2 - 234] = 82\cdot 6481 = 2\cdot 41 \cdot 6481$.
Since both 2 and 41 are prime numbers, the third prime must be 6481.

Example 4. What is the value of

$$\frac{2016^3 - 2\cdot 2016^2 \cdot 2017 + 3\cdot 2016\cdot 2017^2 - 2017^3 + 1}{2016\cdot 2017}\ ?$$

Solution: 2016.
Note: $(a-b)^3 = a^3 - 3\cdot a^2 \cdot b + 3\cdot a\cdot b^2 - b^3$.

$$\frac{2016^3 - 2\cdot 2016^2 \cdot 2017 + 3\cdot 2016\cdot 2017^2 - 2017^3 + 1}{2016\cdot 2017}$$

$$= \frac{2016^3 - 3\cdot 2016^2 \cdot 2017 + 3\cdot 2016\cdot 2017^2 - 2017^3 + 2016^2\cdot 2017 + 1}{2016\cdot 2017}$$

$$= \frac{(2016-2017)^3 + 2016^2\cdot 2017 + 1}{2016\cdot 2017} = \frac{-1 + 2016^2\cdot 2017 + 1}{2016\cdot 2017} = \frac{2016^2\cdot 2017}{2016\cdot 2017}$$

$= 2016$.

Example 5. Find $m^3 + \dfrac{1}{m^3}$ if $m + \dfrac{1}{m} = 3$.

Solution: 18.
We know that $(x+y)^3 = x^3 + 3x^2y + 3xy^2 + y^3 = x^3 + y^3 + 3xy(x+y)$.
So $x^3 + y^3 = (x+y)^3 - 3xy(x+y)$ (1)
Substituting in $x = m$ and $y = \dfrac{1}{m}$ into (1) gives us:

$$m^3+\frac{1}{m^3}=(m+\frac{1}{m})^3-3m\times\frac{1}{m}(m+\frac{1}{m})=3^3-3\times 3=18.$$

Example 6. Find $m^6+\frac{1}{m^6}$ if $m+\frac{1}{m}=4$.

Solution: 2702.

We know that $m^2+\frac{1}{m^2}=\left(m+\frac{1}{m}\right)^2-2=4^2-2=14.$

$$m^6+\frac{1}{m^6}=\left(m^2+\frac{1}{m^2}\right)\left(m^4+\frac{1}{m^4}-1\right)$$

$$=\left(m^2+\frac{1}{m^2}\right)\left[\left(m^2+\frac{1}{m^2}\right)^2-3\right]=14\left(14^2-3\right)=2702.$$

Example 7. Find $m^6+\frac{1}{m^6}$ if $y=\sqrt{m^2-3m+1}+\sqrt{3m-1-m^2}$, where both m and y are real numbers.

Solution: 322.

Since y is given to be a real number, the expressions under the square roots must be greater than or equal to 0. Therefore,

$$\begin{cases} m^2-3m+1\ge 0 \\ 3m-1-m^2\ge 0 \Rightarrow m^2-3m+1\le 0 \end{cases}$$

Since m^2-3m+1 must be both greater than or equal to 0 and less than or equal to 0, $m^2-3m+1=0 \quad \Rightarrow \quad m+\frac{1}{m}=3 \quad (m\ne 0)$.

$$m^3+\frac{1}{m^3}=(m+\frac{1}{m})^3-3m\times\frac{1}{m}(m+\frac{1}{m})=3^3-3\times 3=18.$$

$$m^6+\frac{1}{m^6}=(m^3+\frac{1}{m^3})^2-2=(18)^2-2=324-2=322.$$

Example 8. (1991 ARML) Three distinct positive integers are in arithmetic progression. If the sum of their cubes is divided by the sum of the three numbers, the quotient is 81. If the numbers are arranged in increasing order, compute the "middle" number.

Solution: 7.
Method 1 (official solution):
Call the integers $a - d$, a, and $a + d$.

Then $[(a-d)^3 + a^3 + (a+d)^3]/[(a-d) + a + (a+d)]$
$= [3a^3 + 6ad^2]/3a$
$= a^2 + 2d^2 = 81.$

Clearly a must be odd, but less than 10. Testing $a = 1$ or 5, we get irrational d's. Now $a = 3$ implies $d = \pm 6$, producing a negative term in the progression. Furthermore, $a = 9$ implies $d = 0$, so the terms aren't distinct. Only $a = 7$ works. Since $d = \pm 4$, the terms are 3, 7, 11.

Method 2 (our solution):
Call the integers $a - d$, a, and $a + d$.

Then $[(a-d)^3 + a^3 + (a+d)^3]/[(a-d) + a + (a+d)] = 81$ (1)

By Identity (4.2), $(x+y)^3 + (x-y)^3 = 3x^3 + 6xy^2$, (1) can be written as
$(3a^3 + 6ad^2 + a^3)/3a = 81 \quad \Rightarrow \quad a^2 + 2d^2 = 81 \quad \Rightarrow \quad (9-a)(9+a) = 2d^2$
The following system of equations works:
$(9 - a) = 2$
$(9 + a) = d^2$
Solving we get $d = \pm 4$ and $a = 7$.

Example 9. (1985 ARML) Compute $\lfloor (4+\sqrt{15})^3 \rfloor$, where the brackets denote the Greatest Integer Function.

Solution: 1,207.
Method 1 (our solution):

Note that if $a = 4 - \sqrt{15}$, then $0 < a < 1$. Now let
$b = (4+\sqrt{15})^3 + (4-\sqrt{15})^3$.
Expanding and simplifying leads to $b = 488$. Then $(4+\sqrt{15})^3 = 488 - a^3$, which is between 487 and 488. The answer is 487.

Note:
This is a tie breaker problem. The answer (1,207) published in the book ARML - NYSML Contests 1989-1994 was wrong.

Method 2 (our solution):
Let $x = 4+\sqrt{15}$ and $y = 4-\sqrt{15}$.
$x + y = (4+\sqrt{15}) + (4-\sqrt{15}) = 8$.
$xy = (4+\sqrt{15})(4-\sqrt{15}) = 16 - 15 = 1$.
$x^2 + y^2 = (x+y)^2 - 2xy = 64 - 2 = 62$.
$x^3 + y^3 = (x+y)(x^2 - xy + y^2) = 8(62-1) = 488$.
$(4+\sqrt{15})^3 + (4-\sqrt{15})^3 = 488$.
$(4+\sqrt{15})^3 = 488 - (4-\sqrt{15})^3$.
We know that $0 < 4-\sqrt{15} < 1$, so $0 < \left(4-\sqrt{15}\right)^3 < 1$.
The greatest positive integer not exceeding $\left(4+\sqrt{15}\right)^3$ is $488 - 1 = 487$.

Example 10. What is the value of $(4+2\sqrt{3})^{3/2} - (4-2\sqrt{3})^{3/2}$?

Solution: 20.
Method 1:
Let $a = (4+2\sqrt{3})^{1/2} = [(\sqrt{3})^2 + 2\times\sqrt{3}\times 1 + 1^2]^{1/2} = \sqrt{3}+1$ and
$b = (4-2\sqrt{3})^{1/2} = \sqrt{3}-1$.
We would like to find the value of $(4+2\sqrt{3})^{3/2} - (4-2\sqrt{3})^{3/2}$
Note that $a^3 - b^3 = (a-b)(a^2+ab+b^2)$
$= (a-b)(a^2 - 2ab + b^2 + 2ab + ab) = (a-b)[(a-b)^2 + 3ab]$.

$(4+2\sqrt{3})^{3/2}-(4-2\sqrt{3})^{3/2}=2[2^2+3(\sqrt{3}+1)((\sqrt{3}-1)=2[4+3(3-1)]=20.$

Method 2:
Let $a=(4+2\sqrt{3})^{1/2}$ and $b=(4-2\sqrt{3})^{1/2}$.
We wish to find $a^3-b^3=(a-b)(a^2+ab+b^2)$.

We can easily calculate the values of the expressions of a^2+b^2 and ab:
$a^2+b^2=(4+2\sqrt{3})+(4-2\sqrt{3})=8$.
$ab=[(4+2\sqrt{3})]^{1/2}[(4-2\sqrt{3})]^{1/2}=(4^2-2^2\times 3)^{1/2}=4^{1/2}=2$.

Now we wish to find the value of $a-b$.
We know that $(a-b)^2=a^2-2ab+b^2=(a^2+b^2)-2ab=8-2\times 2=4 \Rightarrow$
$a-b=2$.
Therefore $a^3-b^3=(a-b)(a^2+ab+b^2)=2\times(8+2)=20$.

Example 11. If both a and b are positive real numbers with $\frac{1}{a}-\frac{1}{b}-\frac{1}{a+b}=0$, find the value of $\left(\frac{b}{a}\right)^3+\left(\frac{a}{b}\right)^3$.

Solution: $2\sqrt{5}$.

From our given equation, we have $\frac{1}{a}-\frac{1}{b}=\frac{1}{a+b}$.
Multiplying both sides of the above equation by $a+b$ gives us
$\frac{b}{a}-\frac{a}{b}=1$.

Since $\frac{b}{a}+\frac{a}{b}=\sqrt{(\frac{b}{a}-\frac{a}{b})^2+4\cdot\frac{b}{a}\cdot\frac{a}{b}}=\sqrt{5}$, $\frac{b}{a}+\frac{a}{b}-\sqrt{5}=0$.

So $(\frac{b}{a})^3+(\frac{a}{b})^3+(-\sqrt{5})^3=3\cdot\frac{b}{a}\cdot\frac{a}{b}\cdot(-\sqrt{5})$, or $(\frac{b}{a})^3+(\frac{a}{b})^3=2\sqrt{5}$.

Example 12: Factor $(x-y)^3+(y-z)^3+(z-x)^3$.

Solution: $(x-y)^3+(y-z)^3+(z-x)^3=3(x-y)(y-z)(z-x)$

Our fifth cubic identity is

$$a^3+b^3+c^3-3abc=\frac{1}{2}(a+b+c)\left[(a-b)^2+(b-c)^2+(c-a)^2\right].$$

Observe that if $a+b+c=0$, then $a^3+b^3+c^3=3abc$.

Because $(x-y)+(y-z)+(z-x)=0$, we obtain the factorization

$(x-y)^3+(y-z)^3+(z-x)^3=3(x-y)(y-z)(z-x)$.

Example 13. (1985 NYML) Let $P(x) = 0$ be the polynomial equation of least possible degree, with rational coefficients, having $\sqrt[3]{7}+\sqrt[3]{49}$ as a root. Compute the product of all of the roots of $P(x) = 0$.

Solution: 56.

Method 1 (official method):

If $x=\sqrt[3]{7}+\sqrt[3]{49}$, then $x^3=7+3\sqrt[3]{7^2}\times\sqrt[3]{49}+3\sqrt[3]{7}\times\sqrt[3]{49^2}+49=$

$=56+3\sqrt[3]{7}\times\sqrt[3]{49}(3\sqrt[3]{7}+\sqrt[3]{49})$ so $x^3=56+21x$. Thus $P(x)=x^3-21x-56$, and the product we seek is 56.

Method 2 (our method):

Let $x=\sqrt[3]{7}+\sqrt[3]{49}$, then $x+(-\sqrt[3]{7})+(-\sqrt[3]{49})=0$.

By **Identity 6.** If $a + b + c = 0$, then $a^3 + b^3 + c^3 = 3abc$

So $x^3+(-\sqrt[3]{7})^3+(-\sqrt[3]{49})^3=3x\times(-\sqrt[3]{7})\times(-\sqrt[3]{49})\quad\Rightarrow$

$x^3+(-7)+(-49)=21x \qquad \Rightarrow \qquad x^3-21x-56=0$.

By Vieta's Theorem, the product of the roots is 56.

Example 14. (1978 ARML) Find the smallest root of $(x-3)^3+(x+4)^3=(2x+1)^3$.

Solution: – 4.

Method 1 (official solution):

Let $a = x - 3$, $b = x + 3$. Then $a^3+b^3=(a+b)^3 \qquad \Rightarrow \qquad 0=3ab(a+b)$.

$a = 0 \Rightarrow \quad x = 3;\ b = 0 \Rightarrow \quad x = -4;\ a + b = 0 \quad \Rightarrow \quad x = -\frac{1}{2}$.

The smallest root is – 4.

Method 2 (our solution):
Let $a = x - 3$, $b = x + 3$, $c = -2x - 3$,
We see that $a + b + c = 0$.
By **Identity 6,** $(x - 3)^3 + (x + 4)^3 + (-2x - 1)^3 = 0 = (x - 3)(x + 4)(-2x - 1)$.

Solving we get $x = 3$, $x = -4$, or $x = -\frac{1}{2}$. The smallest root is – 4.

Example 15. (NC Math Contest) Find the product of all distinct real solutions of the equation $(x^2 - 3)^3 - (4x + 6)^3 + 216 = 18(4x + 6)(3 - x^2)$. If this equation has any repeated solutions, use them only once in the product.

Solution: 9.
The equation is actually $a^3 + b^3 + c^3 = 3abc$, where $a = x^2 - 3$, $b = -(4x + 6)$, and $c = 6$.
We know that if $a^3 + b^3 + c^3 = 3abc$, then $a + b + c = 0$ or
$[(a - b)^2 + (b - c)^2 + (c - a)^2] = 0$.

Therefore we have $a + b + c = 0 \Rightarrow (x^2 - 3) - (4x + 6) + 6 = 0 \Rightarrow x^2 - 4x - 3 = 0$.
The product of these two roots is – 3 (Note: two roots are $2 - \sqrt{7}$ and $2 + \sqrt{7}$).

$[(a - b)^2 + (b - c)^2 + (c - a)^2] = 0 \quad \Rightarrow \quad a = b = c$
$(x^2 - 3) = -(4x + 6) = 6$

The only solution is $x = -3$.
The product of all the real roots is $(-3)(-3) = 9$.
Note that this was the last problem in the contest.

Example 16. How many triples of solutions to the system of equations if x, y, and z are distinct integers.

$$\begin{cases} x+y+z=0 \\ x^3+y^3+z^3=-36 \end{cases}$$

Solution: 6.

Since $x+y+z=0$ and $x^3+y^3+z^3=-36$,

By **Identity 6,** $x^3+y^3+z^3=3xyz=-36 \quad \Rightarrow xyz=-12$.

x, y, and *z* must be two positive integers and one negative integer and must also sum to be zero.

There are 6 triples of such answers:

(1, 3, – 4), (3, 1, – 4), (1, – 4, 3), (– 4, 1, 3), (3, – 4, 1), (– 4, 3, 1).

Example 17. If *a, b,* and *c* are real numbers, with $a+b+c=2\sqrt{3}$, and $a^2+b^2+c^2=4$, find the value of $(a-2b+c)^{2013}$.

Solution: 0.

Since $(a+b+c)^2=(2\sqrt{3})^2$, expanding gives us

$a^2+b^2+c^2+2(ab+bc+ca)=12$.

Since $a^2+b^2+c^2=4$, $ab+bc+ca=4 \quad \Longrightarrow \quad a^2+b^2+c^2=ab+bc+ca$.

So $\frac{1}{2}\left[(a-b)^2+(b-c)^2+(c-a)^2\right]=0$.

Therefore, we have: $a-b=0, b-c=0, c-a=0$.

Or $a=b=c$.

And so $(a-2b+c)^{2013}=(a-2a+a)^{2013}=0$.

Example 18. (AMC) Determine the number of ordered pairs of integers (*m*, *n*) for which $mn \geq 0$ and $m^3+n^3+99mn=33^3$.

Solution: 35.

Method 1 (official solution):

Let $m + n = s$. Then $m^3 + n^3 + 3mn(m + n) = s^3$. Subtracting the given equation from the latter yields

$$s^3 - 33^3 = 3mns - 99mn.$$

It follows that $(s - 33)(s^2 + 33s + 33^2 - 3mn) = 0$, hence either $s = 33$ or $(m + n)^2 + 33(m + n) + 33^2 - 3mn = 0$. The second equation is equivalent to $(m - n)^2 + (m + 33)^2 + (n + 33)^2 = 0$, whose only solution, $(-33,-33)$, qualifies. On the other hand, the solutions to $m + n = 33$ satisfying the required conditions are (0, 33), (1, 32), (2, 31), . . . , (33, 0), of which there are 34. Thus there are 35 solutions altogether.

Method 2 (our solution):
Rewrite $m^3 + n^3 + 99mn = 33^3$ as $m^3 + n^3 - 33^3 = -99mn$.

$$a^3 + b^3 + c^3 = m^3 + n^3 - (-33)^3 = m^3 + n^3 - 33^3$$
$$3abc = 3mn(-33) = -99mn.$$

We see that $a = m$, $b = n$, and $c = -33$.

Since $a^3 + b^3 + c^3 = 3abc$, we are sure that either

$a + b + c = 0$ (1)

or $(a-b)^2 + (b-c)^2 + (c-a)^2 = 0$ (2)

Equation (1) becomes $33 + (-m) + (-n) = 0 \Rightarrow \quad m + n = 33$ (3)

There are 34 solutions to equation (3): $(0,33)$, $(1,32)$, $\cdots$, $(33,0)$.

Equation (2) becomes $(m-n)^2 + (m+33)^2 + (n+33)^2 = 0$. (4)

Equation (4) only has one solution: $(-33, -33)$.
In total, there are $34 + 1 = 35$ ordered pairs of integers (m, n).
Note: This was the last problem in the 1999 test.

Example 19. (AMC) The sum of $\sqrt[3]{5+2\sqrt{13}} + \sqrt[3]{5-2\sqrt{13}}$ equals

(A). $\frac{3}{2}$. (B). $\frac{\sqrt[3]{65}}{4}$. (C). $\frac{1+\sqrt[6]{13}}{4}$. (D). $\sqrt[3]{2}$. (E). None of these.

Solution: (E).

Method 1 (official solution):

Let $a=\sqrt[3]{5+2\sqrt{13}}$, $b=\sqrt[3]{5-2\sqrt{13}}$, and $x = a + b$. Then

$x^3 = a^3 + 3a^2b + 3ab^2 + b^3$

$x^3 = a^3 + b^3 + 3ab(a+b)$

$x^3 = 10 + 3\sqrt[3]{-27}x$

The last equation is equivalent to $x^3 + 9x - 10 = 0$ or ($(x-1)(x^2+x+10)=0$, whose only real solution is $x = 1$.

Method 2 (our solution):

Let $\sqrt[3]{5+2\sqrt{13}} + \sqrt[3]{5-2\sqrt{13}} = x$, then $\sqrt[3]{5+2\sqrt{13}} + \sqrt[3]{5-2\sqrt{13}} - x = 0$.

So $(\sqrt[3]{5+2\sqrt{13}})^3 + (\sqrt[3]{5-2\sqrt{13}})^3 + (-x)^3 = 3\cdot\sqrt[3]{5+2\sqrt{13}}\cdot\sqrt[3]{5-2\sqrt{13}}\cdot(-x)$.

$x^3 = (5+2\sqrt{13}) + (5-2\sqrt{13}) + 3\cdot\sqrt[3]{(5+2\sqrt{13})(5-2\sqrt{13})}x = 10 - 9x$

The above equation becomes: $x^3 + 9x - 10 = 0$

Factoring gives $(x-1)(x^2+x+10) = 0$.

We see that $(x^2+x+10) = (x+\frac{1}{2})^2 + \frac{39}{4} > 0$, so $x - 1 = 0$, or $x = 1$.

Example 20. If $x+y+z=6$, $x^2+y^2+z^2=14$ and $x^3+y^3+z^3=36$, find the value of xyz.

Solution: 6.

We know that $(x+y+z)^2 = x^2+y^2+z^2+2xy+2xz+2yz$.

$36 = 2\times 14 + 2(xy+yz+zx) \Rightarrow \qquad (xy+yz+zx) = 11$.

We also know that $x^3+y^3+z^3-3xyz = (x+y+z)(x^2+y^2+z^2-xy-yz-zx)$

$36 - 3xyz = (6)(14-11) \qquad \Rightarrow \qquad xyz = \frac{1}{3}(36-18) = 6$.

Example 21. Compute $(3x+4y+5z)^2$ if $x^2-yz=3$, $y^2-zx=4$, and $z^2-xy=5$, where *a, b, c, x, y, z* are real numbers.

Solution: 36.

Let $d = 3x+4y+5z$

$d = (x^2-yz)x+(y^2-zx)y+(z^2-xy)z$

$= x^3-xyz+y^3-xyz+z^3-xyz = x^3+y^3+z^3-3xyz$.

Squaring both sides of equation $x^2-yz=3$: $(x^2-yz)^2 = 9 \Rightarrow$

$x^4-2x^2yz+y^2z^2=9$ (1)

Multiplying $y^2-zx=4$ and $z^2-xy=5$: $y^2z^2-xy^3-xz^3+x^2yz=20$ (2)

(1) – (2): $x^4+xy^3+xz^3-3x^2yz=-11 \qquad \Rightarrow \qquad x(x^3+y^3+z^3-3xyz)=-11$

$\Rightarrow \qquad dx = -11$ (3)

Similarly, $\quad dy = 1$ (4)

$dz = 13$ (5)

(3) × 3 + (4) × 4 + (5) × 5: $3dx+4dy+5dz = -11\times 3+1\times 4+13\times 5 \Rightarrow$

$d(3x+4y+5z) = 36 \Rightarrow (3x+4y+5z)^2 = 36$.

PROBLEMS

Problem 1. Compute $\dfrac{2017^3-1007^3-1000^3}{2017\times 1007\times 1000}$.

Problem 2. Calculate: $\dfrac{1999^3-1000^3-999^3}{1999\times 1000\times 999}$.

Problem 3. Compute the largest prime factor of $7^{12}+5^{12}-2\cdot 35^6$.

Problem 4. The number (11^6+1) is the product of four primes. Compute the largest of these primes.

Problem 5. What is the value of $\dfrac{13^3+3\cdot 13\cdot 14^2-14^3+1}{13\cdot 14}$?

Problem 6. Compute $r^3+\dfrac{1}{r^3}$ if $r+\dfrac{1}{r}=\sqrt{2}$.

Problem 7. Find $a^6+\dfrac{1}{a^6}$ if $a+\dfrac{1}{a}=\sqrt{3}$.

Problem 8. Find $m^3-\dfrac{1}{m^3}$ if $y=\sqrt{m^2-m-1}+\sqrt{m+1-m^2}$, where both m and y are real numbers.

Problem 9. Both a and b are real numbers with
$\left(m^3+\dfrac{1}{m^3}-a\right)^2+\left(m+\dfrac{1}{m}-b\right)^2=0$. Prove: $b(b^2-3)=a$.

Problem 10. Find the greatest positive integer not exceeding $\left(\sqrt{7}+\sqrt{3}\right)^6$.

Problem 11. Find the greatest positive integer not exceeding $\left(\sqrt{7}+\sqrt{5}\right)^6$.

Problem 12. Factor $(ax-by)^3+(by-cz)^3+(cz-ax)^3$.

Problem 13. Find $(a+b)(b+c)(c+a)+abc$ if $a+b+c=0$.

Problem 14. Calculate: $\sqrt[3]{2+\sqrt{5}}+\sqrt[3]{2-\sqrt{5}}$.

Problem 15. Solve for x: $\sqrt[3]{5+x}+\sqrt[3]{4-x}=3$.

Problem 16. If $x=\sqrt[3]{a+\sqrt{a^2+b^3}}-\sqrt[3]{\sqrt{a^2+b^3}-a}$, show that $x^3+3bx=2a$.

Problem 17. If both x and y are real numbers with $x^3+y^3=a^3$ $(a>0)$, find the range of $x+y$.

Problem 18. Find the value of $\dfrac{a^2}{bc}+\dfrac{b^2}{ca}+\dfrac{c^2}{ab}$ if $a+b+c=0$ and $abc\neq 0$.

Problem 19. If $x+y+z=1$, $x^2+y^2+z^2=2$ and $x^3+y^3+z^3=3$, find the value of xyz.

Problem 20. x, y, and z are positive integers with $x^3-y^3-z^3=3xyz$ and $x^2=2(y+z)$. Find the value of $xy+yz+zx$.

Problem 21. (1979 ARML) Find the lease value of x which satisfies $\sqrt[3]{3x-5}+\sqrt[3]{2x-4}=\sqrt[3]{5x-9}$.

Problem 22. (AMC) If x is a number satisfying the equation $\sqrt[3]{x+9}-\sqrt[3]{x-9}=3$, then x^2 is between
(A) 55 and 65 (B) 65 and 75 (C) 75 and 85 (D) 85 and 95 (E) 95 and 105.

Problem 23. Compute $(x+y)^3$ if $(x-1)^3+2016(x-1)=-1$, and $(y-1)^3+2016(y-1)=1$, where x and y are real numbers.

Problem 24. (1993 ARML) The number $(7^{12} + 4^{12})$ is the product of three 4-digit primes, exactly one of which is greater than 2,626. Compute this largest prime factor.

SOLUTIONS

Problem 1. Solution: 3.
Let $a = 2017$, $b = -1007$, and $c = -1000$.
Since $a+b+c=2017+(-1007)+(-1000)=0$, $a^3+b^3+c^3=3abc$.

$$2017^3+(-1007)^3+(-1000)^3=3\cdot 2017\cdot(-1007)\cdot(-1000)$$

$$\frac{2017^3-1007^3-1000^3}{2017\times 1007\times 1000}=\frac{3\cdot 2017\cdot(-1007)\cdot(-1000)}{2017\times 1007\times 1000}=3.$$

Problem 2. Solution: 3.
$a = 1999$, $b = -1000$, and $c = -999$.
Since $a+b+c=1999+(-1000)+(-999)=0$, so $a^3+b^3+c^3=3abc$.

$$1999^3+(-1000)^3+(-999)^3=3\cdot 1999\cdot(-1000)\cdot(-999)$$

$$\frac{1999^3-1000^3-999^3}{1999\times 1000\times 999}=\frac{3\cdot 1999\cdot(-1000)\cdot(-999)}{1999\times 1000\times 999}=3.$$

Problem 3. Solution: 109.
This is $(7^6-5^6)^2=(48^3-25^3)^2=[(49-25)(7^2+7\times 5+5^2)]^2=[24\times(49+35+25)]^2=(24\times 109)^2$. Thus the answer is 109.

Problem 4. Solution: 1,117.
Using the fact that $x^3+1=(x+1)(x^2-x+1)$,we have $11^6+1=(11^2)^3+1=(11^2+1)(11^4-11^2+1)=122\cdot 14521=2\cdot 61\cdot 13\cdot 1117$. From the given information, it must be true that 1117 is a prime, and that must be the correct answer.

Problem 5. Solution: 39.
Note: $(a-b)^3=a^3-3\cdot a^2\cdot b+3\cdot a\cdot b^2-b^3$.

$$\frac{13^3+3\cdot 13\cdot 14^2-14^3+1}{13\cdot 14}$$

$$=\frac{13^3-3\cdot 13^2\cdot 14+3\cdot 13\cdot 14^2-14^3+3\cdot 13^2\cdot 14+1}{13\cdot 14}$$

$$=\frac{(13-14)^3+3\cdot 13^2\cdot 14+1}{13\cdot 14}=\frac{-1+3\cdot 13^2\cdot 14+1}{13\cdot 14}=\frac{3\cdot 13^2\cdot 14}{13\cdot 14}=39.$$

Problem 6. Solution: $-\sqrt{2}$.

We know that $r^3+\frac{1}{r^3}=\left(r+\frac{1}{r}\right)\left(r^2-1+\frac{1}{r^2}\right)$, and $\left(r+\frac{1}{r}\right)^2=r^2+2+\frac{1}{r^2}=2$.

The second equation gives us $r^2+\frac{1}{r^2}=0 \Rightarrow r^2-1+\frac{1}{r^2}=-1$.

Therefore, $r^3+\frac{1}{r^3}=(r+\frac{1}{r})(-1)=-\sqrt{2}$.

Problem 7. Solution: – 2.

$$a^3+\frac{1}{a^3}=(a+\frac{1}{a})[(a+\frac{1}{a})^2-3]=\sqrt{3}[(\sqrt{3})^2-3]=0$$

$$a^6+\frac{1}{a^6}=(a^3+\frac{1}{a^3})^2-2=(0)^2-2=-2.$$

Problem 8. Solution: 4.

Since y is given to be a real number, the expressions under the square roots must be greater than or equal to 0. Therefore,

$$\begin{cases} m^2-m-1\ge 0 \\ m+1-m^2\ge 0 \Rightarrow m^2-m-1\le 0 \end{cases}$$

Since m^2-m-1 must be both greater than or equal to 0 and less than or equal to 0, $m^2-m-1=0 \quad \Rightarrow \quad m-\frac{1}{m}=1 \quad (m\ne 0)$.

$$m^3-\frac{1}{m^3}=\left(m-\frac{1}{m}\right)\left(m^2+\frac{1}{m^2}+1\right)=\left(m-\frac{1}{m}\right)\left[\left(m-\frac{1}{m}\right)^2+3\right]=4.$$

Problem 9. Solution: $b(b^2-3)$.

Since the square of a number is always greater than or equal to 0, in order for the sum of two squares to be 0, $m^3+\frac{1}{m^3}-a=0$ and $m+\frac{1}{m}-b=0$.

$m^3+\frac{1}{m^3}=a$ and $m+\frac{1}{m}=b$

So $a = m^3 + \frac{1}{m^3} = \left(m + \frac{1}{m}\right)(m^2 - m\left(\frac{1}{m}\right) + \frac{1}{m^2})$

$= \left(m + \frac{1}{m}\right)\left[\left(m + \frac{1}{m}\right)^2 - 3\right] = b(b^2 - 3)$.

Problem 10. Solution: 7039.

Let $x = \sqrt{7} + \sqrt{3}$ and $y = \sqrt{7} - \sqrt{3}$.

$x + y = (\sqrt{7} + \sqrt{3}) + (\sqrt{7} - \sqrt{3}) = 2\sqrt{7}$.

$xy = (\sqrt{7} + \sqrt{3})(\sqrt{7} - \sqrt{3}) = 7 - 3 = 4$.

$x^2 + y^2 = (x + y)^2 - 2xy = 20$

$x^6 + y^6 = (x^2 + y^2)^3 - 3(x^2 + y^2) \cdot x^2 \cdot y^2 = 7040$.

$(\sqrt{7} + \sqrt{3})^6 + (\sqrt{7} - \sqrt{3})^6 = 7040$.

$(\sqrt{7} + \sqrt{3})^6 = 7040 - (\sqrt{7} - \sqrt{3})^6$.

We know that $0 < \sqrt{7} - \sqrt{3} < 1$, so $0 < \left(\sqrt{7} - \sqrt{3}\right)^6 < 1$.

The greatest positive integer not exceeding $\left(\sqrt{7} + \sqrt{3}\right)^6$ is 7040 – 1 = 7039.

Problem 11. Solution: 13535.

Let $x = \sqrt{7} + \sqrt{5}$ and $y = \sqrt{7} - \sqrt{5}$.

$x + y = (\sqrt{7} + \sqrt{5}) + (\sqrt{7} - \sqrt{5}) = 2\sqrt{7}$.

$xy = (\sqrt{7} + \sqrt{5})(\sqrt{7} - \sqrt{5}) = 7 - 5 = 2$.

$x^2 + y^2 = (x + y)^2 - 2xy = 24$

$x^6 + y^6 = (x^2 + y^2)^3 - 3(x^2 + y^2) \cdot x^2 \cdot y^2 = 13536$.

$(\sqrt{7} + \sqrt{5})^6 + (\sqrt{7} - \sqrt{5})^6 = 13536$.

$(\sqrt{7} + \sqrt{5})^6 = 13536 - (\sqrt{7} - \sqrt{5})^6$.

We know that $0 < \sqrt{7} - \sqrt{5} < 1$. So $0 < \left(\sqrt{7} - \sqrt{5}\right)^6 < 1$.

The greatest positive integer not exceeding $\left(\sqrt{7} + \sqrt{5}\right)^6$ is 13536 – 1 = 13535.

Problem 12. Solution:
$(ax-by)^3+(by-cz)^3+(cz-ax)^3=3(ax-by)(by-cz)(cz-ax)$.

Observe that if $a+b+c=0$, then $a^3+b^3+c^3=3abc$ is true.

Because $(ax-by)+(by-cz)+(cz-ax)=0$, we have the following factorization:
$(ax-by)^3+(by-cz)^3+(cz-ax)^3=3(ax-by)(by-cz)(cz-ax)$.

Problem 13. Solution: 0.
Since $a+b+c=0$, $a+b=-c$, $b+c=-a$, and $c+a=-b$.
$(a+b)(b+c)(c+a)+abc=(-c)(-a)(-b)+abc=-abc+abc=0$.

Problem 14. Solution: 1.
Let $\sqrt[3]{2+\sqrt{5}}+\sqrt[3]{2-\sqrt{5}}=x$. Then $\sqrt[3]{2+\sqrt{5}}+\sqrt[3]{2-\sqrt{5}}-x=0$.

So $(\sqrt[3]{2+\sqrt{5}})^3+(\sqrt[3]{2-\sqrt{5}})^3+(-x)^3=3\cdot\sqrt[3]{2+\sqrt{5}}\cdot\sqrt[3]{2-\sqrt{5}}\cdot(-x)$
$\Rightarrow x^3=(2+\sqrt{5})+(2-\sqrt{5})+3\cdot\sqrt[3]{(2+\sqrt{5})(2-\sqrt{5})}x$.
$\sqrt[3]{(2+\sqrt{5})(2-\sqrt{5})}=\sqrt[3]{2^2-(\sqrt{5})^2}=\sqrt[3]{4-5}=\sqrt[3]{-1}=-1$.

Substituting in -1 for x, the above equation becomes: $x^3=4-3x$ or
$x^3+3x-4=0$.

We can easily see that 1 is an answer in this cubic, so we have
$(x-1)(x^2+x+4)=0$.
Either $(x^2+x+4)=0$ or $x-1=0$.
Because $(x^2+x+4)=(x+\frac{1}{2})^2+\frac{15}{4}>0$, $x-1=0$, or $x=1$.
Hence $\sqrt[3]{2+\sqrt{5}}+\sqrt[3]{2-\sqrt{5}}=1$.

Problem 15. Solution: 3 and – 4.

The original equation can be written as $\sqrt[3]{5+x}+\sqrt[3]{4-x}-3=0$.

Therefore $(\sqrt[3]{5+x})^3+(\sqrt[3]{4-x})^3+(-3)^3=3\cdot\sqrt[3]{5+x}\cdot\sqrt[3]{4-x}\cdot(-3)$

Or $\sqrt[3]{(5+x)(4-x)}=2$ $\Longrightarrow$ $(5+x)(4-x)=8$

Solving gives us: $x_1=3$, and $x_2=-4$.

Problem 16. Solution:

Since $x-\sqrt[3]{a+\sqrt{a^2+b^3}}+\sqrt[3]{\sqrt{a^2+b^3}}=0$,

$x^3+(-\sqrt[3]{a+\sqrt{a^2+b^3}})^3+(\sqrt[3]{\sqrt{a^2+b^3}-a})^3=3\cdot x\cdot(-\sqrt[3]{a+\sqrt{a^2+b^3}})\cdot(\sqrt[3]{\sqrt{a^2+b^3}-a})$

Simplifying: $x^3-2a=-3bx$ $\Longrightarrow$ $x^3+3bx=2a$.

Problem 17. Solution: $0<x+y\le\sqrt[3]{4}a$.

Since $x^3+y^3=a^3(a>0)$, $(x+y)(x^2-xy+y^2)>0$.

Because x and y can't be zero at the same time, $(x-\frac{y}{2})^2+\frac{3}{4}y^2>0$.

So we have $x+y>0$.

Letting $x+y=t$, we have $x+y-t=0$.

So we have $x^3+y^3+(-t)^3=3xy\cdot(-t)$.

We also know that $x^3+y^3=a^3$, $y=t-x$, so $a^3+(-t)^3=3x(t-x)\cdot(-t)$.

Simplifying we get: $3tx^2-3t^2x+t^3-a=0$.

Since x is a real number, $\Delta\ge0$.

$(-3t^2)^2-4\cdot3t\cdot(t^3-a^3)\ge0$.

Solve for t: $t\le\sqrt[3]{4}a$ $\Rightarrow$ $x+y\le\sqrt[3]{4}a$

$0<x+y\le\sqrt[3]{4}a$.

Problem 18. Solution: 3.

Method 1:

$$\frac{a^2}{bc}+\frac{b^2}{ca}+\frac{c^2}{ab}=\frac{a^3+b^3+c^3}{abc}$$

$$\frac{a^2}{bc}+\frac{b^2}{ca}+\frac{c^2}{ab}==\frac{a^3+b^3+c^3-3abc+3abc}{abc}$$

$$=\frac{(a+b+c)(a^2+b^2+c^2-ab-bc-ca)+3abc}{abc}=\frac{3abc}{abc}=3$$

Method 2:

Let $a = 2$, $b = c = -1$ such that $a + b + c = 0$.

$$\frac{a^2}{bc}+\frac{b^2}{ca}+\frac{c^2}{ab}=3.$$

Problem 19. Solution: $\frac{1}{6}$.

We know that $(x+y+z)^2=x^2+y^2+z^2+2xy+2xz+2yz$.

$$1^2=2+2(xy+yz+zx) \qquad \Rightarrow \qquad (xy+yz+zx)=-\frac{1}{2}.$$

We also know that $x^3+y^3+z^3-3xyz=(x+y+z)(x^2+y^2+z^2-xy-yz-zx)$

$$3-3xyz=(1)[2-(-\frac{1}{2})] \qquad \Rightarrow \qquad xyz=\frac{1}{6}.$$

Problem 20. Solution: 5.

We have

$$x^3-y^3-z^3-3xyz=x^3+(-y)^3+(-z)^3-3x\cdot(-y)\cdot(-z)$$

$$=(x-y-z)[x^2+(-y)^2+(-z)^2-x(-y)-x(-z)-(-y)(-z)]$$

$$=\frac{1}{2}(x-y-z)[(x-y)^2+(-y+z)^2+(-z-x)^2]$$

$$=\frac{1}{2}(x-y-z)[(x-y)^2+(y-z)^2+(z+x)^2]$$

Since *x, y,* and *z* are positive integers, $(x-y)^2+(y-z)^2+(z+x)^2 \neq 0$.

Therefore, we have $x-y-z=0$, which can be written as

$x = y + z$ (1)

We are also given that $x^2 = 2(y+z)$ (2)

Squaring (1), we get: $x^2 = (y + z)^2$ (3)

Setting equations (2) and (3) equal to each other, we have

$(y + z)^2 = 2(y + z)$ (4)

Since both *y* and *z* are positive integers, $y + z \neq 0$, and so we can divide both sides of (4) by $y + z$:

$y + z = 2$ (5)

Since both *y* and *z* are positive integers, we know that $y = z = 1$.

$x = y + z = 2$.

$xy+yz+zx=2\times1+1\times1+1\times2=5$.

Problem 21. Solution: $\frac{5}{3}$.

Method 1 (official solution):

Let $u^3 = 3x - 5$, $v^3 = 2x - 4$. Then $u + v = (u^3 + v^3)^{1/3}$ or $u^3 + 3uv(u + v) + v^3 = u^3 + v^3$ or $3uv(u + v) = 0$. If $u = 0$, $x = 5/3$. If $v = 0$, $x = 2$. If $u + v = 0$, $x = 9/5$. The least value of *x* is 5/3.

Method 2 (our solution):

The original equation can be written as $\sqrt[3]{3x-5}+\sqrt[3]{2x-4}-\sqrt[3]{5x-9}=0$.

Therefore $\left(\sqrt[3]{3x-5}\right)^3+\left(\sqrt[3]{2x-4}\right)^3-\left(\sqrt[3]{5x-9}\right)^3$

$=3\cdot(\sqrt[3]{3x-5})\cdot(\sqrt[3]{2x-4})\cdot(-\sqrt[3]{5x-9})$.

$(3x-5)+(2x-4)-(5x-9)=3\cdot(\sqrt[3]{3x-5})\cdot(\sqrt[3]{2x-4})\cdot(-\sqrt[3]{5x-9})$

$3\cdot(\sqrt[3]{3x-5})\cdot(\sqrt[3]{2x-4})\cdot(-\sqrt[3]{5x-9})=0$.

$(3x-5)(2x-4)(5x-9)=0$

So $x_1=\frac{5}{3}$, $x_2=2$, and $x_3=\frac{9}{5}$.

The least value of x is 5/3.

Problem 22. Solution: (C)

This is the last problem on the test. There are two official solutions to the problems. We provided the third solution to the problem.

Let $a=\sqrt[3]{x+9}$, $b=-\sqrt[3]{x-9}$, and $c=-3$.

Because $a+b+c=0$, we have

$(\sqrt[3]{x+9})^3+(-\sqrt[3]{x-9})^3+(-3)^3=3\cdot(\sqrt[3]{x+9})\cdot(-\sqrt[3]{x-9})\cdot(-3)$.

Or $x+9-(x-9)-27=9\cdot(\sqrt[3]{x^2-81}) \quad \Rightarrow \quad -9=9\cdot(\sqrt[3]{x^2-81}) \quad \Rightarrow$

$\sqrt[3]{x^2-81}=-1$.

Cube both sides: $x^2-81=-1$ and $x^2=81-1=80$.

Problem 23. Solution: 8.

$(x-1)^3+2016(x-1)=-1 \qquad (1)$

$(y-1)^3+2016(y-1)=1 \qquad (2)$

(1) + (2): $(x-1)^3+(y-1)^3+2016(x+y-2)=0 \quad \Rightarrow$

$$(x-1+y-1)[(x-1)^2-(x-1)(y-1)+(y-1)^2]+2016(x+y-2)=0$$

$$\Rightarrow (x+y-2)[(x-1)^2-(x-1)(y-1)+(y-1)^2]+2016(x+y-2)=0$$

$$\Rightarrow (x+y-2)[(x-1)^2-(x-1)(y-1)+(y-1)^2+2016]=0$$

$[(x-1)^2-(x-1)(y-1)+(y-1)^2+2016]$

$=[(x-1)^2-(x-1)(y-1)+\frac{(y-1)^2}{4}+\frac{3(y-1)^2}{4}+2016]$

$=[(x-1)-\frac{(y-1)^2}{2}]^2+\frac{3(y-1)^2}{4}+2016>0$

So $(x+y-2)=0 \quad \Rightarrow \quad x+y=2 \quad \Rightarrow \quad (x+y)^3=8$

Problem 24. Solution: 1993.

Noting that $x^3 + y^3 = (x + y)(x^2 - xy + y^2)$, we have

$(7^4)^3 + (4^4)^3 = (7^4 + 4^4)(7^8 - 7^4 \cdot 4^4 + 4^8)$.

The first factor equals 2,657 (if this were not a prime, it would have to be the product of two 4-digit primes, which is impossible). Incidentally, the second factor turns out to be $2617 \cdot 1993$!!

BASIC KNOWLEDGE

In this chapter we are going to show you some important rules of radical operations and several commonly used methods to solve radical equations.

Definition

The symbol $\sqrt[n]{\quad}$ is called a radical sign. The expression $\sqrt[n]{a}$ is a **radical**. The number a is called the radicand and n is a positive integer, called **the index** of the radical $\sqrt[n]{a}$.

When $n = 2$, $\sqrt[2]{\quad}$ is called **the square root**. It is customary to use the notation $\sqrt{\quad}$ instead of $\sqrt[2]{\quad}$ for the positive, or principal, square root. In the expression $\sqrt{a}$, $a \ge 0$ and $\sqrt{a} \ge 0$. $\sqrt{2} \approx 1.414$, $\sqrt{3} \approx 1.732$, and $\sqrt{5} \approx 2.236$.

Radical Operations

(1) $m\sqrt{a} + n\sqrt{a} = (m+n)\sqrt{a}$, $(a \ge 0)$

(2) $(\sqrt{a} + \sqrt{b})(\sqrt{a} - \sqrt{b}) = a - b$, $(a \ge 0, b \ge 0)$

(3) $x\sqrt[n]{a} \pm y\sqrt[n]{a} = (x \pm y)\sqrt[n]{a}$, ($a \ge 0$ if n is even)

(4) The **Product Property:** $\sqrt{ab} = \sqrt{a} \cdot \sqrt{b}$ and $\sqrt[n]{ab} = \sqrt[n]{a} \cdot \sqrt[n]{b}$, ($a \ge 0$, $b \ge 0$ if n is even).

(5) The **Quotient Property** $\sqrt{\dfrac{a}{b}} = \dfrac{\sqrt{a}}{\sqrt{b}}$ and $\sqrt[n]{\dfrac{a}{b}} = \dfrac{\sqrt[n]{a}}{\sqrt[n]{b}}$, ($a \ge 0$, $b > 0$ if n is even).

(6) $(\sqrt[n]{a})^m = \sqrt[n]{a^m}$, $(a \ge 0)$.

(7) $\sqrt[m]{\sqrt[n]{a}} = \sqrt[mn]{a}$, $(a \ge 0)$.

m and n are positive integers, $m, n \ge 2$.

Conjugates

Sometimes, conjugates are used to simplify radical expressions.
$x+\sqrt{y}$ and $x-\sqrt{y}$ are conjugates.

Some other useful conjugates:

$p\sqrt{q}+r\sqrt{s}$ and $p\sqrt{q}-r\sqrt{s}$

$\sqrt[m]{a^n}$ and $\sqrt[m]{a^{m-n}}$

$a\pm\sqrt{b}$ and $a\mp\sqrt{b}$

$m\sqrt{a}\pm n\sqrt{b}$ and $m\sqrt{a}\mp n\sqrt{b}$

$\sqrt[3]{a}\pm\sqrt[3]{b}$ and $\sqrt[3]{a^2}\mp\sqrt[3]{ab}+\sqrt[3]{b^2}$.

Nested Radical Simplification

A nested radical is a radical expression that contains another radical expression.

Some nested radicals can be rewritten in a form that is not nested. Rewriting a nested radical in this way is called **denesting**.

Radical Theorem 1: $\sqrt{a\pm\sqrt{b}}$ can be denested if and only if

$$a>0,\ b>0 \qquad (1)$$

and

$$a^2-b=k^2 \qquad (k>0) \qquad (2)$$

Radical Denesting Formula: If $\sqrt{a \pm \sqrt{b}}$ can be denested, then $\sqrt{a \pm \sqrt{b}}$ =
$\sqrt{\frac{a+\sqrt{a^2-b}}{2}} \pm \sqrt{\frac{a-\sqrt{a^2-b}}{2}} = \sqrt{\frac{a+k}{2}} \pm \sqrt{\frac{a-k}{2}}$.

Proof:

Let $\sqrt{a+\sqrt{b}} = \sqrt{x} + \sqrt{y}$.

Squaring both sides: $a+\sqrt{b} = x + y + 2\sqrt{xy}$.

This gives us $x + y = a$, and $xy = \frac{b}{4}$.

Solving the system of equations for x and y in terms of a and b, we have:

$x = \frac{a+\sqrt{a^2-b}}{2}$ and $y = \frac{a-\sqrt{a^2-b}}{2}$, where ($a > 0$, $b > 0$, $a^2 - b > 0$).

$\therefore \sqrt{a+\sqrt{b}} = \sqrt{\frac{a+\sqrt{a^2-b}}{2}} + \sqrt{\frac{a-\sqrt{a^2-b}}{2}}$

We can prove that $\sqrt{a-\sqrt{b}} = \sqrt{\frac{a+\sqrt{a^2-b}}{2}} - \sqrt{\frac{a-\sqrt{a^2-b}}{2}}$ in a similar fashion.

Example 1. (ARML) Express, in simplest from, the value of
$\sqrt{\frac{3}{4}-\sqrt{\frac{1}{2}}} - \sqrt{\frac{3}{4}+\sqrt{\frac{1}{2}}}$.

Solution: – 1.

Method 1 (official method):

Since the rightmost surd is larger than the leftmost surd, the expression is negative. Then, representing the original expression as x, squaring produces

$x^2 = \frac{3}{4} - \sqrt{\frac{1}{2}} + \frac{3}{4} + \sqrt{\frac{1}{2}} - 2\sqrt{(\frac{3}{4})^2 - \frac{1}{2}} = \frac{3}{4} + \frac{3}{4} - 2 \times \frac{1}{4} = 1$.

Since x is negative, $x = -1$.

Method 2 (our method):
Let $a = 3/4$, $b = 1/2$.
$a^2 - b = (\frac{3}{4})^2 - \frac{1}{2} = \frac{1}{16} = (\frac{1}{4})^2$, $k = 2$.
Therefore the given nested radical can be denested.

By the denesting formula):

$$\sqrt{\frac{3}{4} - \sqrt{\frac{1}{2}}} = \sqrt{\frac{\frac{3}{4} + \frac{1}{4}}{2}} - \sqrt{\frac{\frac{3}{4} - \frac{1}{4}}{2}} = \sqrt{\frac{1}{2}} - \frac{1}{2}.$$

$$\sqrt{\frac{3}{4} + \sqrt{\frac{1}{2}}} = \sqrt{\frac{\frac{3}{4} + \frac{1}{4}}{2}} + \sqrt{\frac{\frac{3}{4} - \frac{1}{4}}{2}} = \sqrt{\frac{1}{2}} + \frac{1}{2}.$$

$$\sqrt{\frac{3}{4} - \sqrt{\frac{1}{2}}} - \sqrt{\frac{3}{4} + \sqrt{\frac{1}{2}}} = \sqrt{\frac{1}{2}} - \frac{1}{2} - (\sqrt{\frac{1}{2}} + \frac{1}{2}) = -1.$$

Example 2. (ARML) If $\sqrt{5 + 2\sqrt{6}}$ were expressed as a decimal to the nearest hundredth, find the digit in the hundredth's place.

Solution: 5.
Method 1 (our solution):
$\sqrt{5 + 2\sqrt{6}} = \sqrt{5 + \sqrt{24}}$
Let $a = 5$, $b = 24$.
$a^2 - b = 5^2 - 24 = 1$, $k = 1$.
Therefore the given nested radical can be denested.

By the denesting formula):

$$\sqrt{\frac{5+1}{2}} + \sqrt{\frac{5-1}{2}} = \sqrt{3} + \sqrt{2} = 1.732 + 1.414 = 3.146.$$

To the nearest hundredth, the value is 3.15. The answer is 5.

Example 3. Simplify $\sqrt{17+12\sqrt{2}}$.

Solution: $3 + 2\sqrt{2}$.

We rewrite the given radical as $\sqrt{17+12\sqrt{2}} = \sqrt{17+\sqrt{288}}$.
Let $a = 17$, $b = 288$.
$a^2 - b = 17^2 - 288 = 289 - 288 = 1$, $k = 1$.
Therefore the given nested radical can be denested.

Method 1 (Completing the square):

$$\sqrt{17+12\sqrt{2}} = \sqrt{3^2+2\times3\times\sqrt{8}+(\sqrt{8})^2} = \sqrt{(3+\sqrt{8})^2} = 3+\sqrt{8} = 3+2\sqrt{2}.$$

Method 2 (Using the denesting formula):

$$\sqrt{17+12\sqrt{2}} = \sqrt{17+\sqrt{288}} = \sqrt{\frac{17+1}{2}} + \sqrt{\frac{17-1}{2}} = 3 + 2\sqrt{2}.$$

Example 4. Simplify: $\sqrt{4-2\sqrt{3}}$.

Solution: $\sqrt{3}-1$

We rewrite the given radical as $\sqrt{4-2\sqrt{3}} = \sqrt{4-\sqrt{12}}$.
Let $a = 4$, $b = 12$.
$a^2 - b = 4^2 - 12 = 4 = 2^2$, $k = 2$.
Therefore the given nested radical can be denested.

Method 1 (Completing the square):

$$\sqrt{4+2\sqrt{3}} = \sqrt{(3+1)-2\sqrt{3\times1}} = \sqrt{(\sqrt{3}-1)^2} = \sqrt{3}-1.$$

Method 2 (using the denesting formula):

$$\sqrt{4-2\sqrt{3}} = \sqrt{4-\sqrt{12}} = \sqrt{\frac{4+2}{2}} - \sqrt{\frac{4-2}{2}} = \sqrt{3} - \sqrt{1} = \sqrt{3}-1.$$

Example 5. (ARML) Find the ordered pair of positive integers (a, b), with $a < b$, for which $\sqrt{1+\sqrt{21+12\sqrt{3}}} = \sqrt{a}+\sqrt{b}$.

Solution: (1, 3).
Method 1 (official solution):
Since $\sqrt{21+12\sqrt{3}} = \sqrt{(3+2\sqrt{3})^2}$, if we let the original expression be called x,
$x^2 = 1+3+2\sqrt{3} = 4+2\sqrt{3} = (1+\sqrt{3})^2$ and $x = 1+\sqrt{3}$. Thus $(a, b) = (1, 3)$.

Method 2 (our solution):
Squaring both sides of the given equation, we get
$1+\sqrt{21+12\sqrt{3}} = a+b+2\sqrt{ab} \quad \Rightarrow \quad \sqrt{21+12\sqrt{3}} = (a+b-1)+2\sqrt{ab}$.
We can write $\sqrt{21+12\sqrt{3}}$ as $\sqrt{21+\sqrt{3\times 12^2}} = \sqrt{21+\sqrt{432}}$.
$21^2 - 432 = 1$. Since 1 is a square number, so
$\sqrt{21+12\sqrt{3}} = \sqrt{21+2\sqrt{36\times 3}} = \sqrt{21+2\sqrt{108}}$
$= \sqrt{12+2\sqrt{12\times 9}+9} = \sqrt{(\sqrt{12}+\sqrt{9})^2} = \sqrt{12}+\sqrt{9} = 3+2\sqrt{3}$

Therefore $(a+b-1)+2\sqrt{ab} = 3+2\sqrt{3}$.
We have $a+b-1=3$ and $ab=3$.

Since a and b are positive integers and $a < b$, the only possible values are $a = 1$ and $b = 3$.

Example 6. (ARML) Compute the numerical value of $\sqrt{4+\sqrt{7}} - \sqrt{4-\sqrt{7}}$.

Solution: $\sqrt{2}$.
Method 1:
Let $y = \sqrt{4+\sqrt{7}} - \sqrt{4-\sqrt{7}}$.
Squaring both sides:
$y^2 = (4+\sqrt{7})+(4-\sqrt{7})-2(\sqrt{4+\sqrt{7}})(\sqrt{4-\sqrt{7}}) = 8-2\sqrt{9} = 8-6 = 2$.

Therefore $\sqrt{4+\sqrt{7}}-\sqrt{4-\sqrt{7}}=\sqrt{2}$.

Method 2 (our solution):
We see that $a = 4$, $b = 7$, and $a^2 - b = 4^2 - 7 = 9 = 3^2$. $k = 3$.

Therefore the given nested radical can be denested.

$$\sqrt{4+\sqrt{7}}=\sqrt{\frac{4+3}{2}}+\sqrt{\frac{4-3}{2}}=\sqrt{\frac{7}{2}}+\sqrt{\frac{1}{2}}.$$

$$\sqrt{4-\sqrt{7}}=\sqrt{\frac{4+3}{2}}-\sqrt{\frac{4-3}{2}}=\sqrt{\frac{7}{2}}-\sqrt{\frac{1}{2}}.$$

$$\sqrt{4+\sqrt{7}}-\sqrt{4-\sqrt{7}}=\sqrt{\frac{7}{2}}+\sqrt{\frac{1}{2}}-(\sqrt{\frac{7}{2}}-\sqrt{\frac{1}{2}})=2\times\sqrt{\frac{1}{2}}=\sqrt{2}$$

Example 7. Find $x^6-2\sqrt{2}x^5-3x^4-x^3+2\sqrt{5}x^2-4x+\sqrt{5}$ if $x=\sqrt{5}+\sqrt{2}$.

Solution: $-\sqrt{2}$.

$x^2 - 2\sqrt{2}x - 3 = 0$

$x^2 - 2\sqrt{5}x + 3 = 0$

$x^4(x^2 - 2\sqrt{2}x - 3) - x(x^2 - 2\sqrt{5}x + 3) - x + \sqrt{5} = 0 - 0 - (\sqrt{5} + \sqrt{2}) + \sqrt{5}$
$= -\sqrt{2}$.

Example 8. Simplify $\sqrt[3]{20+14\sqrt{2}}+\sqrt[3]{20-14\sqrt{2}}$.

Solution: 4.
Method 1:
Let $x=\sqrt[3]{20+14\sqrt{2}}+\sqrt[3]{20-14\sqrt{2}}$.

Cubing both sides:

$\left(\sqrt[3]{20+14\sqrt{2}}\right)^3 + 3\left(\sqrt[3]{20+14\sqrt{2}}\right)^2 \times (\sqrt[3]{20-14\sqrt{2}}) + 3(\sqrt[3]{20+14\sqrt{2}}) \times$

$\left(\sqrt[3]{20-14\sqrt{2}}\right)^2 + \left(\sqrt[3]{20-14\sqrt{2}}\right)^3 = x^3.$

Or $20+14\sqrt{2} + 3(\sqrt[3]{20^2-(14\sqrt{2})^2} \times (\sqrt[3]{20+14\sqrt{2}} + \sqrt[3]{20-14\sqrt{2}}) + 20-14\sqrt{2} =$ x^3

Or $40 + 3\times \sqrt[3]{8} \times (x) = x^3 \Rightarrow x^3 - 6x - 40 = 0 \quad \Rightarrow \quad (x-4)(x^2+4x+10) = 0.$

Since $x^2 + 4x + 10 = (x+2)^2 + 6 > 0$, $x = 4$.

Method 2:

Let $\sqrt[3]{20+14\sqrt{2}} + \sqrt[3]{20-14\sqrt{2}} = x$, then $\sqrt[3]{20+14\sqrt{2}} + \sqrt[3]{20-14\sqrt{2}} - x = 0$.

So $(\sqrt[3]{20+14\sqrt{2}})^3 + (\sqrt[3]{20-14\sqrt{2}})^3 + (-x)^3 = 3\cdot\sqrt[3]{20+14\sqrt{2}}\cdot\sqrt[3]{20-14\sqrt{2}}\cdot(-x)$.

$$x^3 = (20+14\sqrt{2}) + (20-14\sqrt{2}) + 3\cdot\sqrt[3]{(20+14\sqrt{2})(20-14\sqrt{2})}x = 40+6x$$

The above equation becomes: $x^3 - 6x - 40 = 0$

Factoring gives $(x-4)(x^2+4x+10) = 0$.

We see that $(x^2+4x+10) = (x+2)^2 + 6 > 0$, so $x - 4 = 0$, or $x = 4$.

Example 9. Find $\sqrt{x^2+y^2-2xy+4x-4y+4} + \sqrt{1-2x+x^2} - \sqrt{y^2-4y+4}$ if $0 < x < 1 < y < 2$.

Solution: 1.

$\sqrt{x^2+y^2-2xy+4x-4y+4} + \sqrt{1-2x+x^2} - \sqrt{y^2-4x+4}$

$= \sqrt{(x-y+2)^2} + \sqrt{(1-x)^2} - \sqrt{(y-2)^2} = |x-y+2| + |1-x| - |y-2|.$

Since $0 < x < 1 < y < 2$, we know that $x - y + 2 > 0$, $1 - x > 0$, and $y - 2 < 0$.

So, $|x-y+2|$ becomes $x-y+2$, $|1-x|$ becomes $1-x$, and $|y-2|$ becomes $2-y$. The answer is then $(x-y+2)+(1-x)-(2-y)=1$.

Example 10. If $\sqrt[3]{\sqrt[3]{16}-2} = \sqrt[3]{a} + \sqrt[3]{b} + \sqrt[3]{c}$, where a, b, and c are rational numbers, compute $a+b+c$.

Solution: $\frac{1}{3}$.

Let $t=\sqrt[3]{16}$. $t^3=16$.

$(t+2)^3=t^3+6t^2+12t+8=16+6t^2+12t+8=6(t^2+2t+4)$

Multiplying the above equation by $(t-2)$:

$(t-2)(t+2)^3=6(t^2+2t+4)(t-2)=6(t^3-8)=6(16-8)=48$.

So $(t-2)=\dfrac{48}{(t+2)^3}$.

$$\sqrt[3]{\sqrt[3]{16}-2}$$

$$=\sqrt[3]{(t-2)}=\sqrt[3]{\frac{48}{(t+2)^3}}=\frac{2\cdot\sqrt[3]{6}}{t+2}=\frac{2\cdot\sqrt[3]{6}}{\sqrt[3]{16}+2}=\frac{2\cdot\sqrt[3]{6}\cdot(\sqrt[3]{16^2}-\sqrt[3]{16}\cdot\sqrt[3]{8}+\sqrt[3]{8^2})}{(\sqrt[3]{16}+\sqrt[3]{8})(\sqrt[3]{16^2}-\sqrt[3]{16}\cdot\sqrt[3]{8}+\sqrt[3]{8^2})}$$

$$=\frac{2\cdot\sqrt[3]{6}\cdot(\sqrt[3]{16^2}-\sqrt[3]{16}\cdot\sqrt[3]{8}+\sqrt[3]{8^2})}{16+8}=\frac{\sqrt[3]{6}\cdot(\sqrt[3]{16^2}-\sqrt[3]{16}\cdot\sqrt[3]{8}+\sqrt[3]{8^2})}{12}$$

$$=\frac{\sqrt[3]{6\cdot 16^2}-\sqrt[3]{6\cdot 16\cdot 8}+\sqrt[3]{6\cdot 8^2}}{12}$$

$$=\sqrt[3]{\frac{6\cdot 16^2}{12^3}}-\sqrt[3]{\frac{6\cdot 16\cdot 8}{12^3}}+\sqrt[3]{\frac{6\cdot 8^2}{12^3}}=\sqrt[3]{\frac{8}{9}}-\sqrt[3]{\frac{4}{9}}+\sqrt[3]{\frac{2}{9}}$$

Hence $a+b+c=\sqrt[3]{\frac{8}{9}}-\sqrt[3]{\frac{4}{9}}+\sqrt[3]{\frac{2}{9}}=\frac{8}{9}-\frac{4}{9}+\frac{2}{9}=\frac{6}{9}=\frac{1}{3}$.

Example 11. Solve $\sqrt{x+1}+2=0$.

Solution:

Since $\sqrt{x+1} \ge 0$, then $\sqrt{x+1} + 2 \ge 2$.

No matter what value we choose for x, $\sqrt{x+1} + 2$ will not equal 0. Therefore, there is no solution to the given equation.

Example 12. Solve $\sqrt{\dfrac{x}{1-x}} + \sqrt{\dfrac{1-x}{x}} = \dfrac{13}{6}$.

Solution: $x_1 = \dfrac{4}{13}$ and $x_2 = \dfrac{9}{13}$.

Let $\sqrt{\dfrac{x}{1-x}} = y$. Taking the reciprocal gives us $\sqrt{\dfrac{1-x}{x}} = \dfrac{1}{y}$.

Substituting $\dfrac{1}{y}$ for $\sqrt{\dfrac{1-x}{x}}$ and y for $\sqrt{\dfrac{x}{1-x}}$ into the given equation, we have

$$y + \frac{1}{y} = \frac{13}{6}.$$

This can be simplified into the quadratic: $6y^2 - 13y + 6 = 0$.

Solving for y using the quadratic formula, we get $y_1 = \dfrac{2}{3}$; $y_2 = \dfrac{3}{2}$.

Thus, $\sqrt{\dfrac{x}{1-x}} = \dfrac{2}{3} \quad \Rightarrow \quad x_1 = \dfrac{4}{13}$.

Or $\sqrt{\dfrac{x}{1-x}} = \dfrac{3}{2} \quad \Rightarrow \quad x_2 = \dfrac{9}{13}$.

Substituting in $x_1 = \dfrac{4}{13}$ and $x_2 = \dfrac{9}{13}$ back into the original equation, we can confidently say that these are indeed the solutions.

Example 13. Find the sum of the real roots of the equation $x^2 + 12x + 16 = 2\sqrt{x^2 + 12x + 19}$.

Solution: -12.

Let $y = x^2 + 12x + 16$.
The original equation can be written as $y = 2\sqrt{y+3}$.
Squaring both sides: $y^2 = 4(y+3) \quad \Rightarrow \quad y^2 - 4y - 12 = 0$.

Solve for y: $y_1 = 6$ or $y_2 = -2$ (extraneous root).

Therefore $x^2 + 12x + 16 = 6 \quad \Rightarrow \quad x^2 + 12x + 10 = 0$.

$$x_{1,2} = \frac{-12 \pm \sqrt{(-12)^2 - 4\times 10}}{2} = \frac{-12 \pm 2\sqrt{26}}{2} = -6 \pm \sqrt{26}.$$

The sum of the roots is $x_1 + x_2 = -12$.

Note that we will give two more solutions to this problem in Example 18.

Example 14. Solve $\sqrt{x^2 + 5x - 2} - \sqrt{x^2 + 5x - 5} = 1$.

Solution: $x_1 = 1$ and $x_2 = -6$.
Let $u = \sqrt{x^2 + 5x - 2}$, $v = \sqrt{x^2 + 5x - 5}$.

$$u - v = 1 \qquad (1)$$
$$u^2 - v^2 = 3 \qquad (2)$$
(2) ÷ (1): $$u + v = 3 \qquad (3)$$

From (1) and (3), we can solve for u and v to get $u = 2$ and $v = 1$, satisfying $u \ge 0$, $v \ge 0$.

$\sqrt{x^2 + 5x - 2} = 2 \quad \Rightarrow \quad x_1 = 1, x_2 = -6.$

We can check that both $x_1 = 1$ and $x_2 = -6$ are indeed the solutions by plugging these values back into the original equation and seeing that the left hand side equals the right hand side.

Note (a): If we had used the value of v to find x, the results would have been the same.

(b): IMPORTANT! We needed to make sure that both $u \geq 0$ and $v \geq 0$.

Example 15. Solve $\sqrt[3]{2-x} + \sqrt{x-1} = 1$.

Solution: $x_1 = 2$, $x_2 = 1$, and $x_3 = 10$.
Let $u = \sqrt[3]{2-x}$, and $v = \sqrt{x-1}$.
We have:

$$u + v = 1 \qquad (1)$$
$$u^3 + v^2 = 1 \qquad (2)$$

From (1), we have $v = 1 - u$. Substituting in $1 - u$ for v into (2), we get $u^3 + u^2 - 2u = 0$.
The three solutions to this cubic equation are $u_1 = 0$, $u_2 = 1$, $u_3 = -2$.
Plugging in these values into (1) to solve for v, we get
$v_1 = 1$, $v_2 = 0$ and $v_3 = 3$. These three values satisfy $v \geq 0$.

Since $x = 2 - u^3$,
$x_1 = 2 - 0 = 2$,
$x_2 = 2 - 1 = 1$, and
$x_3 = 2 + 8 = 10$.

We can check that these three values are indeed the solutions by plugging these values back into the original equation and seeing that the left hand side equals the right hand side.

Note: Here, we only needed to ensure that $v \geq 0$.

Example 16. Solve $\sqrt{2x+1} + 2\sqrt{x-1} = 4$.

Solution: $x = \frac{53}{2} - 4\sqrt{38}$.

The average value of $\sqrt{2x+1}$ and $2\sqrt{x-1}$ is 2.

Therefore we can let

$\sqrt{2x+1} = 2 + t$ and $2\sqrt{x-1} = 2 - t$ where ($-2 \le t \le 2$).

Squaring these two equations gives us the following two equations:

$2x + 1 = 4 + 4t + t^2$ (1)
$4(x - 1) = 4 - 4t + t^2$ (2)

$2 \times (1) - (2)$:
$6 = 4 + 12t + t^2 \Rightarrow t = -6 \pm \sqrt{38}$.

Since $-2 \le t \le 2$, the only solution for t is $t = -6 + \sqrt{38}$.

So $\sqrt{2x+1} = -4 + \sqrt{38} \Rightarrow x = \frac{53}{2} - 4\sqrt{38}$.

We can check that $x = \frac{53}{2} - 4\sqrt{38}$ is indeed the solution by plugging it back into the original equation and seeing that the left hand side equals the right hand side.

Example 17. Solve $\sqrt{x - \frac{5}{x}} - \sqrt{5 - \frac{5}{x}} = x$.

Solution: $\frac{1}{2}(1 + \sqrt{21})$.

The average value of $\sqrt{x - \frac{5}{x}}$ and $-\sqrt{5 - \frac{5}{x}}$ is $\frac{1}{2}x$.

We can let

$\sqrt{x - \frac{5}{x}} = \frac{1}{2}x + t$ (1)

$-\sqrt{5 - \frac{5}{x}} = \frac{1}{2}x - t$ (2)

$(1)^2 - (2)^2$: $x - 5 = 2xt \Rightarrow t = \frac{1}{2}(1 - \frac{5}{x})$.

So $\sqrt{x-\frac{5}{x}} = \frac{1}{2}x + \frac{1}{2}(1-\frac{5}{x})$, or $(x-\frac{5}{x}) - 2\sqrt{x-\frac{5}{x}} + 1 = 0 \Rightarrow (\sqrt{x-\frac{5}{x}} - 1)^2 = 0$.

Thus, $x-\frac{5}{x} = 1 \Rightarrow x^2 - x - 5 = 0$.

Solving for x: $x = \frac{1}{2}(1 \pm \sqrt{21})$.

We can check that $x = \frac{1}{2}(1+\sqrt{21})$ is the only solution by plugging it into our original equation and seeing that the left hand side equals the right hand side.

Example 18. Find the sum of the real roots of the equation
$x^2 + 12x + 16 = 2\sqrt{x^2+12x+19}$.

Solution: -12.
Method 1:
Rewrite the original equation as
$x^2 + 12x + 16 - 2\sqrt{x^2+12x+19} = 0$.
Or $(\sqrt{x^2+12x+19})^2 - 2\sqrt{x^2+12x+19} - 3 = 0$.

$(\sqrt{x^2+12x+19} + 1)(\sqrt{x^2+12x+19} - 3) = 0$.

We have $\sqrt{x^2+12x+19} = -1$ (extraneous) or $\sqrt{x^2+12x+19} = 3$.

Squaring both sides of $\sqrt{x^2+12x+19} = 3$:

$x^2 + 12x + 19 = 9 \Rightarrow x^2 + 12x + 10 = 0$

Since the discriminant of the quadratic $\Delta = 12^2 - 4 \times 10 > 0$, the two roots are real and by Vieta's Theorem, the sum of two roots is then -12.

Method 2:

Rewrite the original equation as $x^2 + 12x + 19 - 2\sqrt{x^2+12x+19} + 1 = 4$.

Or $(\sqrt{x^2+12x+19} - 1)^2 = 4$.

Take the square root of both sides: $\sqrt{x^2+12x+19} - 1 = \pm 2$.

We have $\sqrt{x^2+12x+19} - 1 = 2$, or $\sqrt{x^2+12x+19} - 1 = -2$ (extraneous).

So $\sqrt{x^2+12x+19} - 1 = 2$, we have $\sqrt{x^2+12x+19} = 3$.

Squaring both sides of $\sqrt{x^2+12x+19} = 5$:

$x^2 + 12x + 19 = 9 \Rightarrow x^2 + 12x + 10 = 0$.

Since $\Delta = 12^2 - 4 \times 10 > 0$, by Vieta's Theorem, the sum of two roots is then -12.

Example 19. Solve $\sqrt{3x+1} - \sqrt{x+4} = 7$.

Solution: 96.

We see that $\sqrt{3x+1} - \sqrt{x+4} = 7$ (1)

and $(3x + 1) - (x + 4) = 2x - 3$ (2)

(2) ÷ (1): $\sqrt{3x+1} + \sqrt{x+4} = \dfrac{2x-3}{7}$, or $7\sqrt{3x+1} + 7\sqrt{x+4} = 2x - 3$ (3)

Multiplying (1) by 7 and adding it to (3), we get

$7\sqrt{3x+1} = x + 23$.

Squaring both sides of the above equation and factoring yields:

$(x - 5)(x - 96) = 0$ (4)

Solving for x, we have $x = 5$, $x = 96$.

We substitute these two values into the original equation to find that only $x = 96$ works.

Example 20. Find all values of a such that $\dfrac{3}{1-\sqrt{a-2}}+\dfrac{3}{1+\sqrt{a-2}}=6$.

Solution: 2.
First we divide both sides of the equation by 3:

$$\frac{1}{1-\sqrt{a-2}}+\frac{1}{1+\sqrt{a-2}}=2 \qquad (1)$$

We see that $1-\sqrt{a-2}$ and $1+\sqrt{a-2}$ are conjugates and
$(1-\sqrt{a-2})(1+\sqrt{a-2})=3-a$.

Therefore from (1) we have $\dfrac{1+\sqrt{a-2}+1-\sqrt{a-2}}{(1-\sqrt{a-2})(1+\sqrt{a-2})}=2 \quad \Rightarrow \quad \dfrac{2}{3-a}=2$

$$\Rightarrow \quad \frac{1}{3-a}=1 \qquad \Rightarrow \quad 3-a=1 \quad \Rightarrow \quad a=2.$$

We can check that $a=2$ is the solution by plugging it into our original equation and seeing that the left hand side equals the right hand side.

Example 21. Solve $\sqrt{x+5}+\dfrac{3}{\sqrt{x+5}}=2\sqrt{3}$.

Solution: – 2.

We observe that $\sqrt{x+5}>0$ and $\dfrac{3}{\sqrt{x+5}}>0$.

We know that $a+b\geq 2\sqrt{ab}$ $(a>0,\ b>0)$.

In our case, $\sqrt{x+5}+\dfrac{3}{\sqrt{x+5}}\geq 2\sqrt{\sqrt{x+5}\cdot\dfrac{3}{\sqrt{x+5}}}=2\sqrt{3}$.

Equality holds if and only if $\sqrt{x+5}=\dfrac{3}{\sqrt{x+5}}$.

So the original equation is equivalent to $x+5=3 \quad \Rightarrow \quad x=-2$.
We can check that $x=-2$ is the solution by plugging it into our original equation and seeing that the left hand side equals the right hand side.

Example 22. (ARML) Find all values of x which satisfy

$$\frac{6}{\sqrt{x-8}-9}+\frac{1}{\sqrt{x-8}-4}+\frac{7}{\sqrt{x-8}+4}+\frac{12}{\sqrt{x-8}+9}=0.$$

Solution: 17 or 44.

Method 1 (official solution):

Let $y=\sqrt{x-8}$ (noting that y is positive). Then

$$(y-3)(\frac{18}{y^2-8}+\frac{1}{y^2-16})=0.$$

If $y = 3$, then $x = 17$. If $y \neq 3$, then $18(y^2-16)+8(y^2-81)=0$. The only positive solution of this equation is $y = 6$, from which $x = 44$.

Note the typo in the official solution: $(y-3)(\frac{18}{y^2-8}+\frac{1}{y^2-16})=0$ should be

$$(y-3)(\frac{18}{y^2-81}+\frac{1}{y^2-16})=0.$$

Method 2 (our solution):

The original equation can be written as:

$$(\frac{6}{\sqrt{x-8}-9}+\frac{12}{\sqrt{x-8}+9})+(\frac{1}{\sqrt{x-8}-4}+\frac{7}{\sqrt{x-8}+4})=0 \Rightarrow$$

$$\frac{6(\sqrt{x-8}+9)+12(\sqrt{x-8}-9)}{(\sqrt{x-8}-9)(\sqrt{x-8}+9)})+\frac{\sqrt{x-8}+4+7(\sqrt{x-8}-4)}{(\sqrt{x-8}-4)(\sqrt{x-8}+4)}=0$$

$$\Rightarrow \quad \frac{18\sqrt{x-8}-54}{x-89}+\frac{8\sqrt{x-8}-24}{x-24}=0$$

$$\Rightarrow \quad \frac{18(\sqrt{x-8}-3)}{x-89}+\frac{8(\sqrt{x-8}-3)}{x-24}=0$$

$$\Rightarrow \quad \frac{9(\sqrt{x-8}-3)}{x-89}+\frac{4(\sqrt{x-8}-3)}{x-24}=0$$

$$\Rightarrow \quad (\sqrt{x-8}-3)(\frac{9}{x-89}+\frac{4}{x-24})=0.$$

We have either $(\sqrt{x-8}-3)=0 \quad \Rightarrow \quad x=17;$

or $\dfrac{9}{x-89}+\dfrac{4}{x-24}=0 \quad \Rightarrow \quad x=44.$

Example 23. The value of x which satisfies $\sqrt{4x+4}-\sqrt{3x-3}=\sqrt{2x+2}-\sqrt{x-1}$ is $(a-\sqrt{3}-\sqrt{8})/(b-\sqrt{3}+\sqrt{8})$. Find the ordered pair of numbers (a, b).

Solution: (5, –1).

Rearranging, $(\sqrt{x+1})(2-\sqrt{2})=(\sqrt{x-1})(\sqrt{3}-1)$. Squaring,

$$(x+1)(6-4\sqrt{2})=(x-1)(4-2\sqrt{3}) \quad \Rightarrow \quad (x+1)(3-2\sqrt{2})=(x-1)(2-\sqrt{3})$$

$$\Rightarrow \quad 3x+3-2\sqrt{2}x-2\sqrt{2}=2x-2-\sqrt{3}x+\sqrt{3}$$

$$\Rightarrow \quad 2-\sqrt{3}+3-2\sqrt{2}=2x-\sqrt{3}x-3x+2\sqrt{2}x$$

$$\Rightarrow \quad 5-\sqrt{3}-2\sqrt{2}=-x-\sqrt{3}x+2\sqrt{2}x$$

$$\Rightarrow \quad 5-\sqrt{3}-2\sqrt{2}=(-1-\sqrt{3}+2\sqrt{2})x$$

$$\Rightarrow \quad x=\frac{5-\sqrt{3}-2\sqrt{2}}{-1-\sqrt{3}+2\sqrt{2}}=\frac{5-\sqrt{3}-\sqrt{8}}{-1-\sqrt{3}+\sqrt{8}}.$$

so $(a, b) = (5, -1)$.

PROBLEMS

Problem 1. Simplify $\sqrt{5+2\sqrt{6}} - \sqrt{5-2\sqrt{6}}$.

$x^2 = 5+2\sqrt{6}+5-2\sqrt{6}-2\cdot\sqrt{1} = 8 \quad x = 2\sqrt{2}$

Problem 2. If $\sqrt{4+2\sqrt{3}}$ were expressed as a decimal to the nearest hundredth, find the digit in the hundredth's place.

Problem 3. Simplify $\sqrt{9-2\sqrt{14}}$.

Problem 4. Find xyz if $\sqrt{612\sqrt{6}+360\sqrt{10}+340\sqrt{15}+2015} = x\sqrt{3} + y\sqrt{5} + z\sqrt{8}$, where x, y, and z are positive integers.

Problem 5. Compute $\sqrt{9-6\sqrt{2}} - \sqrt{9+6\sqrt{2}}$.

Problem 6. Find $3x^2-5xy+3y^2$ if $x = \dfrac{1}{\sqrt{3}-\sqrt{2}}$ and $y = \dfrac{1}{\sqrt{3}+\sqrt{2}}$.

Problem 7. Simplify $S = \sqrt[3]{2+\sqrt{5}} + \sqrt[3]{2-\sqrt{5}}$.

Problem 8. Simplify: $\sqrt{x^2+6x+9}+\sqrt{x^2-4x+4}$ if $-3 < x < 2$.

Problem 9. Show that $\sqrt[3]{ax^2+by^2+cz^2} = \sqrt[3]{a} + \sqrt[3]{b} + \sqrt[3]{c}$ if $ax^3 = by^3 = cz^3$ and $\dfrac{1}{x} + \dfrac{1}{y} + \dfrac{1}{z} = 1$.

Problem 10. Simplify $\sqrt{2-\sqrt{3}}$.

Problem 11. Find the integer part of $(1+\sqrt{2})^4$.

Problem 12. (ARML) Find all values of $x > 4$ which satisfy $\sqrt{x-4\sqrt{x-4}}+2 = \sqrt{x+\sqrt{4x-4}}-2$.

Problem 13. (ARML) The value of x which satisfies $\sqrt{6x+6}-\sqrt{5x-5}=\sqrt{4x+4}-\sqrt{3x-3}$ is $(a-\sqrt{15}-\sqrt{24})/(b-\sqrt{15}+\sqrt{24})$. Find the ordered pair of numbers (a, b).

Problem 14. Solve $\sqrt{3x-1}+\sqrt{5x-3}+\sqrt{x-1}=2\sqrt{2}$.

Problem 15. Solve $x^2 - \sqrt{x^2-9} = 21$.

Problem 16. Solve $2(x+1) - 2\sqrt{x(x+8)} = \sqrt{x}-\sqrt{x+8}$.

Problem 17. Solve $\sqrt[3]{x+45} - \sqrt[3]{x-16} = 1$.

Problem 18. Solve $x = \sqrt{x-\frac{1}{x}} + \sqrt{1-\frac{1}{x}}$.

Problem 19. Solve $x + \frac{x}{\sqrt{x^2-1}} = 2\sqrt{2}$.

Problem 20. Solve $2x^2 + x\sqrt{3x^2+1} = 4$.

Problem 21. Solve $\sqrt{x^2+5x-2} - \sqrt{x^2+5x-5} = 1$.

Problem 20. Solve $3\sqrt{x^4-2x^2+1} + 2x\sqrt{x^4+2x^2-8} = (x^2+1)^2$.

Problem 23. Solve $\sqrt{2x-3} - 3\sqrt{1-x} = 0$.

Problem 24. Solve $\sqrt[4]{x} + \sqrt[4]{97-x} = 5$.

Problem 25. Solve $\sqrt{x+5} + \sqrt{x-3} = 4$.

Problem 26. Find the sum of the roots of the equation $9 - \sqrt[3]{x} = \dfrac{18}{\sqrt[3]{x}}$.

Problem 27. Solve $\sqrt[3]{45+x} + \sqrt[3]{16-x} = 1$.

Problem 28. (IMO) For which real numbers x do the following equations hold:

(a) $\sqrt{x+\sqrt{2x-1}} + \sqrt{x-\sqrt{2x-1}} = \sqrt{2}$,

(b) $\sqrt{x+\sqrt{2x-1}} + \sqrt{x-\sqrt{2x-1}} = 1$,

(c) $\sqrt{x+\sqrt{2x-1}} + \sqrt{x-\sqrt{2x-1}} = 2$?

SOLUTIONS

Problem 1. Solution: $2\sqrt{2}$.

Method 1:

Let the difference be x with $x > 0$.

$$x^2 = (\sqrt{5+2\sqrt{6}})^2 - 2\sqrt{5+2\sqrt{6}}\,\sqrt{5-2\sqrt{6}} + (\sqrt{5-2\sqrt{6}})^2$$
$$= 5 + 2\sqrt{6} - 2\sqrt{5^2-(2\sqrt{6})^2} + 5 - 2\sqrt{6}$$
$$= 10 - 2\sqrt{25-24} = 10 - 2 = 8.$$

Thus $x = \sqrt{x^2} = \sqrt{8} = 2\sqrt{2}$.

Method 2:

$\sqrt{5+2\sqrt{6}} = \sqrt{5+\sqrt{24}}$

Let $a = 5$, $b = 24$.

$a^2 - b = 5^2 - 24 = 1$, $k = 1$.

Therefore the given nested radical can be denested.

By the denesting formula):

$$\sqrt{\frac{5+1}{2}} + \sqrt{\frac{5-1}{2}} = \sqrt{3} + \sqrt{2}.$$
$$\sqrt{\frac{5+1}{2}} - \sqrt{\frac{5-1}{2}} = \sqrt{3} - \sqrt{2}.$$

$$\sqrt{5+2\sqrt{6}} - \sqrt{5-2\sqrt{6}} = \sqrt{3} + \sqrt{2} - (\sqrt{3} - \sqrt{2}) = 2\sqrt{2}.$$

Problem 2. Solution: 3.

We rewrite the given radical as $\sqrt{4+2\sqrt{3}} = \sqrt{4+\sqrt{12}}$.

Let $a = 4$, $b = 12$.

$a^2 - b = 4^2 - 12 = 4 = 2^2$, $k = 2$.

Therefore the given nested radical can be denested.

Method 1 (Completing the square):

$\sqrt{4+2\sqrt{3}} = \sqrt{(3+1)+2\sqrt{3\times 1}} = \sqrt{(\sqrt{3}+1)^2} = \sqrt{3}+1 = 1.732 + 1 = 2.732.$

To the nearest hundredth, the value is 2.73. The answer is 3.

Method 2 (using the denesting formula):

$\sqrt{4+2\sqrt{3}} = \sqrt{4+\sqrt{12}} = \sqrt{\frac{4+2}{2}} + \sqrt{\frac{4-2}{2}} = \sqrt{3}+\sqrt{1} = \sqrt{3}+1 \ \sqrt{3}+1 = 1.732$

$+ 1 = 2.732.$

To the nearest hundredth, the value is 2.73. The answer is 3.

Problem 3. Solution: $\sqrt{7}-\sqrt{2}$.

We rewrite the given radical as $\sqrt{9-2\sqrt{14}} = \sqrt{9-\sqrt{56}}$.

We see that $a = 9$, $b = 72$, and $a^2 - b = 9^2 - 56 = 25 = 5^2$. $k = 5$.

Therefore the given nested radical can be denested.

Method 1 (Completing the square):

$\sqrt{9-2\sqrt{14}} = \sqrt{(7+2)-2\sqrt{7\times 2}} = \sqrt{(\sqrt{7}-\sqrt{2})^2} = \sqrt{7}-\sqrt{2}.$

Method 2 (Using the denesting formula):

$\sqrt{9-2\sqrt{14}} = \sqrt{9-\sqrt{56}} \ \sqrt{\frac{9+5}{2}} - \sqrt{\frac{9-5}{2}} = \sqrt{7}-\sqrt{2}.$

Problem 4. Solution: 1530.

Expanding $(x\sqrt{3} + y\sqrt{5} + z\sqrt{8})^2$ we get: $3x^2 + 5y^2 + 8z^2 + 2xy\sqrt{15} + 4yz\sqrt{10} + 4zx\sqrt{6}$.

Equating this expression with $\sqrt{612\sqrt{6}+360\sqrt{10}+340\sqrt{15}+2015}$, we see that

$3x^2 + 5y^2 + 8z^2 = 2015$,

$2xy = 340$, $4xz = 612$, and $4yz = 360$.

The last three equations can be simplified into

$xy = 170$, $xz = 153$, and $yz = 90$.

The product of these three expressions can be written as $x^2y^2z^2 = xy \cdot xz \cdot yz = 2^6 \cdot 3^4 \cdot 13^2 \Rightarrow xyz = 1530$.

$x = \dfrac{xyz}{xy} = \dfrac{1530}{90} = 17$ and similarly $y = 10$ and $z = 9$.

We can check that indeed $3x^2 + 5y^2 + 8z^2 = 2015$.

Thus, $xyz = 17 \times 10 \times 9 = 1530$.

Problem 5. Solution: $2\sqrt{3}$.

We can rewrite the given radical as $\sqrt{9+6\sqrt{2}} = \sqrt{9+\sqrt{72}}$.

We see that $a = 9$, $b = 72$, and $a^2 - b = 9^2 - 72 = 9 = 3^2$. Therefore the given nested radical can be denested.

Method 1: By the formula, we have

$$\sqrt{9+\sqrt{72}} = \sqrt{\frac{9+\sqrt{9^2-72}}{2}} + \sqrt{\frac{9-\sqrt{9^2-72}}{2}} = \sqrt{6}+\sqrt{3}.$$

Similarly, $\sqrt{9-6\sqrt{2}} = \sqrt{9-\sqrt{72}} = \sqrt{\dfrac{9+\sqrt{9^2-72}}{2}} - \sqrt{\dfrac{9-\sqrt{9^2-72}}{2}} = \sqrt{6}-\sqrt{3}$.

Thus $\sqrt{9-6\sqrt{2}} - \sqrt{9+6\sqrt{2}} = \sqrt{6}+\sqrt{3} - (\sqrt{6}-\sqrt{3}) = 2\sqrt{3}$.

Method 2:

$$\sqrt{9-6\sqrt{2}} = \sqrt{9-2\sqrt{18}} = \sqrt{6-2\sqrt{18}+3} = \sqrt{(\sqrt{6})^2 - 2\sqrt{6}\times\sqrt{3} + (\sqrt{3})^2} = \sqrt{6}-\sqrt{3}$$

Similarly, $\sqrt{9+6\sqrt{2}} = \sqrt{6}+\sqrt{3}$.

Thus $\sqrt{9-6\sqrt{2}} - \sqrt{9+6\sqrt{2}} = \sqrt{6}+\sqrt{3} - (\sqrt{6}-\sqrt{3}) = 2\sqrt{3}$.

Problem 6. Solution: 25.

$$x = \frac{1}{\sqrt{3}-\sqrt{2}} = \frac{\sqrt{3}+\sqrt{2}}{(\sqrt{3}-\sqrt{2})(\sqrt{3}+\sqrt{2})} = \sqrt{3} + \sqrt{2}$$

$$y = \frac{1}{\sqrt{3}+\sqrt{2}} = \frac{\sqrt{3}-\sqrt{2}}{(\sqrt{3}+\sqrt{2})(\sqrt{3}-\sqrt{2})} = \sqrt{3} - \sqrt{2}$$

$\therefore x + y = 2\sqrt{3}$ and $xy = (\sqrt{3})^2 - (\sqrt{2})^2 = 1$.

$3x^2 - 5xy + 3y^2 = 3(x^2 + y^2) - 5xy = 3(x + y)^2 - 11xy$.

Substituting in the values that we calculated for $x + y$ and xy, we get

$3(x + y)^2 - 11xy = 3(2\sqrt{3})^2 - 11 = 25$.

Problem 7. Solution: 1.

Let $\sqrt[3]{2+\sqrt{5}} = a$, $\sqrt[3]{2-\sqrt{5}} = b$.

We get $S = a + b$.

Cubing both sides: $S^3 = (a + b)^3 = a^3 + b^3 + 3ab(a + b) = 4 + 3 \times (-1)S = 4 - 3S$.

$\therefore S^3 + 3S - 4 = 0$, $(S - 1)(S^2 + S + 4) = 0$.

Since the quadratic $S^2 + S + 4 = 0$ has no real solutions, the only answer is $S = 1$.

Problem 8. Solution: 5.

$\sqrt{x^2+6x+9} + \sqrt{x^2-4x+4} = |x+3| + |x-2|$.

Since $-3 < x < 2$, then $x + 2 > 0$ and $x - 2 < 0$.

Therefore, $|x+3|$ can be written as $x + 3$ and $|x-2|$ can be written as $-(x - 2)$.

$x + 3 - (x - 2) = x + 3 - x + 2 = 5$.

Problem 9. Solution:

Let $ax^3 = by^3 = cz^3 = t$.

Then $ax^2 = \frac{t}{x}$, $by^2 = \frac{t}{y}$, $cz^2 = \frac{t}{z}$.

$$\sqrt[3]{ax^2+by^2+cz^2} = \sqrt[3]{\frac{t}{x}+\frac{t}{y}+\frac{t}{z}} = \sqrt[3]{(\frac{1}{x}+\frac{1}{y}+\frac{1}{z})t}.$$

We know that $\frac{1}{x} + \frac{1}{y} + \frac{1}{z} = 1$.

Therefore

$\sqrt[3]{ax^2+by^2+cz^2} = (\frac{1}{x}+\frac{1}{y}+\frac{1}{z})\sqrt[3]{t} = \frac{1}{x}\sqrt[3]{ax^3}+\frac{1}{y}\sqrt[3]{by^3}+\frac{1}{z}\sqrt[3]{cz^3}$

$= \sqrt[3]{a}+\sqrt[3]{b}+\sqrt[3]{c}$.

Problem 10. Solution: $\frac{\sqrt{6}-\sqrt{2}}{2}$.

Method 1 (Completing the square):

$$\sqrt{2-\sqrt{3}} = \sqrt{\frac{2+\sqrt{2^2-3}}{2}} - \sqrt{\frac{2-\sqrt{2^2-3}}{2}} = \sqrt{\frac{3}{2}} - \sqrt{\frac{1}{2}} = \frac{\sqrt{6}-\sqrt{2}}{2}.$$

Method 2 (Using the denesting formula):

$$\sqrt{2-\sqrt{3}} = \sqrt{\frac{2+\sqrt{2^2-3}}{2}} - \sqrt{\frac{2-\sqrt{2^2-3}}{2}} = \sqrt{\frac{3}{2}} - \sqrt{\frac{1}{2}} = \frac{\sqrt{6}-\sqrt{2}}{2}.$$

Problem 11. Solution: 33.

Method 1:

$(1+\sqrt{2})^4 = [(1+\sqrt{2})^2]^2 = (3+2\sqrt{2})^2 = 17+12\sqrt{2}$.

We know that $\sqrt{2} \approx 1.414 \quad \Rightarrow \quad 1.41 < \sqrt{2} < 1.415$.

So $16.92 < 12\sqrt{2} < 16.98 \quad \Rightarrow \quad 33.92 < 17 + 12\sqrt{2} < 33.98$.

Therefore the integer part of $(1+\sqrt{2})^4$ is 33.

Method 2:

$(1+\sqrt{2})^4 = [(1+\sqrt{2})^2]^2 = (3+2\sqrt{2})^2$.

We also know that

$(3+2\sqrt{2})^2 + (3-2\sqrt{2})^2$

$= 9+12\sqrt{2}+8+9-12\sqrt{2}+8 = 34$.

Since $0 < 3-2\sqrt{2} < 1$ and $0 < (3-2\sqrt{2})^2 < 1$, we can conclude that the integer part of $(1+\sqrt{2})^4$ is 33.

Problem 12. Solution: $x \geq 8$.

Method 1 (official solution):

$\sqrt{x-4\sqrt{x-4}} = \sqrt{(\sqrt{x-4})^2 - 4\sqrt{x-4}+4} = \sqrt{(\sqrt{x-4}-2)^2} = \left|\sqrt{x-4}-2\right|$.

Similarly,

$\sqrt{x+4\sqrt{x-4}} = \sqrt{(\sqrt{x-4})^2 + 4\sqrt{x-4}+4} = \sqrt{(\sqrt{x-4}+2)^2} = \left|\sqrt{x-4}+2\right|$.

We must show $\left|\sqrt{x-4}+2\right| - \left|\sqrt{x-4}-2\right| = 4$. This last equation is satisfied by all $x \ge 8$.

Method 2 (our solution):

$\sqrt{x+4\sqrt{x-4}} = \sqrt{(\sqrt{x-4})^2 + 4\sqrt{x-4}+4} = \sqrt{(\sqrt{x-4}+2)^2} = \left|\sqrt{x-4}+2\right|$.

Since $x > 4$, $\left|\sqrt{x-4}+2\right| = \sqrt{x-4}+2$.

The original equation becomes: $\sqrt{x-4\sqrt{x-4}} + 2 = \sqrt{x-4} + 2 - 2 \quad \Rightarrow$

$\sqrt{x-4\sqrt{x-4}} = \sqrt{x-4} - 2$.

Since $\sqrt{x-4\sqrt{x-4}} \ge 0$, $\sqrt{x-4} - 2 \ge 0 \quad \Rightarrow \quad \sqrt{x-4} \ge 2 \quad \Rightarrow \quad x-4 \ge 4 \Rightarrow \quad x \ge 8$.

Problem 13. Solution: (9, –1).

Rearranging, $(\sqrt{x}+1)(\sqrt{6}-2) = (\sqrt{x}-1)(\sqrt{5}-\sqrt{3})$. Squaring, $(x+1)(10-4\sqrt{6}) = (x-1)(8-2\sqrt{15})$. This equation is linear in x. Solving, $x = (9-\sqrt{15}-\sqrt{24})/(-1-\sqrt{15}+\sqrt{24})$, so $(a, b) = (9, -1)$.

Problem 14. Solution: 1.

Since $3x - 1 \ge 0$, $x \ge \frac{1}{3}$.

Since $5x - 3 \ge 0$, $x \ge \frac{3}{5}$.

Since $x - 1 \ge 0$, $x \ge 1$.

Therefore the domain is $x \ge 1$ as shown in the figure below.

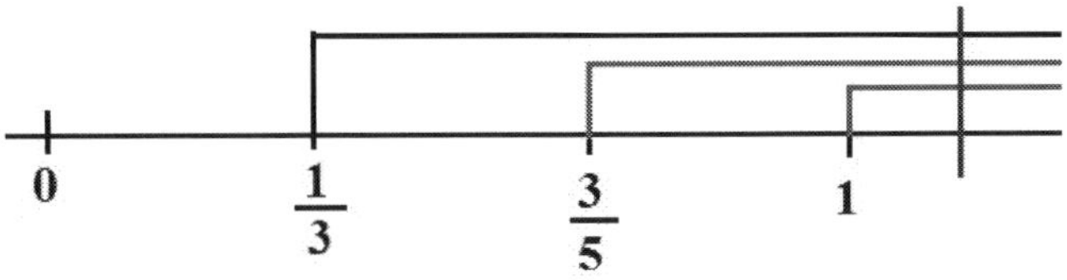

When $x \ge 1$, we have
$\sqrt{3x-1} \ge \sqrt{2}$, $\sqrt{5x-3} \ge \sqrt{2}$, and $\sqrt{x-1} \ge 0$.

Therefore $\sqrt{3x-1} + \sqrt{5x-3} + \sqrt{x-1} \ge 2\sqrt{2}$.

The equality holds if and only if $x = 1$.
We can check this by plugging it into the original equation and seeing that the left hand side equals the right hand side.

Problem 15. Solution: 5, –5.
Let $\sqrt{x^2-9} = y$. We have $x^2 = y^2 + 9$.

Substituting this into the given equation we have $y^2 - y - 12 = 0$.
Solving the quadratic equation for y, we get: $y_1 = 4$, $y_2 = -3$.

We have $\sqrt{x^2-9} = 4$ or $\sqrt{x^2-9} = -3$ (extraneous).
Solving $\sqrt{x^2-9} = 4$ for x: $x_1 = 5$, $x_2 = -5$.

We can check that both $x_1 = 5$ and $x_2 = -5$ are the solutions by plugging it into the original equation and seeing that the left hand side equals the right hand side.

Problem 16. Solution: 1.
Let $\sqrt{x} - \sqrt{x+8} = y$.

Squaring both sides we get:
$y^2 = x + x + 8 - 2\sqrt{x(x+8)}$.

Therefore $2x + 2 - 2\sqrt{x(x+8)} = y^2 - 6$.

The original equation can be written as $y^2 - 6 = y$.

Solving for y: $y_1 = 3$, $y_2 = -2$.
We have $\sqrt{x} - \sqrt{x+8} = 3$ or $\sqrt{x} - \sqrt{x+8} = -2$.
Since $\sqrt{x} < \sqrt{x+8}$, $\sqrt{x} - \sqrt{x+8} = 3$ cannot be true, so we only solve $\sqrt{x} - \sqrt{x+8} = -2$. We get $x = 1$.

We can check that that $x = 1$ is the solution by plugging it into the original equation and seeing that the left hand side equals the right hand side.

Problem 17. Solution: 80, –109.

Let $u = \sqrt[3]{x+45}$, and $v = \sqrt[3]{x-16}$.

$$u - v = 1 \qquad (1)$$
$$u^3 - v^3 = 61 \qquad (2)$$
$$(2) \div (1): u^2 + uv + v^2 = 61 \qquad (3)$$

From (1) and (3), we get $v_1 = 4$, $v_2 = -5$.

Since $v^3 = x - 16$, $x = v^3 + 16$.
$x_1 = 64 + 16 = 80$, $x_2 = -125 + 16 = -109$.

We can check that both $x_1 = 80$ and $x_2 = -109$ are the solutions by plugging it into the original equation and seeing that the left hand side equals the right hand side.

Note: We do not need to check to make sure that $u \ge 0$ and $v \ge 0$, since $x + 45$ or $x - 16$ can be negative.

Problem 18. Solution: $x = \dfrac{1+\sqrt{5}}{2}$

Let $\sqrt{x - \dfrac{1}{x}} = u$ and $\sqrt{1 - \dfrac{1}{x}} = v$.

We have $u + v = x$.

Since $u - v = \dfrac{u^2 - v^2}{u + v}$, $u - v = \dfrac{x - \frac{1}{x} - 1 + \frac{1}{x}}{x} = 1 - \dfrac{1}{x}$.

Then we get $2u = x + 1 - \dfrac{1}{x} \Rightarrow 2u = u^2 + 1$.

Therefore $u = 1$ ($u = -1$ is extraneous) and $x - \dfrac{1}{x} = 1$.

Solving $x - \dfrac{1}{x} = 1$ we get $x = \dfrac{1 \pm \sqrt{5}}{2}$ ($x = \dfrac{1 - \sqrt{5}}{2}$ is extraneous since x must be positive).

We can check that $x = \dfrac{1 + \sqrt{5}}{2}$ is a solution by plugging it into the original equation and seeing that the left hand side equals the right hand side.

Problem 19. Solution: $\sqrt{2}$.

The average value of x and $\dfrac{x}{\sqrt{x^2 - 1}}$ is $\sqrt{2}$.

Therefore we let

$x = \sqrt{2} + t$ and $\dfrac{x}{\sqrt{x^2 - 1}} = \sqrt{2} - t$.

$$x^2 = 2 + 2\sqrt{2}\,t + t^2 \qquad (1)$$

$$\frac{x^2}{x^2 - 1} = 2 - 2\sqrt{2}\,t + t^2 \qquad (2)$$

From (1), we have: $x^2 - 1 = 1 + 2\sqrt{2}\,t + t^2$ (3)

From (2), we have: $\dfrac{1}{x^2 - 1} = 1 - 2\sqrt{2}\,t + t^2$ (4)

(3) × (4): $1 = (1 + 2\sqrt{2}\,t + t^2)(1 - 2\sqrt{2}\,t + t^2)$.

Simplifying: $t^4 - 6t^2 = 0$.
Solving for t: $t = 0$ or $t = \pm\sqrt{6}$.
So $x = \sqrt{2}$ or $x = \sqrt{2} \pm \sqrt{6}$.

We see that only $x = \sqrt{2}$ is a solution after plugging these two values into the original equation and seeing that the left hand side equals the right hand side.

Problem 20. Solution: $x = 1$ and $x = -4$.

Multiply both sides of the given equation by 2:
$4x^2 + 2x\sqrt{3x^2+1} = 8$.
Then, add 1 to both sides:
$x^2 + 2x\sqrt{3x^2+1} + 3x^2 + 1 = 9$.
The original equation can then be written as
$(x+\sqrt{3x^2+1})^2 = 9$.
We have $x+\sqrt{3x^2+1} = 3 \quad \Rightarrow \quad x = 1$ or $x = -4$.
We also have $x+\sqrt{3x^2+1} = -3 \quad \Rightarrow \quad x = -1$ or $x = 4$.

We can check that both $x = 1$ and $x = -4$ are the solutions by plugging it into the original equation and seeing that the left hand side equals the right hand side.

Problem 21. Solution: 1, – 6.
We are given the equation $\sqrt{x^2+5x-2} - \sqrt{x^2+5x-5} = 1$ (1)

Rationalizing the left hand side by multiplying it by $\dfrac{\sqrt{x^2+5x-2}+\sqrt{x^2+5x-5}}{\sqrt{x^2+5x-2}+\sqrt{x^2+5x-5}}$

= 1, we get: $\dfrac{3}{\sqrt{x^2+5x-2}+\sqrt{x^2+5x-5}} = 1$

$\Rightarrow \sqrt{x^2+5x-2}+\sqrt{x^2+5x-5} = 3.$ (2)

[(1) + (2)]/2: $\sqrt{x^2+5x-2} = 2$ (3)
[(2) – (1)]/2: $\sqrt{x^2+5x-5} = 1$ (4)

Solving (3) for x: $x = 1$ or $x = -6$.
Solving (4) for x: $x = 1$ or $x = -6$.

We can check that both $x = 1$ and $x = -6$ are the solutions by plugging them into the original equation and seeing that the left hand side equals the right hand side.

Problem 22. Solution: 2.
The original equation can be rewritten as
$3\sqrt{(x^2+1)^2-4x^2} + 2x\sqrt{(x^2+1)^2-9} = (x^2+1)^2$.

Let $f(x) = 3$, $g(x) = 2x$, $h(x) = (x^2 + 1)^2$.

The original equation has the same solutions as $9 + 4x^2 = (x^2 + 1)^2$, $(x \ge 0)$.
$x^4+2x^2+1=9+4x^2 \Rightarrow \quad x^4-2x^2-8=0 \quad \Rightarrow \quad (x^2-1)-9=0$
$\Rightarrow \quad (x^2-1-3)(x^2-1+3)=0$
There is one solution $x = 2$.

Problem 23. Solution: No solutions.
Since $2x - 3 \ge 0$, $x \ge \dfrac{3}{2}$.
Since $1-x \ge 0, x \le 1$.

There exists no such value for x satisfying both the inequalities listed above. Therefore there is no solution to the given equation.

Problem 24. Solution: 16, 81.

Let $u = \sqrt[4]{x}$, $v = \sqrt[4]{97-x}$.
$u + v = 5$ (1)
$u^4 + v^4 = 97$ (2)

We know that
$u^4 + v^4 = (u + v)^4 - 4uv(u + v)^2 + 2u^2v^2 = 625 - 100uv + 2u^2v^2 = 97$.

Therefore $u^2v^2 - 50uv + 264 = 0$ (3)
From (1) and (3), we get $u_1 = 2$, $u_2 = 3$ and $v_1 = 3$, $v_2 = 2$, which satisfies $u \ge 0$, $v \ge 0$.

In other words, $\sqrt[4]{x} = 2$ or $\sqrt[4]{x} = 3$.
Solving for x: $x_1 = 16$, $x_2 = 81$.

We can check that both $x_1 = 16$ and $x_2 = 81$ are the solutions by plugging them into the original equation and seeing that the left hand side equals the right hand side.

Problem 25. Solution: 4.
We are given the equation $\sqrt{x+5} + \sqrt{x-3} = 4$ (1)

Rationalizing the left hand side by multiplying it by $\dfrac{\sqrt{x+5}-\sqrt{x-3}}{\sqrt{x+5}+\sqrt{x-3}}$, we get:

$$\frac{8}{\sqrt{x+5}-\sqrt{x-3}} = 4 \Rightarrow \qquad \sqrt{x+5} - \sqrt{x-3} = 2 \qquad (2)$$

(1) + (2): $\sqrt{x+5} = 3$ (3)
(1) – (2): $\sqrt{x-3} = 1$ (4)
Solving (3) for x: $x = 4$.
Solving (4) for x: $x = 4$.

We can check that 4 is the solution by plugging it into the original equation and seeing that the left hand side equals the right hand side.

Problem 26. Solution: 243.
Let $\sqrt[3]{x} = y$.
The given equation can be written as $y^2 - 9y + 18 = 0$.

Solving: $y = 3$ or $y = 6$.
Therefore $x = 3^3$ or 6^3.
The sum is $3^3 + 6^3 = 243$.

Problem 27. Solution: $x_1 = -109$ and $x_2 = 80$.

Method 1:
Let $\sqrt[3]{45+x} = u$, $\sqrt[3]{16-x} = v$

$$\begin{cases} u+v=1, & (1) \\ u^3+v^3=61 & (2) \end{cases}$$

From (1) and (2), we can get $uv = -20$ (3)

From (1) and (3), we get $\begin{cases} u=-4, \\ v=5; \end{cases}$ or $\begin{cases} u=5, \\ v=-4. \end{cases}$

$\therefore \sqrt[3]{16-x} = 5$ or $\sqrt[3]{16-x} = -4$.

Solving we get $x_1 = -109,\ x_2 = 80$.

We can check that both $x_1 = -109$ and $x_2 = 80$ are the solutions by plugging it into the original equation and seeing that the left hand side equals the right hand side.

Method 2:

The given equation can be written as $\sqrt[3]{45+x} + \sqrt[3]{16-x} + \sqrt[3]{-1} = 0$.

Let $a = \sqrt[3]{45+x}$, $b = \sqrt[3]{16-x}$, $c = \sqrt[3]{-1}$.

We observe that $a + b + c = 0$.

Therefore we have $a^3 + b^3 + c^3 = 3abc$.

Or $(45 + x) + (16 - x) + (-1) = 3\sqrt[3]{45+x} \cdot \sqrt[3]{16-x} \cdot \sqrt[3]{-1} \Rightarrow \sqrt[3]{(45+x)(x-16)}$ $= 20$.

Solving for x we get $x_1 = -109,\ x_2 = 80$.

We can check that both $x_1 = -109$ and $x_2 = 80$ are the solutions by plugging it into the original equation and seeing that the left hand side equals the right hand side.

Problem 28. Solution:

$$\sqrt{x+\sqrt{2x-1}} + \sqrt{x-\sqrt{2x-1}} = \frac{1}{\sqrt{2}}(\sqrt{2x+2\sqrt{2x-1}} + \sqrt{2x-2\sqrt{2x-1}})$$

$$= \frac{1}{\sqrt{2}}(\left|\sqrt{2x-1}+1\right| + \left|\sqrt{2x-1}-1\right|)$$

$$= \begin{cases} \dfrac{2\sqrt{2x-1}}{\sqrt{2}} = \sqrt{2}\cdot\sqrt{2x-1}, & \text{if } \sqrt{2x-1} > 1, \text{ or } x > 1; \\ \dfrac{2}{\sqrt{2}} = \sqrt{2}, & \text{if } \sqrt{2x-1} \le 1, \text{ or } \dfrac{1}{2} \le x \le 1. \end{cases}$$

(a) The equation holds for $1/2 \le x \le 1$.
(b) The equation has no solution.
(c) The equation holds for $4x - 2 = 4 \Rightarrow x = 3/2$.

Angle – Measure – Sum Principles – Triangles

Theorem 1. The sum of the measures of the angles of a triangle equals the measure of a straight angle, or 180°. $\angle A + \angle B + \angle C = 180°$

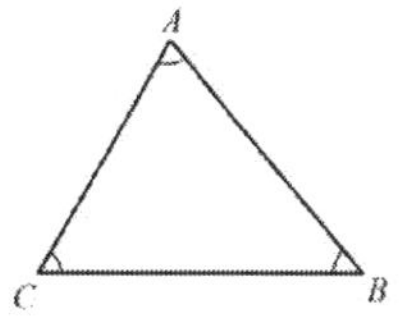

Proof:
We draw the line m parallel to BC, the base of the triangle.
So $\angle C = \angle x$, $\angle B = \angle y$.
Since $\angle A + \angle x + \angle y = 180°$, $\angle A + \angle B + \angle C = 180°$.

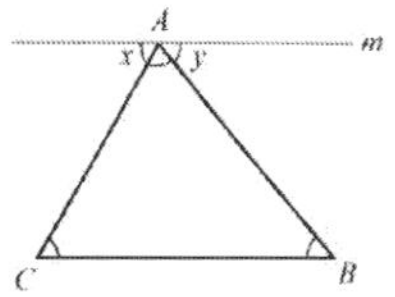

Theorem 2 (The Exterior Angle Theorem): The measure of each exterior angle of a triangle equals the sum of the measures of its two remote nonadjacent interior angles.
$z = a + b;\ x = b + c;\ y = c + a$

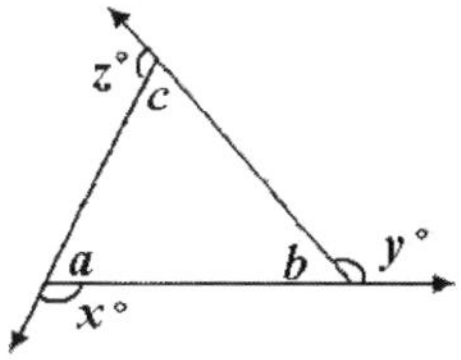

Proof:

$b + y = 180°$ (1)

$a + b + c = 180°$ (2)

(1) – (2): $+ y - (c + a) = 0 \Rightarrow y = c + a$

Similarly we can prove $x = b + c$ and $z = a + b$.

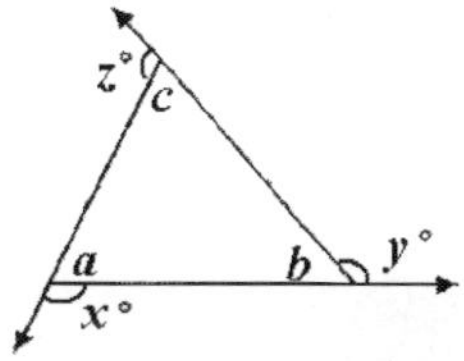

Theorem 3. The sum of the measures of the exterior angles of a triangle equals 360°.
$x + y + z = 360°$

Proof:

$x = b + c$ (1)

$y = a + c$ (2)

$z = a + b$ (3)

$a + b + c = 180°$ (4)

(1) + (2) + (3): $a + b + c + x + y + z = 540°$ (5)

Substituting (4) into (5): $x + y + z = 360°$.

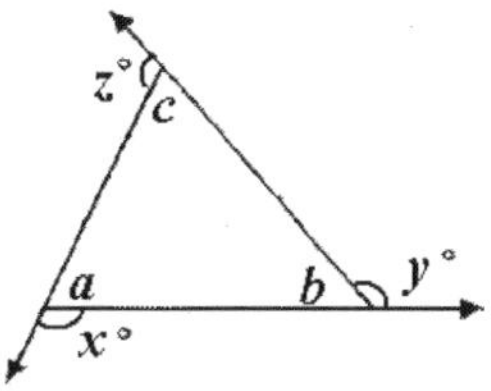

Theorem 4. The four angles in the figure below have the following relationship: $\angle D = \angle A + \angle B + \angle C$.

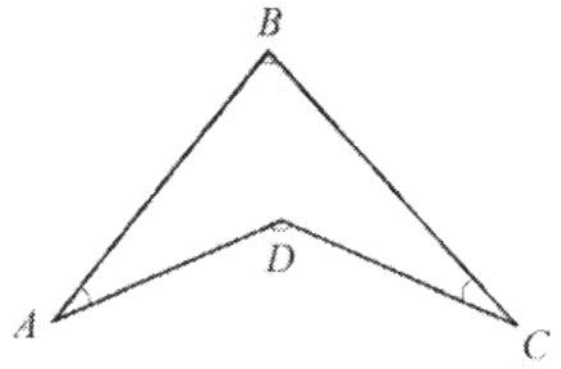

Proof:
Extend AD to meet BC at E.
By **Theorem 2**, $\angle D = \alpha + \angle C$ (1)
By **Theorem 2**, $\alpha = \angle A + \angle B$ (2)
Substituting (2) into (1): $\angle D = \angle A + \angle B + \angle C$.

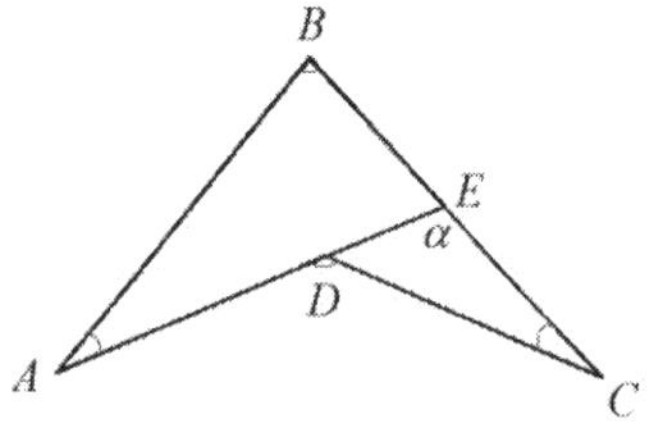

Theorem 5. Triangle ABC has $\angle B > \angle C$. The angle between the altitude and the angle bisector at vertex A is $\frac{1}{2}\angle B - \frac{1}{2}\angle C$.

Proof:
We know that $AE \perp BC$.
So $\angle DAE = 90° - \angle ADE = 90° - (\angle DAC + \angle C)$
$= 90° - \angle C - \frac{1}{2}\angle BAC$
We also know that $\angle BAC = 180° - (\angle B + \angle C)$. So
$\frac{1}{2}\angle BAC = 90° - \frac{1}{2}\angle B - \frac{1}{2}\angle C$.

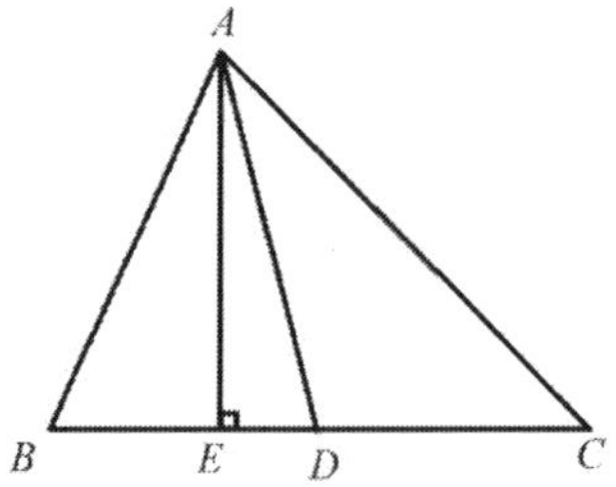

Then $\angle DAE = 90° - \angle C - (90° - \frac{1}{2}\angle B - \frac{1}{2}\angle C) = \frac{1}{2}\angle B - \frac{1}{2}\angle C$.

Theorem 6. The measure of the sum of all interior angles of a regular n-sided polygon is $(n-2)\times 180°$. The measure of an interior angle of a regular n-sided polygon is $\frac{(n-2)\times 180°}{n}$.

Theorem 7.1 If the median to a side of a triangle is one-half of the measure of that side, i.e. $AM = MB = MC$, then triangle ABC is a right triangle with $\angle C = 90°$.

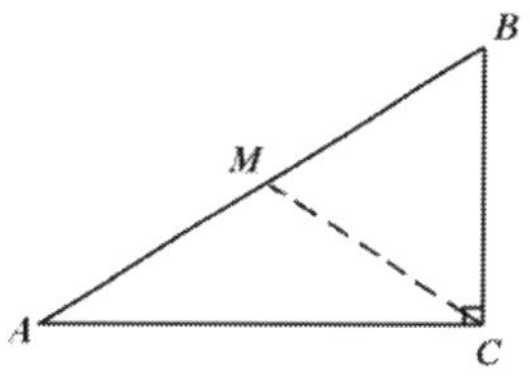

Theorem 7.2 Triangle ABC has three sides with the ratio of the lengths $BC : AB : AC = 1 : \sqrt{3} : 2$, then triangle ABC is a 30 ° – 60 ° - 90 ° right triangle with $\angle A = 30°$.

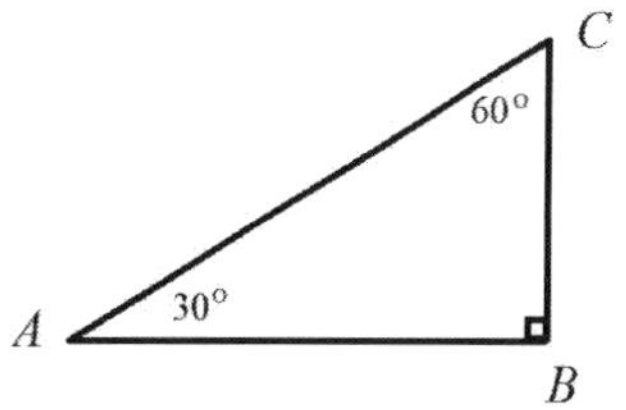

Angle-measurement Principles - Circles

Theorem 8.1. A central angle is measured by its intercepted arc.

$\angle AOB = \overset{\frown}{AB}$

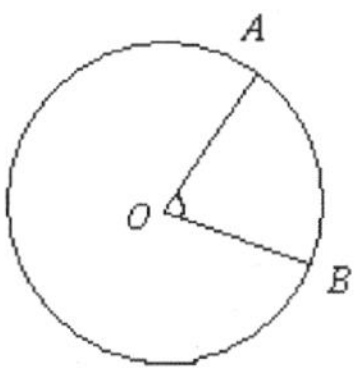

Theorem 8.2. An inscribed angle is measured by one-half its intercepted arc.

$\angle ACB = \frac{1}{2}\overset{\frown}{AB}$

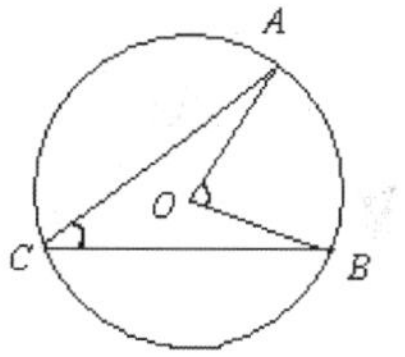

Theorem 9.1. $\angle 1 = \frac{1}{2}(\overset{\frown}{CB} + \overset{\frown}{DB})$

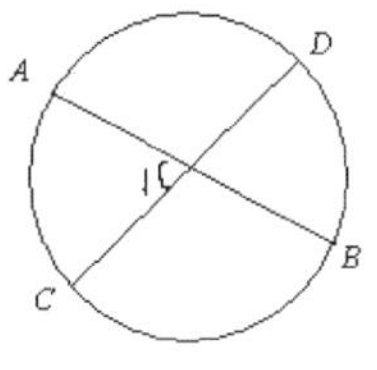

Theorem 9.2. $\angle A = \frac{1}{2}(\overset{\frown}{CB} - \overset{\frown}{DE}) = \frac{1}{2}(b - a)$

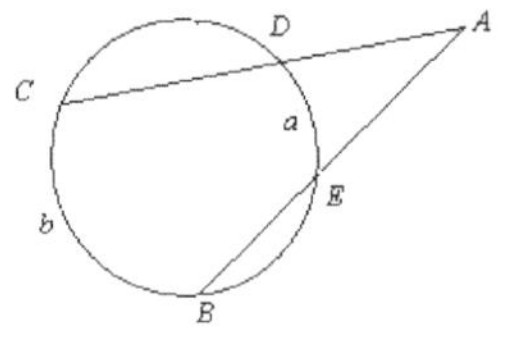

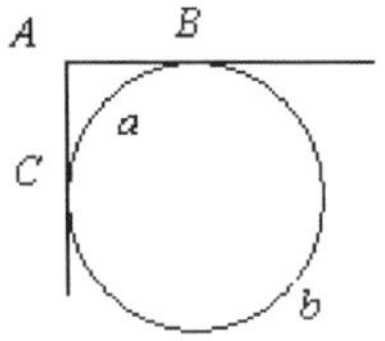

Theorem 10. In the same or congruent circles, congruent inscribed angles have congruent intercepted arcs.

$\angle ADB = \angle ACB$

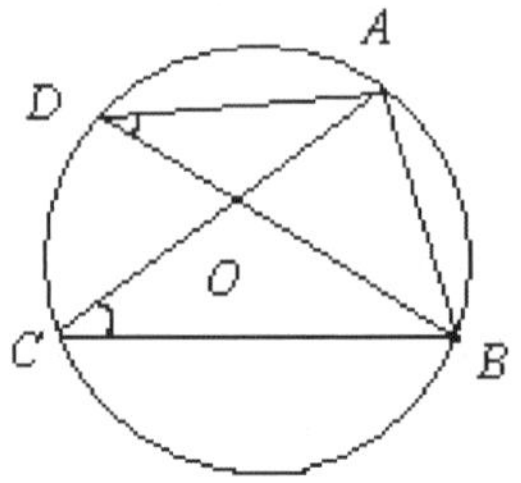

Theorem 11. Opposite angles of an inscribed quadrilateral are supplementary.

$\angle A + \angle C = \angle B + \angle D = 180°.$
$\angle EBC = \angle D$

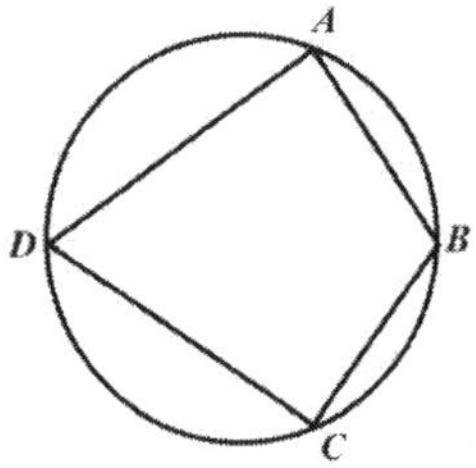

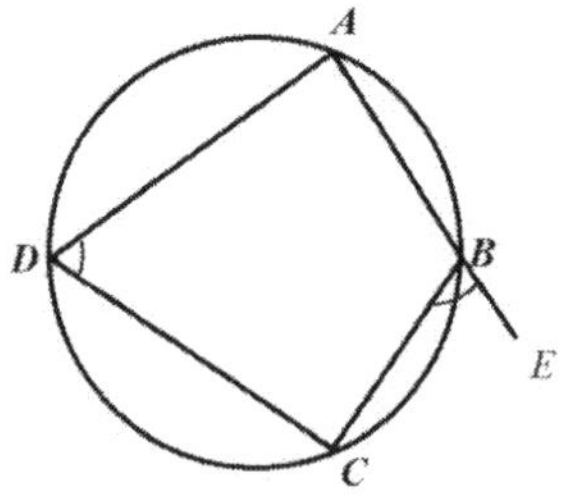

Example 1. (2004 ARML) In the diagram, BD bisects $\angle ABC$ and CE is the trisector of $\angle ACB$ that is closest to BC. If $m\angle A = T$ and $m\angle DBC - m\angle ECB = T/3$, compute the degree measure of $\angle DBC$.

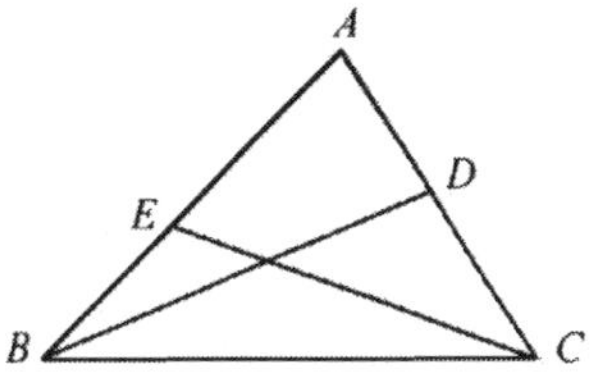

Solution: 36°.
Method 1 (official solution):
Since $2x + 3y + T = 180°$, then $3x + 3y = 180° - T + x$, giving $x + y = 60° + (x - T)/3$. It is given that $x - y = T/3$ so adding the equations yields $2x = 60° + x/3$. Thus, $x = 36°$ and T is irrelevant

Method 2 (our solution):

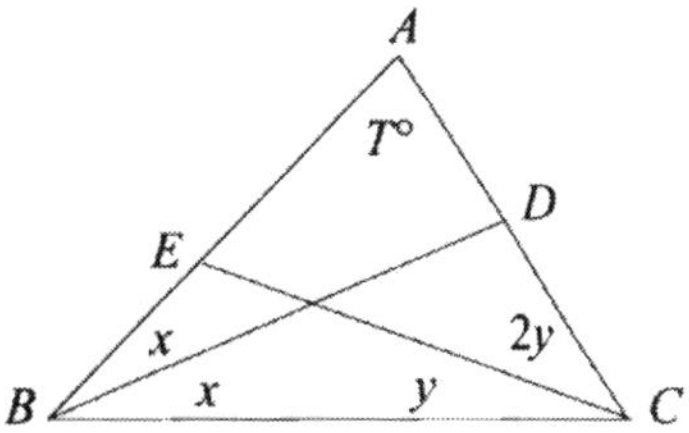

$$2x + 3y + T = 180° \qquad (1)$$

$$x - y = \frac{T}{3} \quad \Rightarrow \quad 3x - 3y = T \qquad (2)$$

$$(1) + (2): \; 5x = 180° \quad \Rightarrow \quad x = 36°.$$

Example 2. (NYML) In a right triangle, the larger acute angle, θ, is 5 times the angle between the altitude and median to the hypotenuse. Compute the number of degrees in θ.

Solution: 50.
Method 1 (official solution):
Since the median is half the hypotenuse, it creates an isosceles triangle whose angles are (θ, θ, and $90 - (\theta/k)$. Setting their sum equal to 180 produces $\theta = 90k/(2k - 1) = 50$.

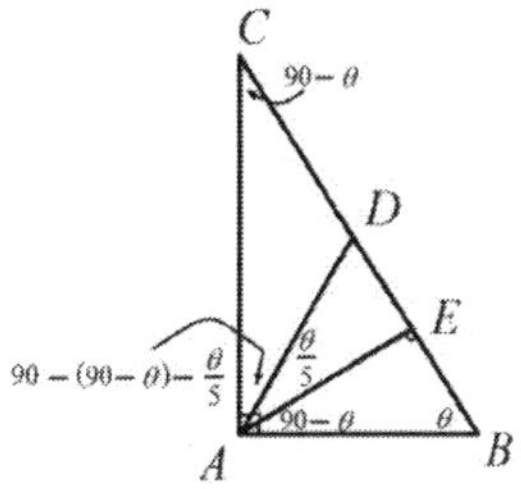

Method 2 (our solution):

Let $\angle B = \theta$, $\angle DAE = \dfrac{\theta}{5}$.

So $\angle BAE = 90 - \theta$, $\angle BCA = 90 - \theta$, and

$\angle DAC = 90-(90-\theta)-\frac{\theta}{5}=\frac{4}{5}\theta$.

Since AD is the median of right triangle ABC, $AD = CD$.

So $\angle DAC = \angle DCA \Rightarrow \frac{4}{5}\theta = 90-\theta \Rightarrow \theta = 50$.

Example 3. (2006 ARML) If $ABCDE$ is a regular pentagon and $MNCD$ is a square, compute the value of $m\angle AMN - m\angle EAM$ in degrees.

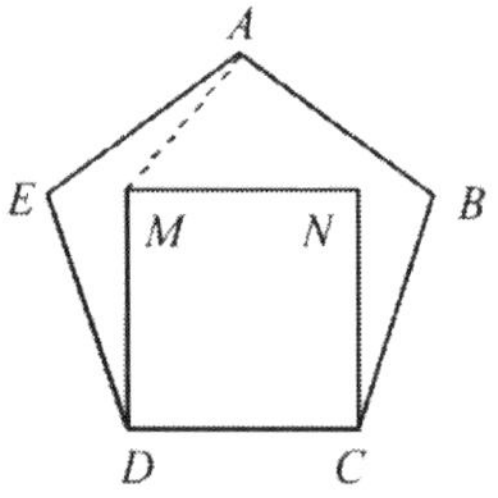

Solution: 36.
Method 1 (official solution):
Draw line PA parallel to MN. Set $m\angle AMN = x$ and $m\angle EAM = y$.

Since $m\angle PAM = m\angle AMN = x$, then $m\angle PAE = x - y$.

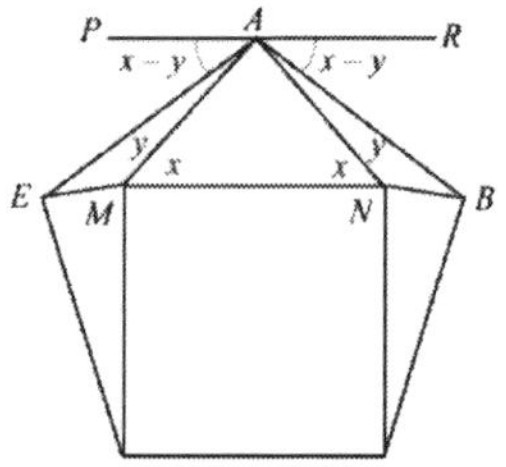

Since $m\angle RAB = x - y$, then $180 = 2(x - y) + 108 \Rightarrow x - y = 36$.

Method 2 (official solution):
Let $m\angle EAM = x$; the other angles are as marked. Note: $m\angle AEM = 27$. Since $m\angle EMA = 180 - (27 + x) = 153 - x$, then $m\angle AMN = 360 - (90 + 81 + 153 - x) = 36 + x$. Thus, $m\angle AMN - m\angle EAM = (36 + x) - x = 36$.

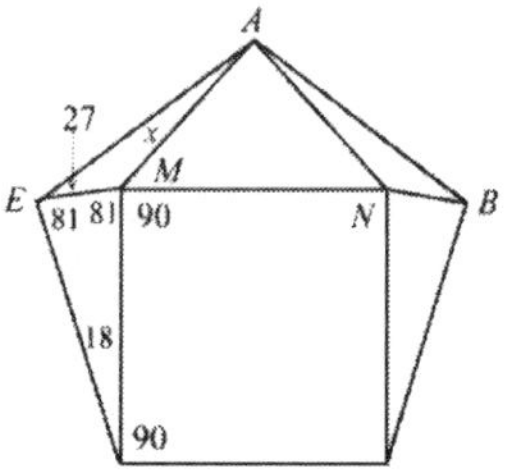

Method 3 (our solution):

Extend AN to meet BC at P. $\angle B = \frac{(5-2)\times 180}{5} = 108°$.

$\angle C = 108 - 80 = 18°$. $\angle CNP = 90 - x$. $\angle CPN = 108 + y$.

The sum of three interior angles of triangle CNP is 180: $18° + 90 - x + 108 + y = 180° \quad \Rightarrow x - y = 36$.

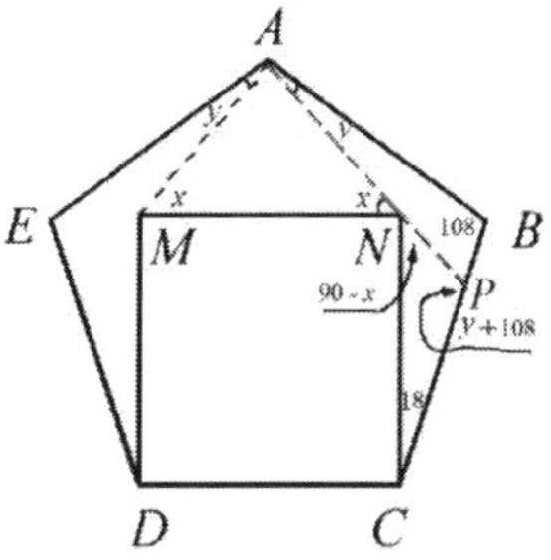

Method 4 (our solution):
Let $m\angle MAN = 108 - 2y$. Then in triangle AMN: $2x + (108 - 2y) = 180$, giving $2x - 2y = 72 \Rightarrow x - y = 36$.

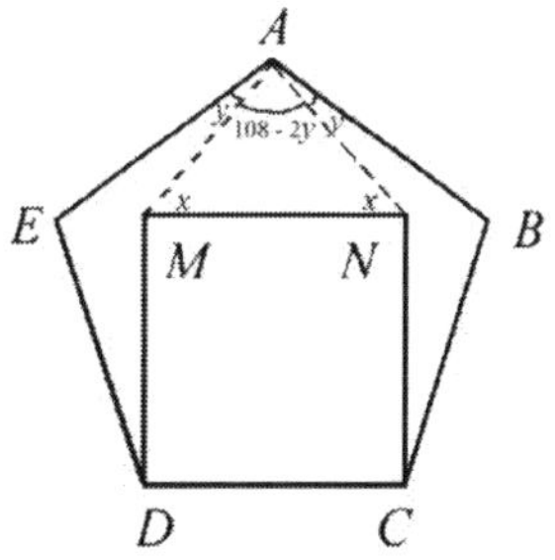

Example 4. (1998 ARML) Let positive integers A, B, and C be the angles of a triangle such that $A \le B \le C$. Determine the number of all the values that C can take on.

Solution: 119.
The maximum of C occurs when $A = B = 1° \Rightarrow C = 178°$.
The minimum of C occurs when $A = B = C = 60°$.
$178 - 60 + 1 = 119$. The number of all the values that C can take on is 119.

Example 5. (1998 ARML) In acute-angled triangle ABC, $m\angle A = (x + 15)°$, $m\angle B = (2x - 6)°$, and the exterior angle at C has measure $(3x + 9)°$. Compute the number of possible integral values of x.

Solution: 20.
Since an exterior angle of a triangle is equal to the sum of the two remote interior angles, we set $3x + 9 = (x + 15) + (2x - 6)$, but that is an identity and is of no help. Since the triangle is acute-angled, we have several conditions to consider. First, $m\angle A < 90° \Rightarrow x + 15° < 90° \Rightarrow x < 75°$. Second, $m\angle B < 90° \Rightarrow 2x - 6 < 90° \Rightarrow x$

$< 48°$. Third, since $\angle C$ is acute, then $3x + 9°$ is obtuse, giving $90° < 3x + 9° < 180° \Rightarrow 27° < x < 57°$. Considering all the conditions, we have $27° < x < 48°$, giving $x \in \{28°, 29°, \ldots, 46°, 47°\}$. Thus, the number of integral values of x is 20.

Example 6. (NYML) In triangle ABC, $\angle B$ is obtuse and $AB > BC$. An angle bisector of an exterior angle at A meets BC at D; an angle bisector of an exterior angle at B meets AC at E. If $AD = AB = BE$, find $m\angle BAC$.

Solution: 12.

Method 1 (official solution):

In figure below, let $m\angle BAC = m\angle BEC = \theta$. Then $m\angle FBE = 2\theta = m\angle EBC$, and also $m\angle DBA = 4\theta = m\angle ADB$. But, $m\angle DAB = (180° - \theta)/2$ and $(180° - \theta)/2 + 4\theta + 4\theta = 180° \Rightarrow \theta = 12°$.

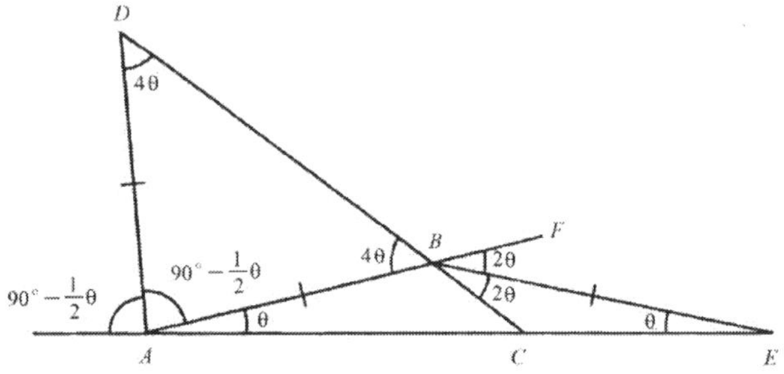

Method 2 (our solution):

In figure below, let $m\angle BAC = m\angle BEC = \theta$. Then $m\angle FBE = 2\theta$.

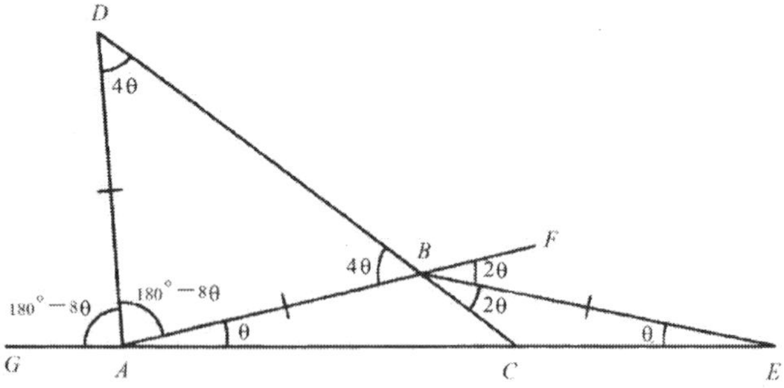

Since BE is the angle bisector of $\angle B$, $m\angle EBC = m\angle FBE = 2\theta$.

Angels $\angle DBA$ and $\angle FBC$ are vertical angles, so $m\angle DBA = 4\theta$. Since $AD = AB$, $m\angle ADB = m\angle DBA = 4\theta$. Thus $m\angle DAB = 180° - 8\theta = m\angle DAG$

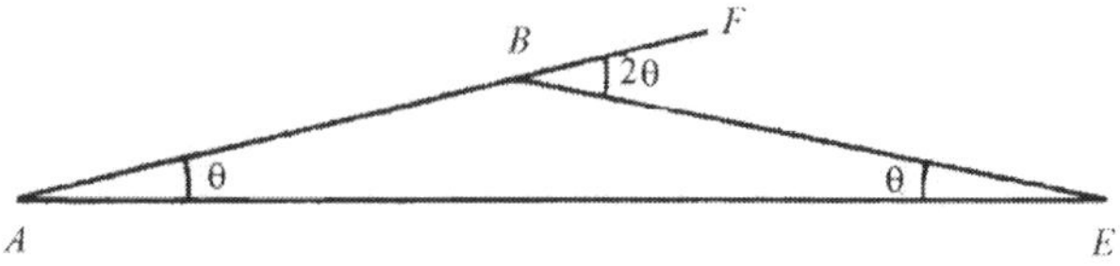

For triangle ABD, we have $180° - 8\theta + 180° - 8\theta + \theta = 180° \Rightarrow \theta = 12°$.

Example 7. (NYML) Two rays begin at point A and form an angle of 43° with one another. Lines l, m, and n (no two of which are parallel) each form an isosceles triangle with the original rays. Compute the largest angle of the triangle formed by lines l, m, and n.

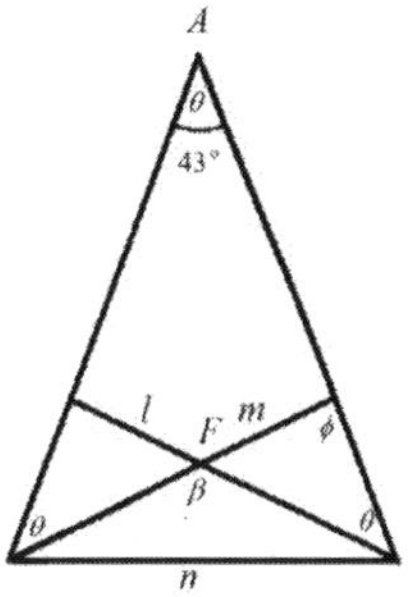

Solution: 129°.
Method 1 (official solution):
Placing the three lines in a convenient position (which does not affect the angles formed), we have $\phi = 2\theta \Rightarrow \beta = 3\theta =$ 129° or 129.

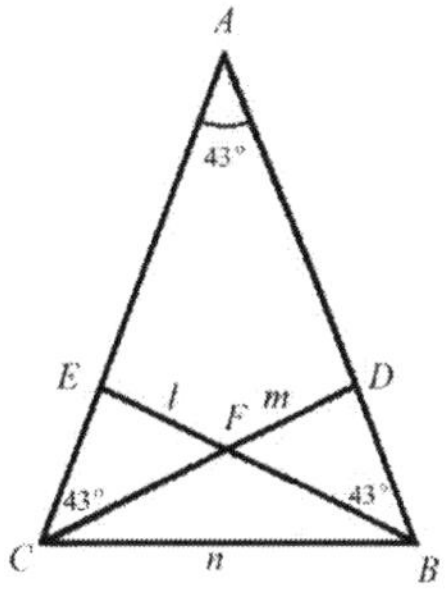

Method 2 (our solution):
$\angle CFB = \angle ACB + \angle ABE + \angle CAB = 43° + 43° + 43°$
$= 3 \times 43° = 129°$.

Example 8. (2006 ARML) If $AB = AC$, BD bisects $\angle ABC$, CD bisects $\angle ACB$, and $m\angle A = 18°$, compute $m\angle BDC$.

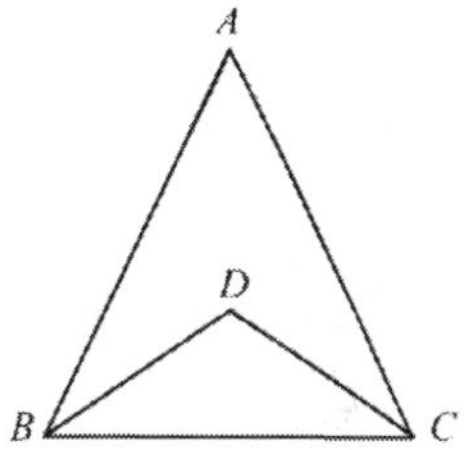

Solution: 99.
Method 1 (official solution):

Set $m\angle A = 4x$,then $m\angle ABC = \angle ACB = \dfrac{180-4x}{2} = 90 - 2x$

$\Rightarrow m\angle DBC = m\angle DCB = 45 - x$.

Thus, $m\angle D = 180 - (90 - 2x) = 90 + 2x$. Since $4x = 18$, then $2x = 9$, so $m\angle D = 99$.

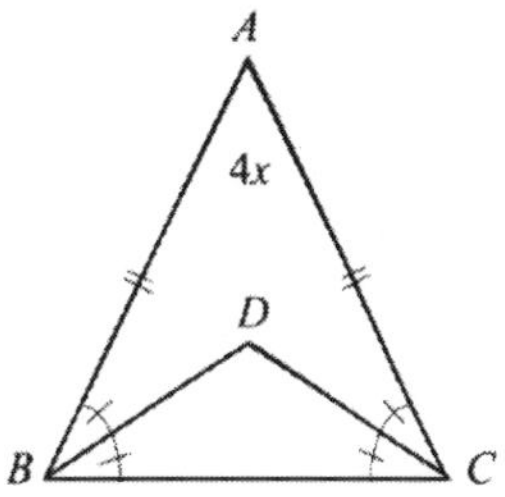

Method 2 (our solution):

By **Theorem 4,** $\angle D = \dfrac{180-18}{4} + \dfrac{180-18}{4} + 18$

$= 36$.

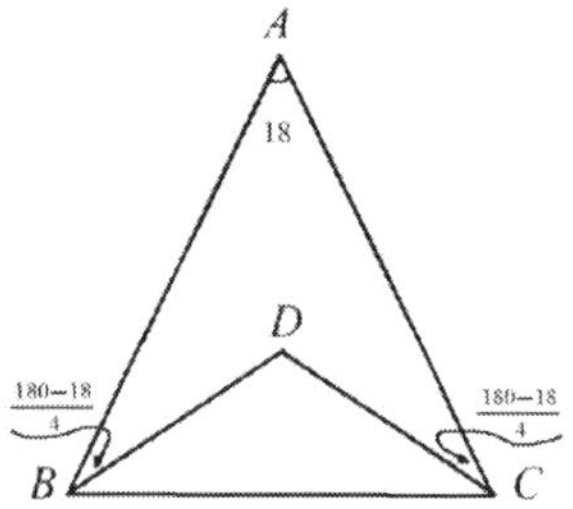

Example 9. In quadrilateral *ABDC*, *BE* and *CF* bisect angles *B* and *C*, respectively, and intersect in point *G*, as shown in the figure. The measure of angle *BDC* is 140° and the measure of angle *BGC* is 110°. Find the measure of angle *A*.

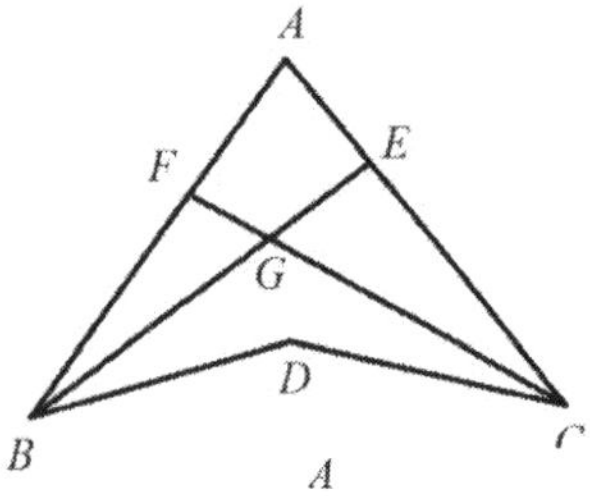

Solution: 80.
By **Theorem 4,**

$140° = 2\alpha + 2\beta + \angle A$ (1)
$110° = \alpha + \beta + \angle A$ (2)
$(2) \times 2$: $220° = 2\alpha + 2\beta + 2\angle A$ (3)
$(3) - (1)$: $80° = \angle A$.

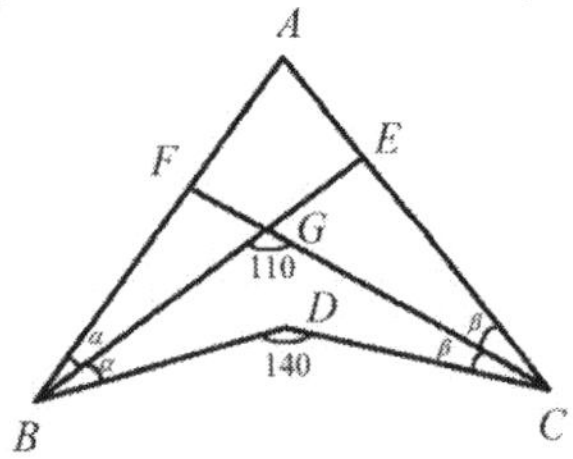

Example 10. In the diagram, *BD* and *BE* trisect $\angle ABC$, and *CP* and *CE* trisect $\angle ACB$. If $m\angle A = 60°$, compute the degree measure of $\angle BPE$.

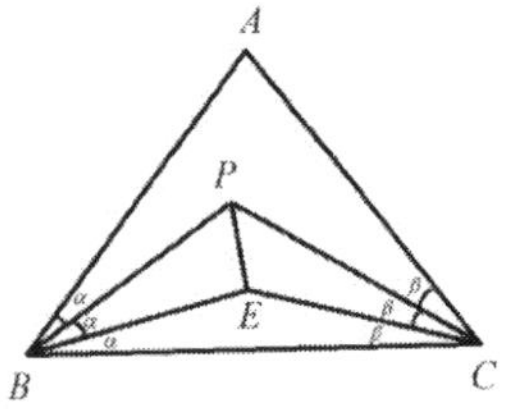

Solution: 50°.
$3(\alpha + \beta) + 60° = 180° \quad \Rightarrow \quad \alpha + \beta = 40°$.

$\angle BPC = \alpha + \beta + 60° = 40° + 60° = 100°$.

If we extend *PE* to meet *BC* at *F*, we know that *PF* is the angle bisector of $\angle BPC$ since these three lines concurrent.

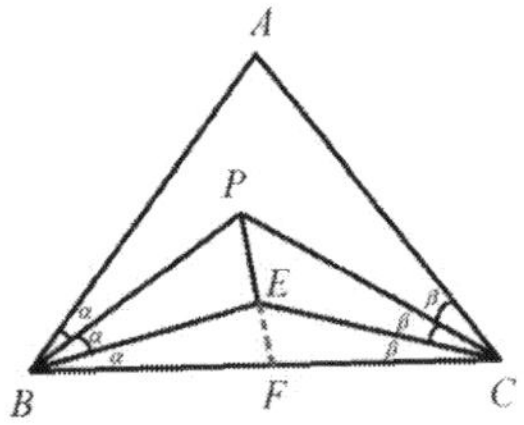

So $\angle BPE = \dfrac{1}{2}\angle BPC = \dfrac{100°}{2} = 50°$

Example 11. In quadrilateral ABCD, extend BA and CD to met at E, extend CB and DA to meet at F. *EG* bisects $\angle BEC$. *FG* bisects $\angle CFD$. $\angle ADC = 60°$. $\angle ABC = 80°$. Find $\angle EGF$.

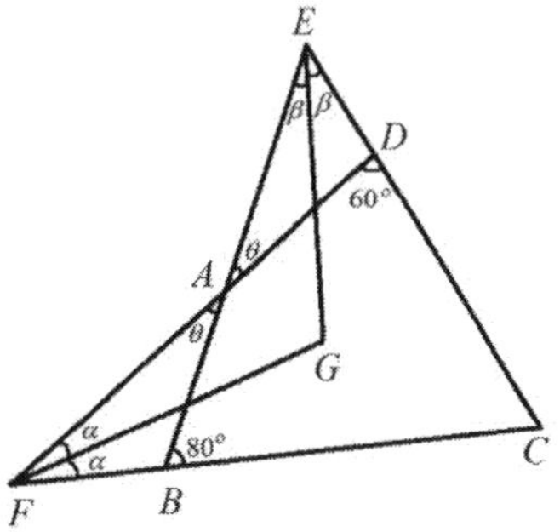

Solution: 110.
By **Theorem 4,**
$\angle EAF = 2\alpha + 2\beta + \angle C$ (1)
$\angle EGF = \alpha + \beta + \angle C$
(2)
Looking at triangle ADE: $60° = \theta + 2\beta$ (3)
Looking at triangle ABF: $80° = 2\alpha + \theta$ (4)
(3) + (4): $140° = 2\alpha + 2\beta + 2\theta$
$\Rightarrow \quad 70° = \alpha + \beta + \theta$ (5)
Rewrite (1) as $180° = 2(\alpha + \beta) + \theta + \angle C$ (6)
(6) – (5): $110° = \alpha + \beta + \angle C = \angle EGF$.

Example 12. Find $\angle 1 + \angle 2 + \angle 3 + \angle 4 + \angle 5 + \angle 6$.

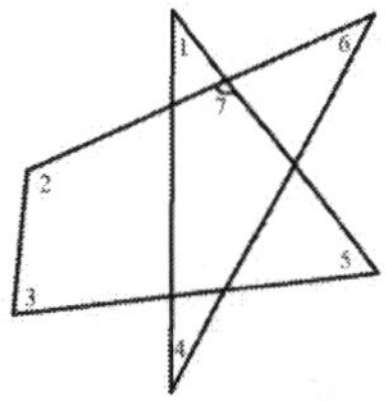

Solution: 360.
We label each corner as shown in the figure.
In quadrilateral *FECH*:
$\angle 2 + \angle 3 + \angle 5 + \angle 7 = 360°$ (1)

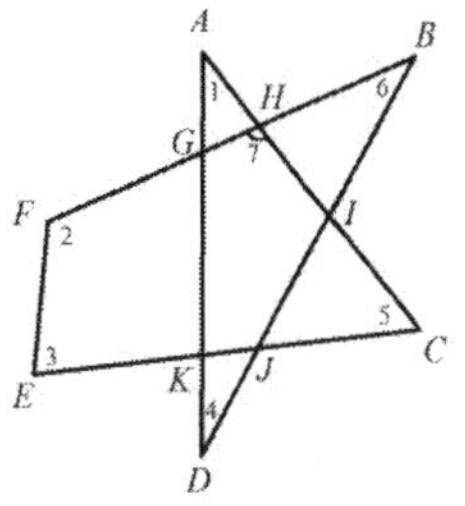

In quadrilateral *ADBH*:
$\angle 7 = \angle 1 + \angle 4 + \angle 6$ (2)
Substituting (2) into (1):
$\angle 1 + \angle 2 + \angle 3 + \angle 4 + \angle 5 + \angle 6 = 360°$.

Example 13. (2012 ARML) Triangle ABC has $m\angle A > m\angle B > m\angle C$. The angle between the altitude and the angle bisector at vertex A is 6°. The angle between the altitude and the angle bisector at vertex B is 18°. Compute the degree measure of angle C.

Solution: 44.

Method 1 (official solution):

Let the feet of the altitudes from A and B be E and D, respectively, and let F and G be the intersection points of the angle bisectors with AC and BC, respectively, as shown below.

Then $m\angle GAE = 6°$ and $m\angle DBF = 18°$. Suppose $m\angle FBC = x°$ and $m\angle CAG = y°$. So $m\angle CAE = (y + 6)°$ and $m\angle CBD = (x + 18)°$. Considering right triangle BDC, $m\angle C = 90° - (x + 18)° = (72 - x)°$, while considering right triangle AEC, $m\angle C = 90° - (y + 6)° = (84 - y)°$. Thus $84 - y = 72 - x$ and $y - x = 12$.

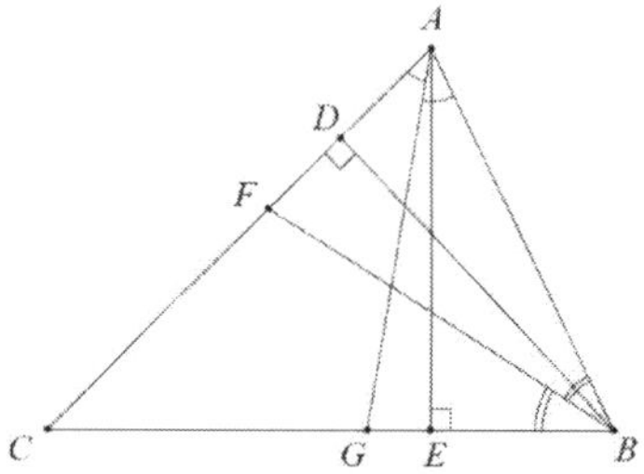

Considering ΔABE, $m\angle EAB = (y - 6)°$ and $m\angle EBA = 2x°$, so $(y - 6) + 2x = 90$, or $2x + y = 96$. Solving the system yields $x = 28$; $y = 40$. Therefore $m\angle A = 80°$ and $m\angle B = 56°$, so $m\angle C = 44°$.

Method 2 (official solution):

From right triangle ABE, $90° = (\frac{1}{2}A - 6°) + B$, and from right triangle ABD, $90° = (\frac{1}{2}B - 18°) + A$. Adding the two equations gives $180° = \frac{3}{2}(A + B) - 24°$, so $A + B = \frac{3}{2} \times 204° = 136°$ and $C = 180° - (A + B) = 44°$.

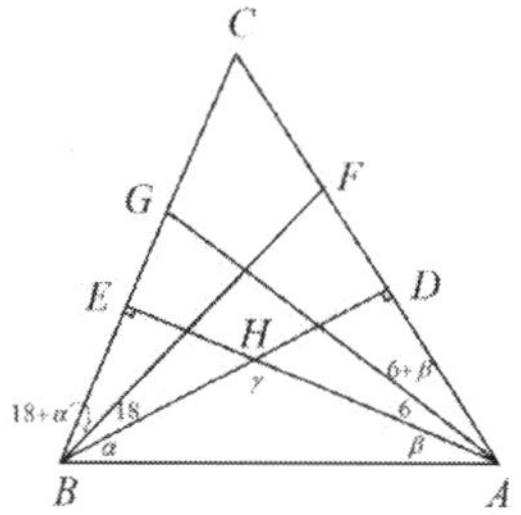

Method 3 (our solution):

We label each angle as follows. We see that quadrilateral $CDHG$ is cyclic.

So $\gamma + \angle C = 180°$ (1)
We also know that
$\gamma = (18+\alpha+18)+(6+\beta+6)+\angle C$ (2)
Looking at triangle *ABH*, we see that
$\gamma+\alpha+\beta = 180°$ (3)
Substituting (3) into (2): $2\gamma - \angle C = 228°$ (4)
Solving the system of equations (1) and (4): $\angle C = 44°$

Method 4 (our solution):

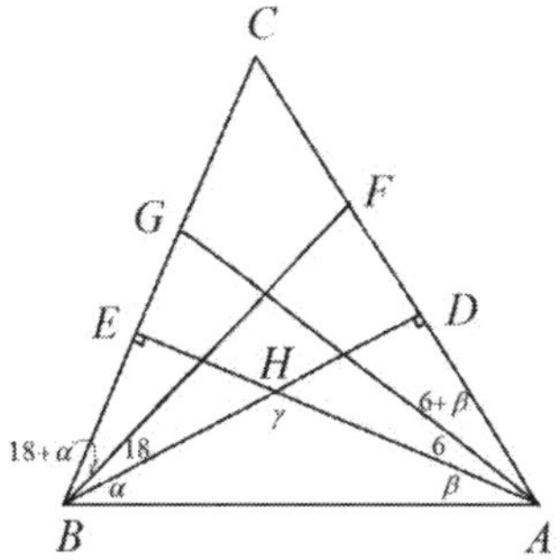

By Theorem 5,

$18° = \frac{1}{2}\angle A - \frac{1}{2}\angle C$ (1)

$6° = \frac{1}{2}\angle B - \frac{1}{2}\angle C$ (2)

(1) + (2): $24° = \frac{1}{2}\angle A + \frac{1}{2}\angle B - \angle C \Rightarrow$

$24° = \frac{1}{2}\angle A + \frac{1}{2}\angle B - \angle C + \frac{1}{2}\angle C - \frac{1}{2}\angle C \Rightarrow$

$24° = \frac{1}{2}(\angle A + \angle B + \angle C) - \angle C - \frac{1}{2}\angle C \Rightarrow$

$24° = \frac{1}{2}(180°) - \frac{3}{2}\angle C \Rightarrow \frac{3}{2}\angle C = 90° - 24° = 66° \Rightarrow$

$\angle C = \frac{2}{3}\times 66 = 44°$.

Example 14. (ARML) If the number of sides of a regular polygon is 8, compute in degrees the positive difference between the sum of the interior angles and the sum of the exterior angles.

Solution: 720°.
The sum of the exterior angles is 360°, the sum of the interior angles is (8 – 2) × 180°, so (8 – 2) × 180° – 360° = 720°.

Example 15. (NYML) In a convex polygon of n sides, one interior angle contains x ° while each of the remaining $n - 1$ interior angles contains 133°. Compute all four possible values for x.

Solution: 8, 55, 102, 149.
The equation $133(n - 1) + x = 180(n - 2)$ implies $x = 47n - 227$.
Since x is between 0 and 180, we can only have $n = 5,6,7,8$ producing $x = 8, 55, 102, 149$.

Example 16. (ARML) In triangle ABC, the perpendicular bisector of AC intersects AC at M and AB at T. If the area of triangle AMT is 1/4 the area of triangle ABC, and $\angle A + \angle C = 128°$, compute the number of degrees in angle A.

Solution: 38°.
Method 1 (official solution):
Draw median BM. Let the area of triangle $AMT = K$, Then the area of triangle $ABC = 4K$, and the area of triangle $BCM = 2K$. Therefore the area of triangle $BMT = K$, so MT must be median of triangle BMA. But that makes M and T midpoints, so MT is parallel to BC, and angle $C = 90°$! Therefore angle $A = 38$.

Method 2 (our solution):
Connect CT.
Since MT is the perpendicular bisector of AC, $TA = TC$ and $S_{\Delta AMT} = S_{\Delta CMT}$.
Since the area of triangle AMT is 1/4 the area of triangle ABC, $S_{\Delta ACT} = S_{\Delta BCT}$. So TC is the median on AD. So $AT = TB = TC$. Then $\angle C = 90°$.
$\angle A + \angle C = 128° \quad \Rightarrow \quad \angle A = 38°$.

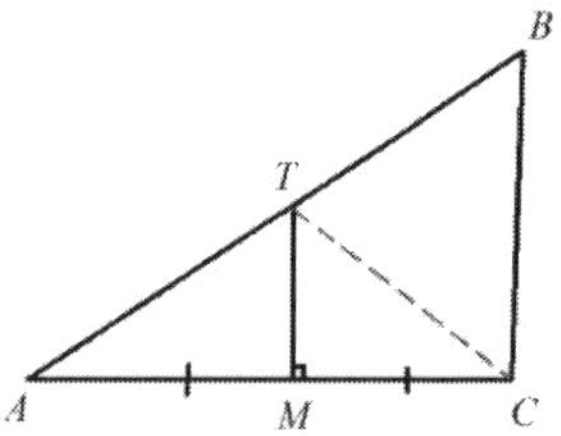

Example 17. (1996 NEAML) The circle shown has a radius of 7, the length of minor arc $\overset{\frown}{AC} = 4\pi$ and m $\angle CEB = 60°$. Find the exact length of minor arc $\overset{\frown}{DB}$.

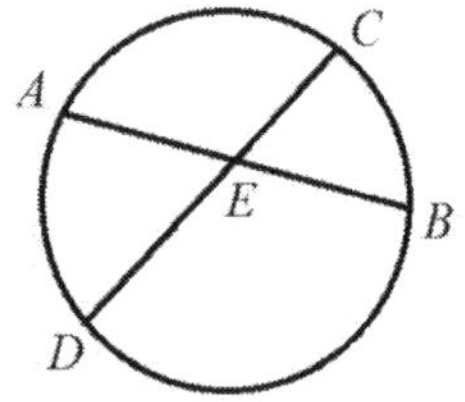

Solution: $\dfrac{16\pi}{3}$.

Method 1 (official solution):

The circumference of the circle is 14π and m $\overset{\frown}{AC}$ = 4π.

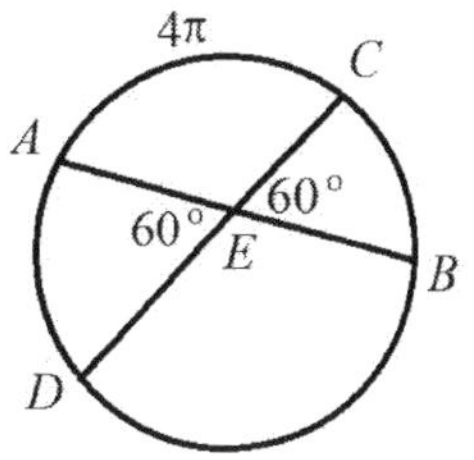

Since m ∠*CEB* = 60°,

$\frac{\overset{\frown}{AD}+\overset{\frown}{CB}}{2} = 60°$ making $\overset{\frown}{AD}+\overset{\frown}{CB}$ equal to one-third of the circumference, The sum of the lengths of the arc is therefore $\frac{14\pi}{3}$.

Thus m $\overset{\frown}{DB}$ = 14π − 4π $-\frac{14\pi}{3} = \frac{16\pi}{3}$.

Method 2 (our solution):

Let *x* be the exact length of minor arc $\overset{\frown}{DB}$. The circumference of the circle is 14π and m $\overset{\frown}{AC}$ = 4π.

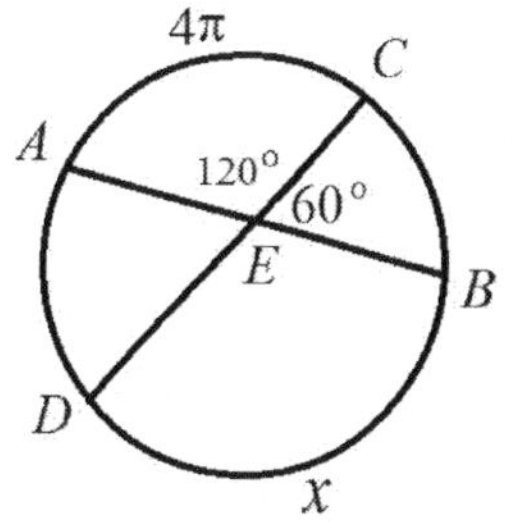

Since m ∠*CEA* = 120°,

$\frac{4\pi + x}{2} = 120° \quad \Rightarrow \quad 4\pi + x = 240°$ making $4\pi + x$ equal to two-third of the circumference, or

$4\pi + x = \frac{2}{3}\times 14\pi \Rightarrow x = \frac{2}{3}\times 14\pi - 4\pi = \frac{16\pi}{3}$.

Example 18. (2002 ARML) *ADOC* is a secant of a circle with center *O*. *A* lies outside the circle and *D* and *C* lie on the circle. *ABE* is also a secant of circle *O* and *B* and *E* are distinct points lying on circle *O*. If *AB* = *BC*, compute, in degrees, the largest possible integer value of the measure of ∠*CAE*.

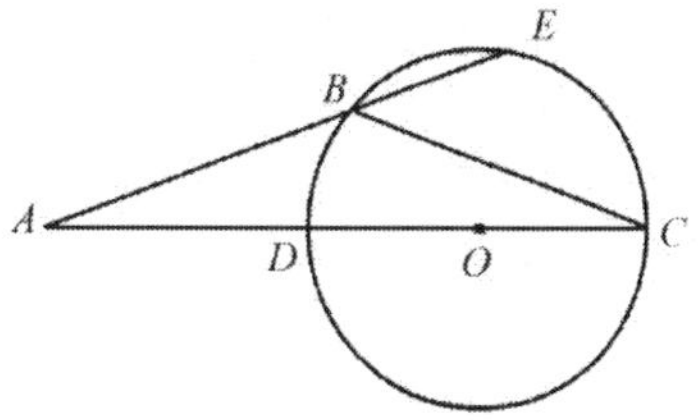

Solution: 29°.

Let $m\angle A = x$. Then $m\angle C = x \Rightarrow m\overset{\frown}{BD} = 2x$ and by the Exterior Angle Theorem, $m\angle EBC = 2x \Rightarrow m\overset{\frown}{EC} = 4x$. Thus, $180° = 2x + m\overset{\frown}{BE} + 4x \Rightarrow 6x < 180°$, making $x < 30° \Rightarrow m\angle A = 29°$.

Example 19. (NYML) In triangle ABC (in the figure below), angle ACB is 50 degrees and angle CBA is 70 degrees. Let D be the foot of the perpendicular from A to BC, O the center of the circle circumscribed about triangle ABC, and E the other end of the diameter (of this circle) which goes through A. Find the angle DAE.

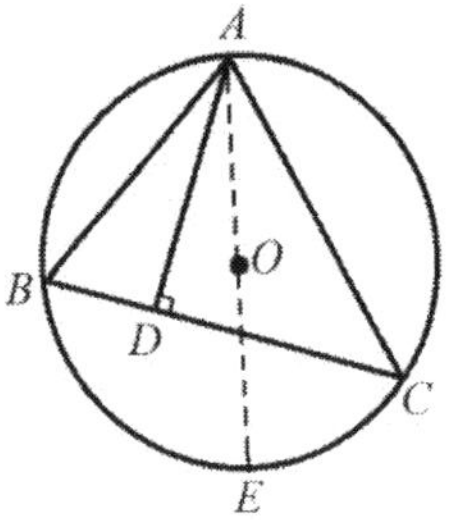

Solution: 20°.

Method 1 (official solution):

Observe, from figure at right:

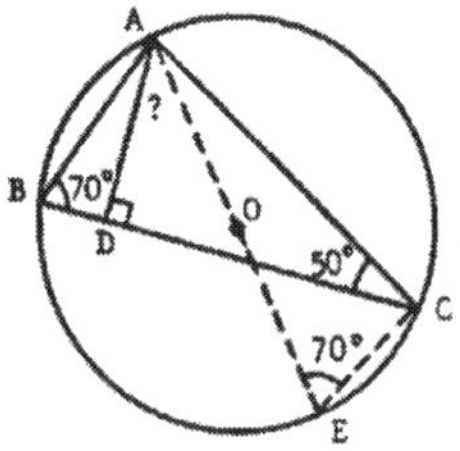

$\angle BAC = 180 - 50 - 70 = 60°$

$\angle ACE = 90°$

$\angle AEC = \dfrac{1}{2} AC\ ) = \angle ABD = 70°$

$\angle BAD = 90 - 70 = 20°$

$\angle EAC = 90 - 70 = 20°$

$\angle DAE = 60 - 20 - 20 = 20°$

The answer is 20°.

Method 2 (our solution):

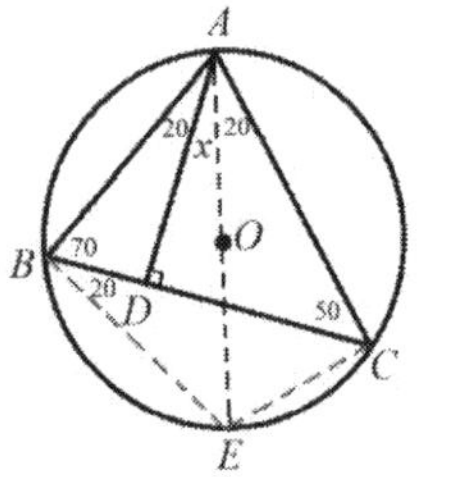

Label each angle as shown in the figure. $\angle BAD = 20°$. $\angle BAC = 180° - 70° - 50° = 60°$. Connect BE and CE. $\angle ABE = 90°$. So $\angle CBE = 90° - 70° = 20°$. $\angle CBE = \angle CAE = 20°$. So $x = 60° - 20° - 20° = 20°$.

Example 20. Let triangle ABC have vertices on a circle. Let $\overline{AD}$ be an altitude of the triangle and let $\overline{AK}$ be a diameter of the circle. If $\angle ABC = 80°$ and $\angle BCA = 64°$, find $\angle DAK$.

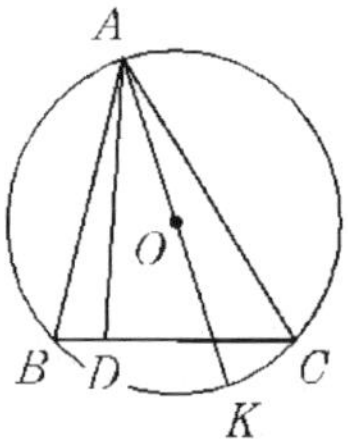

Solution: 16°.

$\angle BAC = 180° - \angle ABC - \angle BCA = 36°$.

Connect CK. $\angle ACK = 90°$ and $\angle AKC = \angle ABC = 80°$.

So $\angle CAK = 180° - \angle ACK - \angle AKC = 10°$.

In right triangle ABD, $\angle BAD = 90° - \angle ABC = 10°$.
Thus $\angle DAK = \angle BAC - \angle BAD - \angle CAK = 16°$.

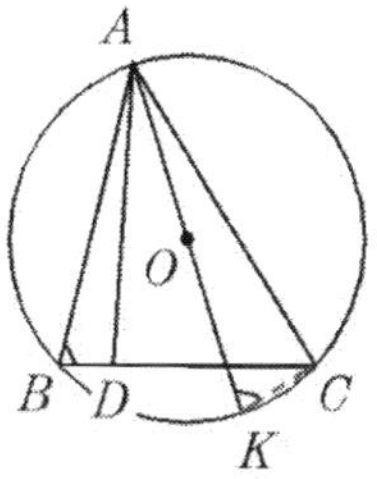

Example 21. (ARML) The bisectors of the angles of quadrilateral $ABCD$ are drawn. They form quadrilateral $EFGH$, as shown, in which $\angle E + \angle F = 193°$. If $\angle A > \angle C$, compute the numerical value of $\angle A - \angle C$. [For clarification, $\angle E$ means $\angle HEF$, $\angle F$ means $\angle EFG$, $\angle A$ means $\angle DAB$, and $\angle C$ means $\angle BCD$.]

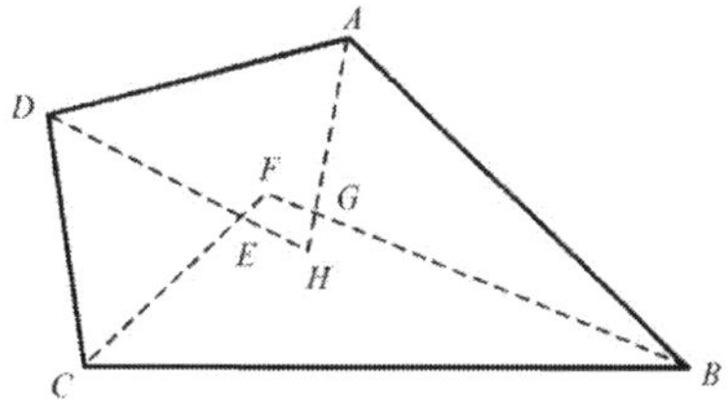

Solution: 26°.
Method 1 (official solution):
The sum of angles CDE, DCE, BAG, and ABG is $\frac{1}{2} \times (360°) = 180°$, so angles E and G must be supplementary. Thus quadrilateral $EFGH$ is cyclic. Let $\angle BAG = a$, $\angle ABG = b$, and $\angle BCF = c$. Then $a + b = 180 - G$ and $b + c = 180 - F$. Therefore $a - c = F - G = F - (180 - E) = E + F - 180$, so $A - C = 2[E + F - 180] = 26$ or 26°. In general, $A - C = 2(E + F) - 360$, and $B - D = 2(E - F)$.

Method 2 (our solution):
We label each angle as shown in the figure.

Since $\angle E + \angle F = 193°$, $m + n = 360° - (\angle E + \angle F) = 167°$.

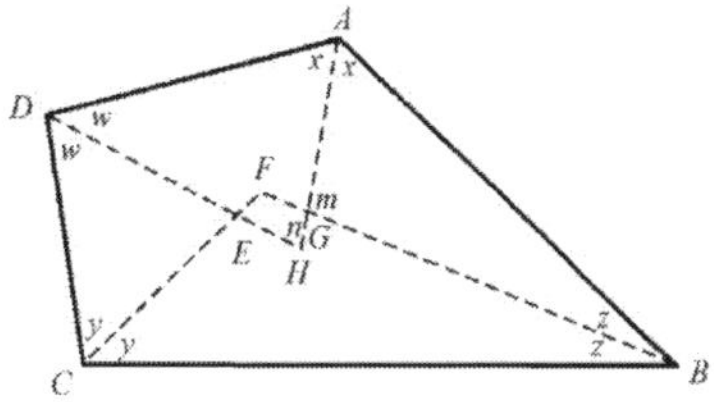

For the four triangles in the figure, we have:

$$x + w + n = 180° \quad (1)$$

$$x + z + m = 180° \quad (2)$$

$y + z + F = 180°$ (3)

$w + y + E = 180°$ (4)

(1) + (2): $2x + w + z + 167 = 360°$ (5)

(3) + (4): $2y + w + z + 193 = 360°$ (6)

(5) + (6): $2(x - y) - 26 = 0 \quad \Rightarrow \quad 2(x - y) = \angle A - \angle C = 26°$.

PROBLEMS

Problem 1: In triangle ABC, $\angle D=30°$. BD bisects $\angle ABC$, and CD bisects $\angle ACE$. Find $\angle A$.

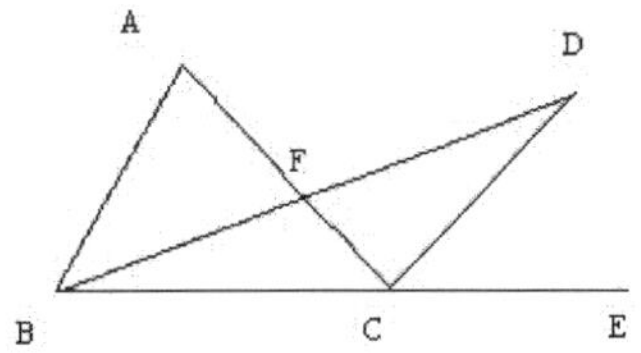

Problem 2. Find the sum of the measures of angles A, B, C, D, and E in the accompanying figure.

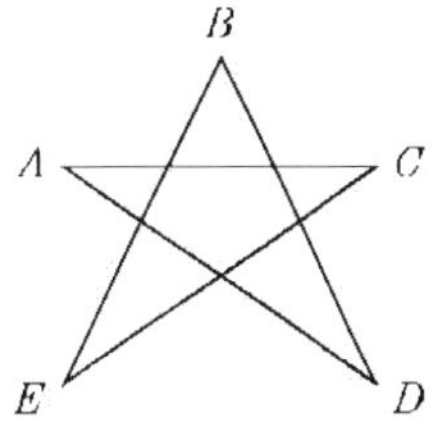

Problem 3. As shown in the figure, ABC is a right triangle with $\angle ACB = 90°$. If $AC = AE$, $BC = BD$, find $\angle ACD + \angle BCE$.

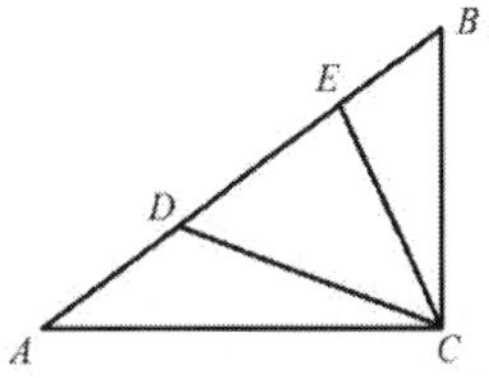

Problem 4. (1997 NEAML) Regular hexagon $ABCDEF$ and square $MNOP$ have the same center and sides of length 1. Points A, M, P, and E are collinear. If $AB//MN$, determine $m\angle MFE$ in degrees.

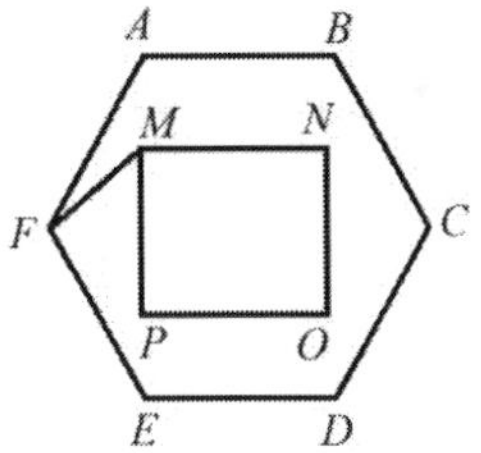

Problem 5. In the figure $l \parallel n$, $\angle 1 = 100°$, and $\angle 2 = 120°$. Find $\angle 3$.

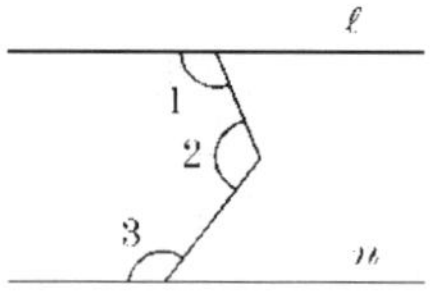

Problem 6. Line k is parallel to line j and $\angle 1$, $\angle 2$, $\angle 3$ and $\angle 4$ form, in that order, an increasing arithmetic sequence of angles with $m\angle 3 < 90°$. If $m\angle 1 = 54°$, compute the largest possible integer value for the measure of $\angle 4$.

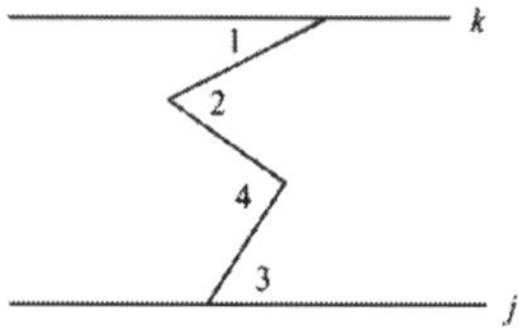

Problem 7. As shown in the figure, two lines AB and CD are parallel. Find $\angle 1 + \angle 2 + \angle 3 + \angle 4 + \angle 5 + \angle 6$.

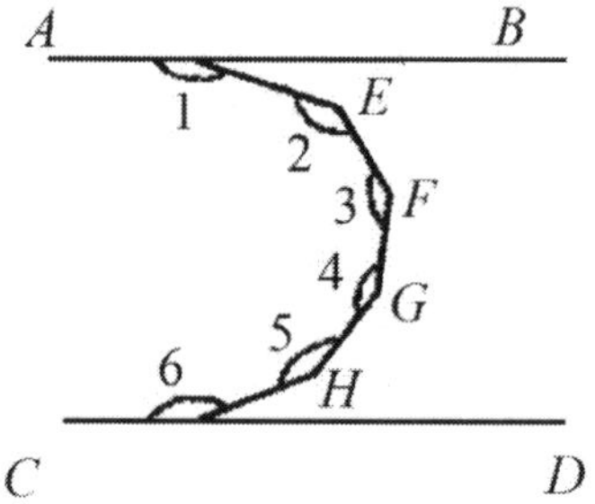

Problem 8. In the diagram, $\angle MBA$, $\angle NAC$, and $\angle OCB$ are exterior angles of triangle ABC. Lines TB and CQ intersect at point Q. Ray BT and ray CQ bisect $\angle MBA$ and $\angle OCB$ respectively. Find the measure of $\angle BQC$ if $\angle CAN = 122°$.

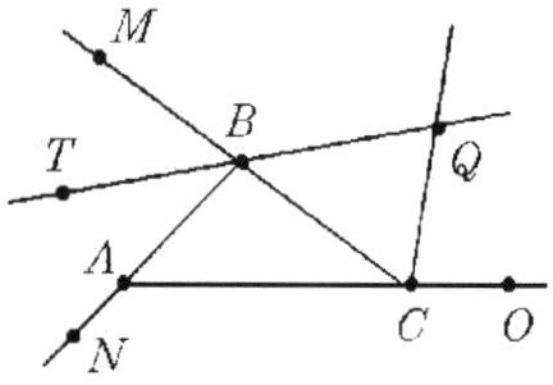

Problem 9. In triangle ABC, $\overline{AD}$ and $\overline{BE}$ bisect angles A and B, respectively, and intersect in point P. The measure of angle ACB is 70°. Find the measure of angle APE.

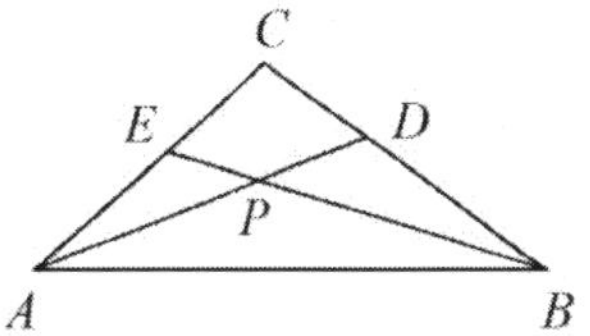

Problem 10. As shown in the figure, O is a point inside triangle ABC. OB bisects $\angle ABC$. OC bisects $\angle ACB$. $\angle BOC = 130\,^\circ$. Find $\angle A$.

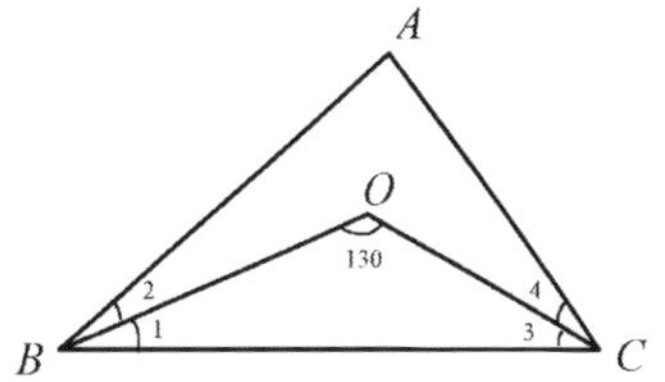

Problem 11. Triangle ABC, $m\angle B = 70^\circ$ and $m\angle C = 34^\circ$. Find the angle between the altitude and the angle bisector at vertex A.

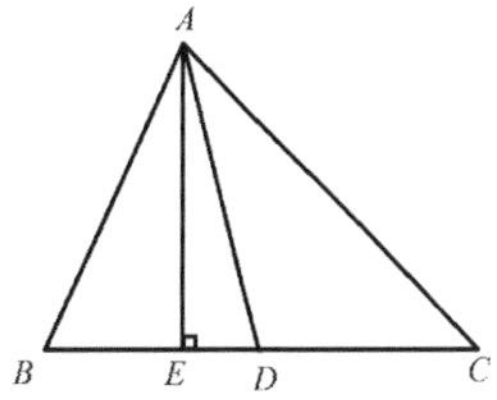

Problem 12. (NYML) The average number of degrees in the angles of a convex polygon 1s 150. How many sides does it have?

Problem 13. In ΔABC, $\angle B = 2\angle A$ and $AB = 2\sqrt{3} = 2BC$. Find AC.

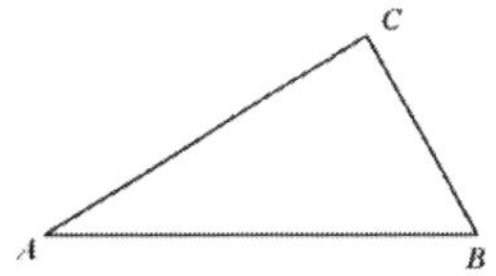

Problem 14. AB and CD are two chords of the circle O intersecting at point P. $\angle APD = 60^\circ$. If the length of arc AD is 3π and the length of arc BC is 5π, find the circle's area. Express your answer in terms of π.

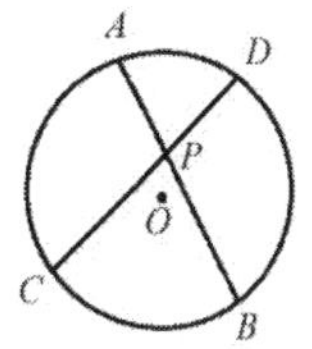

Problem 15. Points *A, B, Q, C* and *D* lie on a circle as shown in the figure. The measure of *BQ* and *QD* are 42° and 38° respectively.
What is the sum of the measures of $\angle P$ and $\angle Q$?

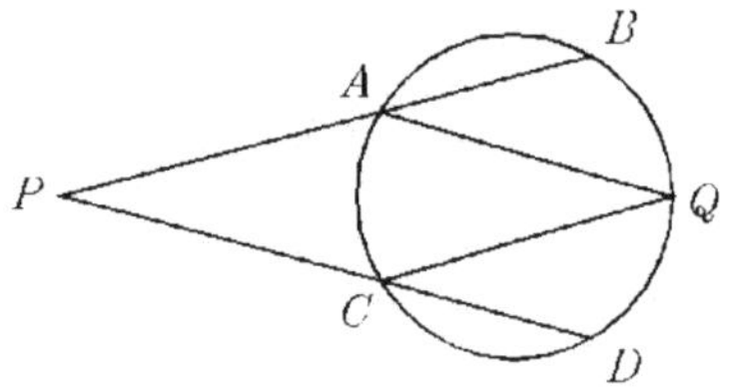

Problem 16. Two rays emanating from point *A* intersect a circle twice as shown. If the arc *BC* covers 25% of the circle's circumference, and $\angle BAC = 25°$, calculate $\angle DPB$.

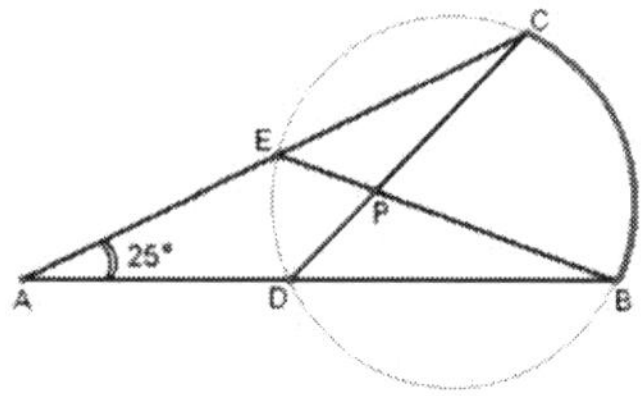

Problem 17. In the figure, $BC = 85°$, $CD = 120°$, $\angle BFC = 70°$ and *E* is the midpoint of arc *AB*. The measure of angle *BPC* is:

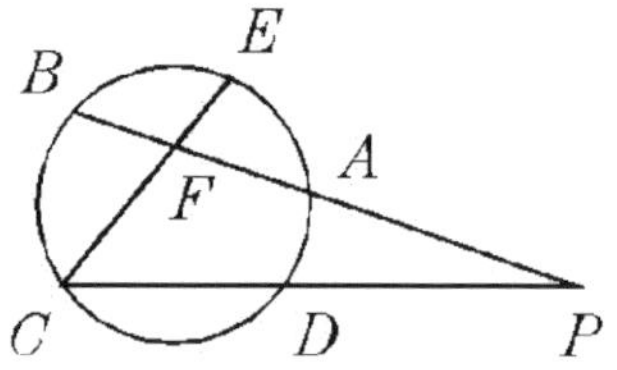

Problem 18. In the circle, $\overline{OA}$ is a radius, $BC = OA$, $\angle AOD$ equals x and $\angle ACO = y$. Which of the following is true?

A. $x = 2y$ B. $x = \dfrac{5y}{2}$ C. $x = 3y$ D. $x = y$ E. $x = 4$

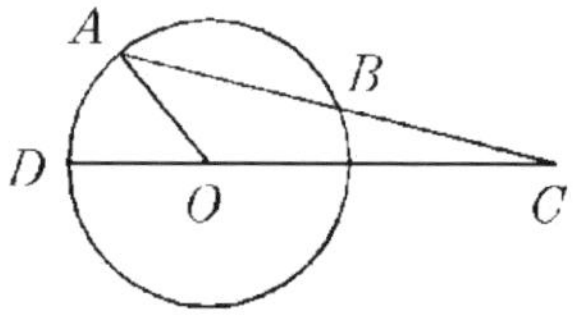

Problem 19. In the figure, the circle is circumscribed about triangle ABC, $\overline{BD}$ is an altitude of the triangle, and $\overline{BK}$ is a diameter of the circle. If $\angle BAC = 70°$ and $\angle BCA = 50°$, find $m\angle DBK$.

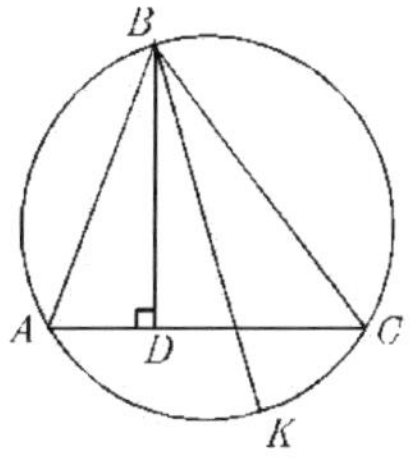

Problem 20. The bisectors of the angles of quadrilateral $ABCD$ are drawn. They form quadrilateral $EFGH$, as shown, in which $\angle EFG - \angle HEF = 19°$. If $\angle ADC > \angle ABC$, compute the numerical value of $\angle ADC - \angle ABC$.

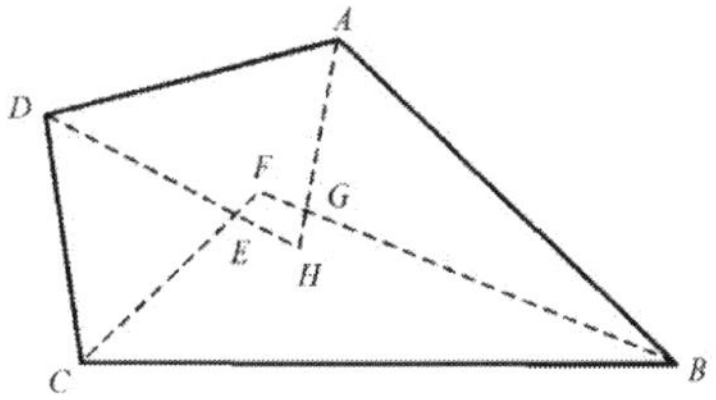

Problem 21. O is the center of two concentric circles as shown. AB and CD are chords of the larger circle and they intersect at E on the smaller circle. CD intersects the smaller circle at F. If $m\overset{\frown}{AC} + m\overset{\frown}{EF} = 73°$, compute $m\overset{\frown}{DB}$.

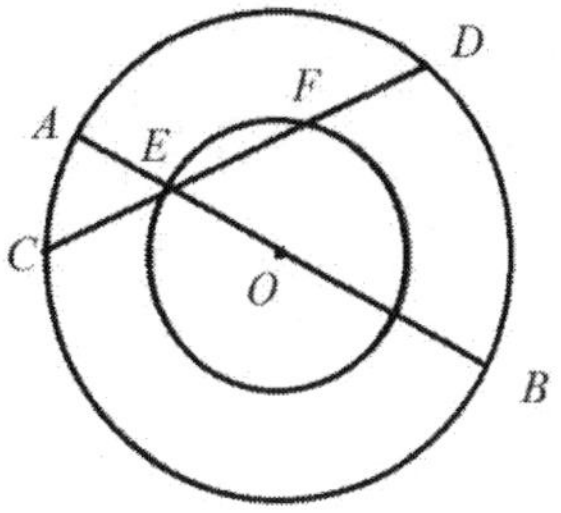

SOLUTIONS:

Problem 1: Solution: 60°.

The exterior angle is the sum of two non-adjacent interior angles. From the figure below,

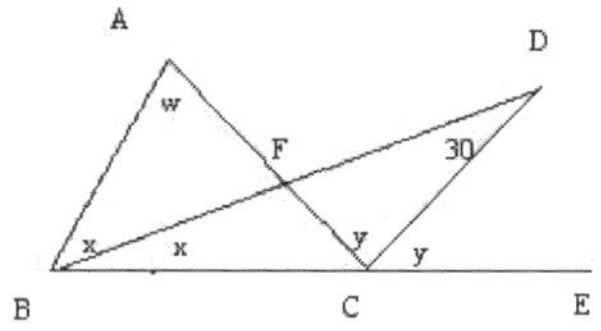

$$2y = 2x + w$$

$$y = x + 30$$

Solve for w by multiplying the second equation by 2 and subtracting the result from the first equation.

$w = 60°$.

Problem 2. Solution: 180.

Draw line l that is parallel to the side AC.

So $\angle 1 = \angle 3$, $\angle 2 = \angle 4$.

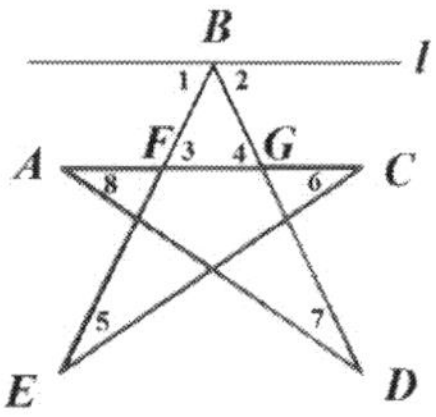

We also see that $\angle 1 + \angle B + \angle 2 = 180°$ (1)

In triangle CEF, by 3.2, $\angle 3 = \angle 5 + \angle 6$.

In triangle ADG, by 3.2, $\angle 4 = \angle 7 + \angle 8$.

That is, $\angle 1 = \angle 5 + \angle 6$ (2)

$\angle 2 = \angle 7 + \angle 8$ (3)

Substituting (2) and (3) into (1): $\angle A + \angle B + \angle C + \angle D + \angle D = 180°$.

Problem 3. Solution: 45°.

Method 1:

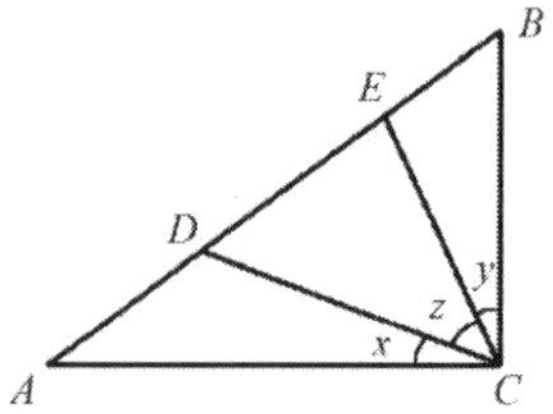

Let $\angle ACD = x, \angle BCE = y$, $\angle BCE = z$.

Since $AC = AE$, $\angle ACE = x + z$

$$= \frac{180° - \angle A}{2} = 90° - \frac{1}{2}\angle A \qquad (1)$$

Since $BC = BD$, $\angle BCD = y + z$

$$= \frac{180° - \angle B}{2} = 90° - \frac{1}{2}\angle B \qquad (2)$$

(1) + (2):

$x + z + y + z = 180° - \frac{1}{2}(\angle A + \angle B)$ (3)

We know that $x + y + z = 90°$ (4)

$\angle A + \angle B = 90°$ (5)

Substituting (4) and (5) into (3):

$90° + z = 180° - \frac{1}{2}(90°) \Rightarrow z = 45°$

$\angle ACD + \angle BCE = x + y = 90° - 45° = 45°$.

Problem 4. Solution: 105.

$\angle FAM = 30°$. ΔAFT is a 30-60-90 right triangle, and given $AF = 1$, then $FQ = 1/2 = MQ$. So $\angle MFQ = 45°$ and $\angle MFQ = 60 + 45 = 105°$.

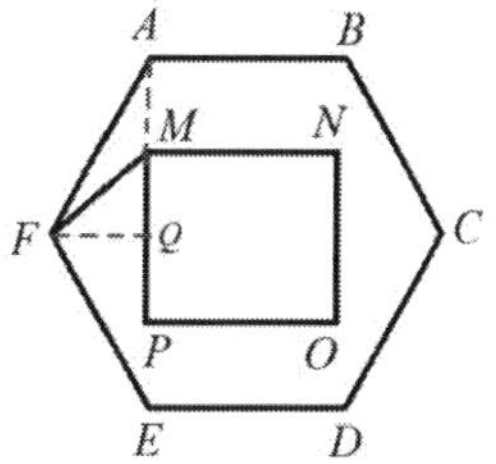

Problem 5. Solution: 140°.

As shown in the figure, extend AB to meet line n at C.

$\angle A = 180° - \angle 1 = 180° - 100° = 80°$.

$\angle BCD = \angle A = 80°$.

$\angle CBD = 180° - \angle 2 = 180° - 120° = 60°$.

By **Theorem 2**, $\angle 3 = \angle BCD + \angle CBD = 60° + 80° = 140°$.

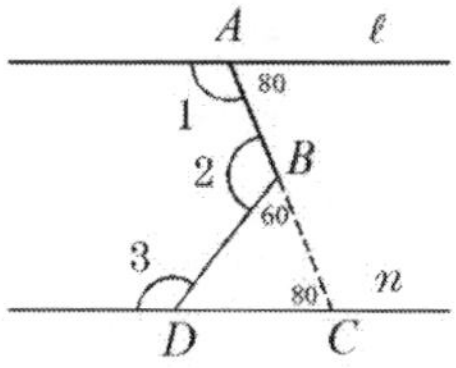

Problem 6. Solution: 107.

Method 1:

The measures of the angles are $m\angle 1 = 54°$, $m\angle 2 = 54° + d$, $m\angle 3 = 54° + 2d$, and $m\angle 4 = 54° + 3d$.

Since $\angle 3$ is acute, $54 + 2d < 90 \Rightarrow d < 18$. So $m\angle 4 < 54 + 3 \times 18 = 108$. So the largest possible integer value for $m\angle 4 = 108 - 1 = 107$.

Method 2:

By drawing lines parallel to lines k and m through the vertices of angles 2 and 4, one can see that $m\angle 4 = d + (50 + 2d) = 50 + 3d$.
Since $\angle 3$ is acute, $54 + 2d < 90 \Rightarrow d < 18$. So $m\angle 4 < 54 + 3 \times 18 = 108$. So the largest possible integer value for $m\angle 4 = 108 - 1 = 107$.

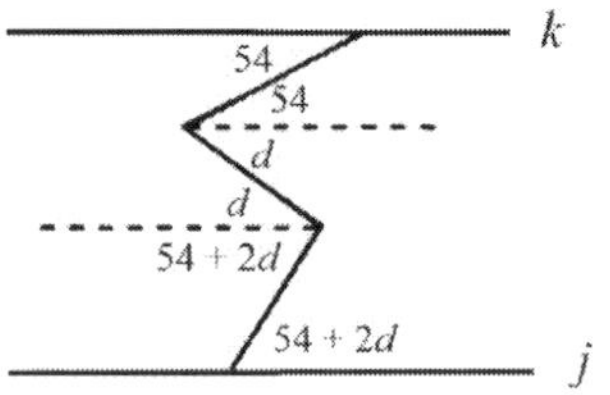

Problem 7. Solution: 900°.
We draw $JEK // MFN // PGQ // SHT // CYD$.

$\angle XEJ + \angle AXE = 180°$ (1)
$\angle JEF + \angle MFE = 180°$ (2)
$\angle MHG + \angle PGF = 180°$ (3)
$\angle PGH + \angle SHG = 180°$ (4)
$\angle SHY + \angle DYH = 180°$ (5)
(1) + (2) + (3) + (4) + (5): $\angle 1 + \angle 2 + \angle 3 + \angle 4 + \angle 5 + \angle 6 = 5 \times 180° = 900°$.

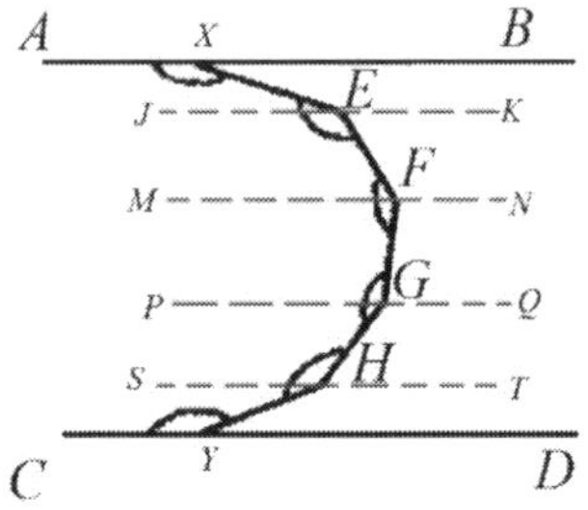

Problem 8. Solution: 61°.
We label some angles as in the figure.
By **Theorem 3**, $y + 2u + 2v = 360°$ (1)
By **Theorem 1,** $u + v + x = 180°$ (2)
Multiplying (2) by 2: $2u + 2v + 2x = 360°$ (3)
(1) – (3): $y = 2x$ $\Rightarrow x = 122/2 = 61°$.

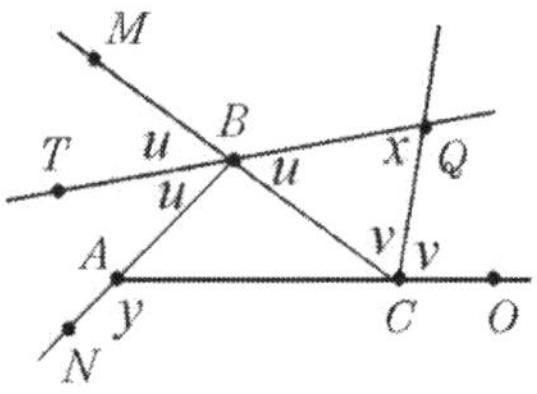

Problem 9. Solution: 55°.
Method 1:
$2x + 2y = 180° - 70° = 110°$ (1)
Dividing both sides of (1) by 2: $x + y = 55°$ (2)
By **Theorem 2**, $\angle APE = m = x + y = 55°$.

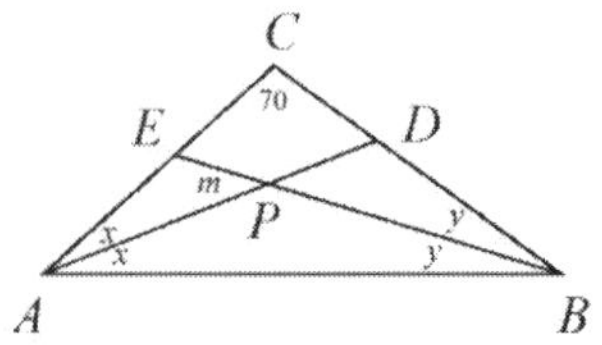

Method 2:
$2x + 2y = 180° - 70° = 110°$ (1)
Dividing both sides of (1) by 2: $x + y = 55°$ (2)
By **Theorem 4,** $\angle APB = 70° + x + y = 70° + 55° = 125°$.

$\angle APE = m = 180^\circ - 125^\circ = 55^\circ$.

Problem 10. Solution: 80.

$$\angle A + \angle B + \angle C = 180^\circ \qquad (1)$$

$$130^\circ = \angle A + \frac{\angle B}{2} + \frac{\angle C}{2}$$

$$\Rightarrow \qquad 2\angle A + \angle B + \angle C = 260^\circ \qquad (2)$$

$(2) - (1)$: $\angle A = 80^\circ$

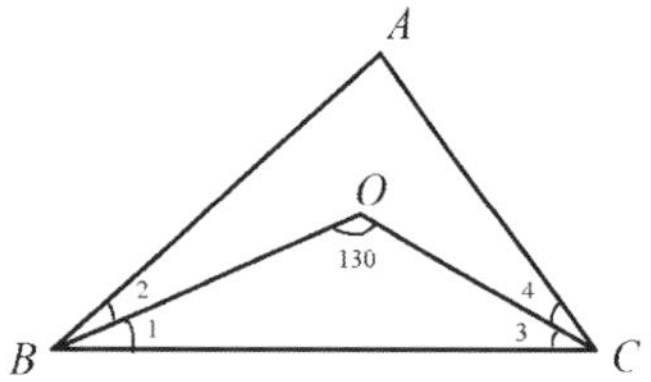

Problem 11. Solution: 18.

$\angle BAC = 180^\circ - (70^\circ + 34^\circ) = 76^\circ$.

Since AD bisects $\angle BAC$, $\angle BAD = 76^\circ/2 = 38^\circ$.

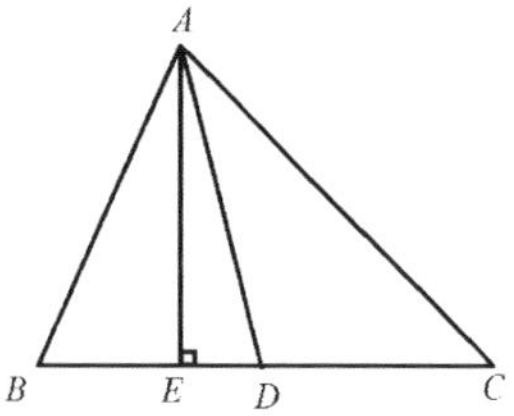

In right triangle ABE, $\angle B = 70^\circ$, so $\angle BAE = 20^\circ$, so $\angle DAE = \angle BAD - \angle BAE = 38^\circ - 20^\circ = 18^\circ$.

Note: $\angle DAE = \frac{1}{2}\angle B - \frac{1}{2}\angle C$.

Problem 12. (NYML) **Solution:** 12.

The angle sum for an n-sided polygon is $(n-2)(180)$. The average equals

$$150 = \frac{(n-2)180}{n} \qquad \Rightarrow \qquad 5n = 6(n-2) \Rightarrow \qquad n = 12.$$

Problem 13. Solution: 3.

Since $AB > BC$, $\angle C > \angle A$.

Draw CD to meet AB at D such that $\angle ACD = \angle A$.

ΔADC is an isosceles triangle and $AD = DC$.

$\angle CDB = \angle ACD + \angle A = 2\angle A = \angle B$

Therefore, ΔBCD is also an isosceles triangle, and so $DC = BC$.

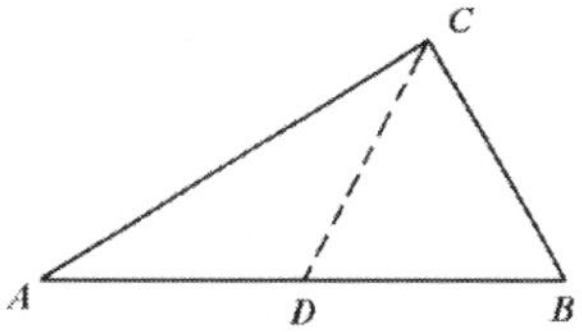

$$AB = AD + DB = 2BC$$

$$\Rightarrow \qquad AD + DB = 2DC = 2AD$$

$$\Rightarrow \qquad AD = DB = DC.$$

This tells us that DC is the median of right triangle ABC with $\angle C = 90^\circ$.

By the Pythagorean Theorem, we have $AB^2 = AC^2 + BC^2 \quad \Rightarrow \quad AC = 3$.

Problem 14. Solution: 144π.

$$\angle APD = \frac{\overset{\frown}{AD} + \overset{\frown}{BC}}{2} = \frac{3\pi + 5\pi}{2} \quad \Rightarrow \quad \overset{\frown}{AD} + \overset{\frown}{BC} = 120^\circ$$ which makes one-third of the circumference, or 8π makes one-third of the circumference. So the circumference is $3 \times 8\pi = 24\pi$. The radius is r and $2\pi r = 24\pi \Rightarrow r = 12$. The area of the circle is $\pi \times 12^2 = 144\pi$.

Problem 15. Solution: 40°.

$$\angle P = \frac{1}{2}(BQ + QD - AC) \quad \Rightarrow \quad \angle P = \frac{1}{2}(42 + 38 - 2\angle Q) \quad \Rightarrow$$

$$\angle P + \angle Q = \frac{1}{2}(42 + 38) = 40^\circ.$$

Problem 16. Solution: 115°.

Since the arc $\overset{\frown}{BC}$ covers 25% of the circle's circumference, $\overset{\frown}{BC} = 90^\circ$.

$\angle CEB = \frac{1}{2}\overset{\frown}{BC} = 45^\circ$. $\angle CDB = \angle CEB = 45^\circ$.

$$\angle A = \frac{1}{2}(\overset{\frown}{BC} - \overset{\frown}{DE}) \quad \Rightarrow \frac{1}{2}(90^\circ - \overset{\frown}{DE}) = 25^\circ \Rightarrow \overset{\frown}{DE} = 90^\circ - 50^\circ = 40^\circ.$$

So $\angle DBE = 40/2 = 20^\circ$.

$\angle DPB = 180^\circ - \angle DBE - \angle CDB = 180^\circ - 20^\circ - 45^\circ = 115^\circ$.

Problem 17. Solution: 20°.

By **Theorem 9.1,** $\angle BFC = 70^\circ = \frac{1}{2}(\overset{\frown}{CB} + \overset{\frown}{AE})$

$\Rightarrow \quad 140^\circ = 85^\circ + \overset{\frown}{AE}$

$\Rightarrow \quad \overset{\frown}{AE} = 55^\circ$. Thus $\overset{\frown}{BE} = 55^\circ$.

So $\overset{\frown}{AD} = 360^\circ - (55^\circ + 55^\circ + 85^\circ + 120^\circ) = 45^\circ$.

By **Theorem 9.2,** $\angle BPC = \frac{1}{2}(\overset{\frown}{CB} - \overset{\frown}{AD}) = \frac{1}{2}(85^\circ - 45^\circ) = 20^\circ$.

Problem 18. Solution: C.

Connect BO. We know that $BC = OA = OB$.
So we label each angle as shown in the figure.
It is clear that $x = 3y$.

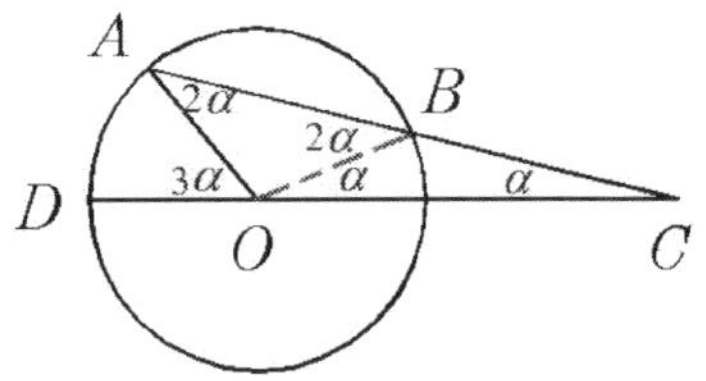

Problem 19. Solution: 20°.

$\angle ABC = 180° - \angle BAC - \angle ACB = 60°$.
Connect CK. $\angle BCK = 90°$ and $\angle BKC = \angle BAC = 70°$.
So $\angle CBK = 180° - \angle BCK - \angle BKC = 20°$.
In right triangle ABD, $\angle ABD = 90° - \angle BAC = 20°$.
Thus $\angle DBK = \angle ABC - \angle ABD - \angle CBK = 20°$.

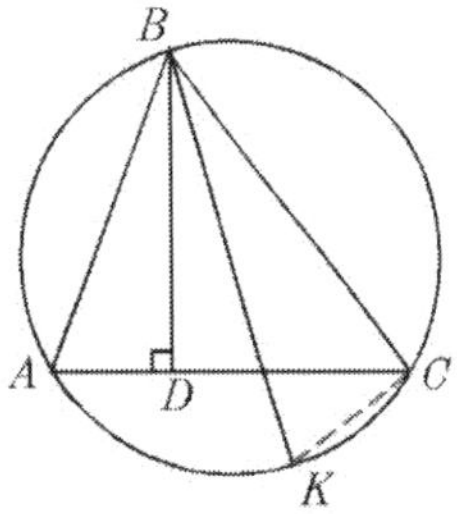

Problem 20. Solution: 38°.

We label each angle as shown in the figure.
The sum of angles CDE, DCE, BAG, and ABG is $\frac{1}{2} \times (360°) = 180°$, so angles E and G must be supplementary. Thus quadrilateral $EFGH$ is cyclic.

Since $\angle EFG - \angle HEF = 19°$, $m - n = 19°$.

For the triangles ADH and ABG in the figure, we have:

$x + w + n = 180°$ (1)
$x + z + m = 180°$ (2)
(1) – (2): $w - z = 19$
$2(w - z) = 19 \times 2 = 38$.

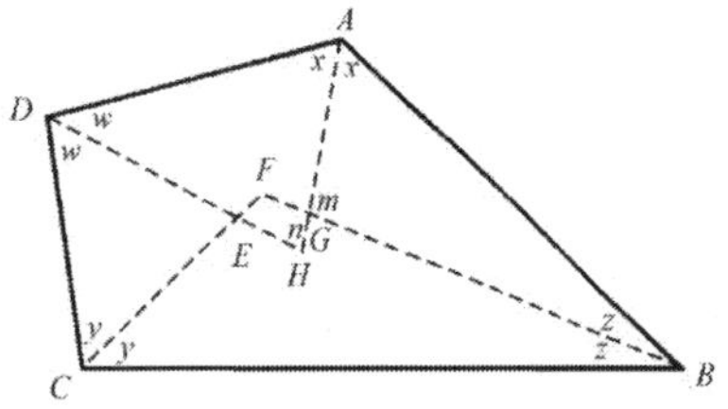

Problem 21. Solution: 107

Connect OE.

$\alpha = \overset{\frown}{EF}$

$\gamma = 180 - \overset{\frown}{EF}$

$\beta = \dfrac{1}{2}\gamma = \dfrac{180 - \overset{\frown}{EF}}{2}$.

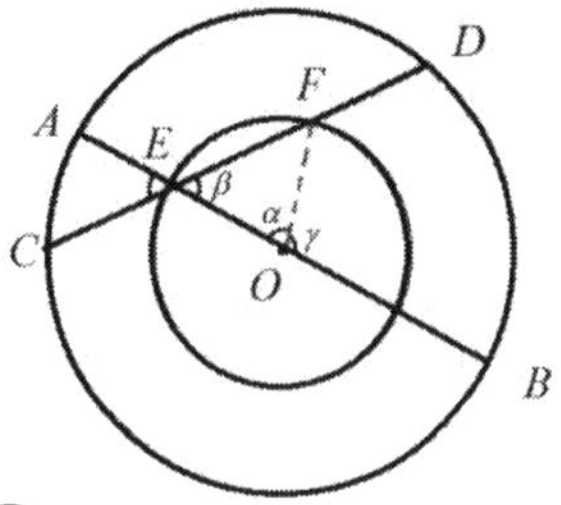

By **Theorem 9.2,** $\beta = \dfrac{\overset{\frown}{AC} + \overset{\frown}{DB}}{2} \Rightarrow \quad 2\beta = \overset{\frown}{AC} + \overset{\frown}{DB}$

$\Rightarrow \qquad \overset{\frown}{DB} = 2\beta - \overset{\frown}{AC} = 180 - \overset{\frown}{EF} - \overset{\frown}{AC} = 180 - (\overset{\frown}{AC} + \overset{\frown}{EF}) = 180 - 73 = 107°$

BASIC KNOWLEDGE

Angle bisector

An angle bisector of a triangle is a segment or ray that bisects an angle and extends to the opposite side. As shown in the figure, AD is the angle bisector of $\angle A$.

$\angle 1 = \angle 2$.

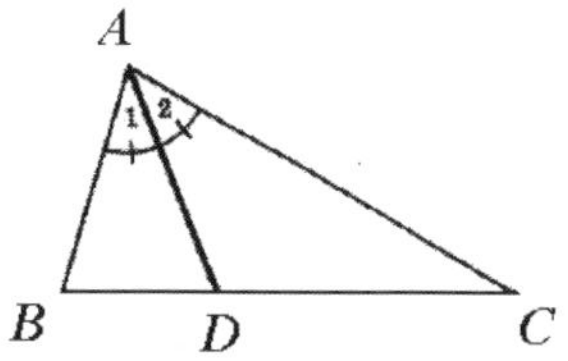

Theorem 1a (The Angle Bisector Theorem)

The angle bisector of a triangle divides the opposite side into segments that are proportional to the adjacent sides.

$$\frac{AB}{AC} = \frac{BD}{CD} \quad \text{or} \quad \frac{AB}{BD} = \frac{AC}{CD}$$

Proof:

Method 1:

Draw $DE \,//\, AB$ through D to meet AC at E.

We know that $AE = ED$ and $\Delta ABC \sim \Delta EDC$.

Therefore: $\dfrac{AB}{AC} = \dfrac{ED}{EC} = \dfrac{AE}{EC} = \dfrac{BD}{CD}$.

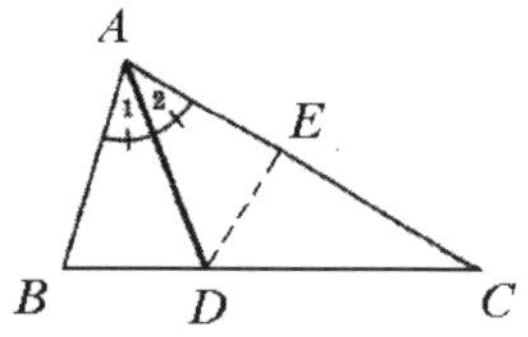

Method 2:

Since ΔABD and ADC share the same vertex, the ratio of their areas is

$$\frac{S_{\Delta ABD}}{S_{\Delta ADC}} = \frac{BD}{CD}.$$

We also know that $\dfrac{S_{\Delta ABD}}{S_{\Delta ADC}} = \dfrac{\frac{1}{2} AB \times AD \times \sin\angle 1}{\frac{1}{2} AD \times AC \times \sin\angle 2} = \dfrac{AB}{AC}$.

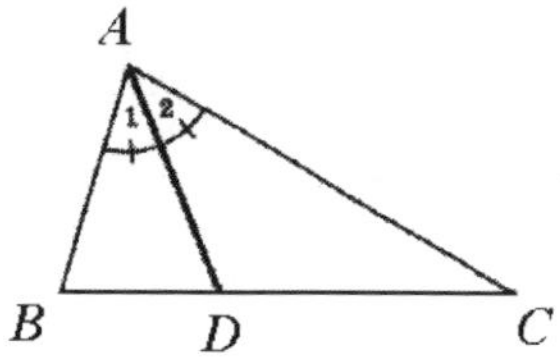

Therefore: $\dfrac{AB}{AC} = \dfrac{BD}{CD}$.

Method 3:

Draw $CE \parallel DA$. CE meets the extension of BA at E.

$BD : DC = BA : AE$.

Since $\angle ACE = \angle 2 = \angle 1 = \angle 3$, $AE = AC$

So $BD : DC = BA : AC$

or $\dfrac{AB}{AC} = \dfrac{BD}{CD}$.

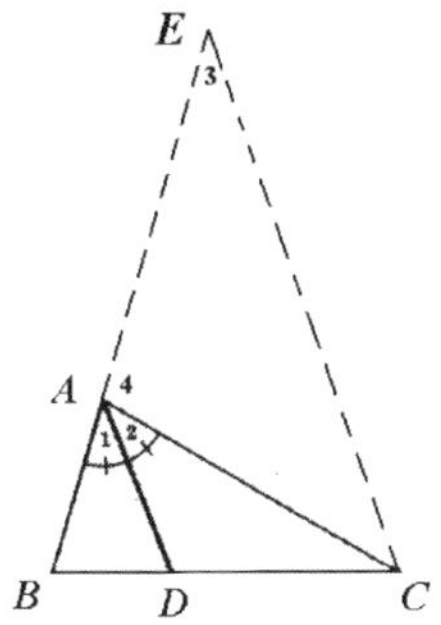

Method 4:

Draw $BE // AC$ so that BE meets the extension of AD at E.

$\angle 1 = \angle 2 = \angle 3$

So $BA = BE$ and $\Delta CAD \sim \Delta BED$

Therefore $CD : DB = AC : BE = AC : AB$, or $\dfrac{AB}{AC} = \dfrac{BD}{CD}$.

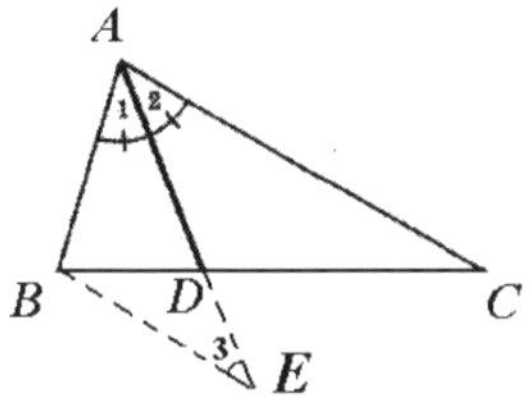

Theorem 1 b (The Angle Bisector Theorem)

In ΔABC, if AD bisects the exterior angle $\angle CAE$ of ΔABC, then

$$\frac{AB}{BD} = \frac{AC}{CD} \quad \text{or} \quad \frac{AB}{AC} = \frac{BD}{CD}$$

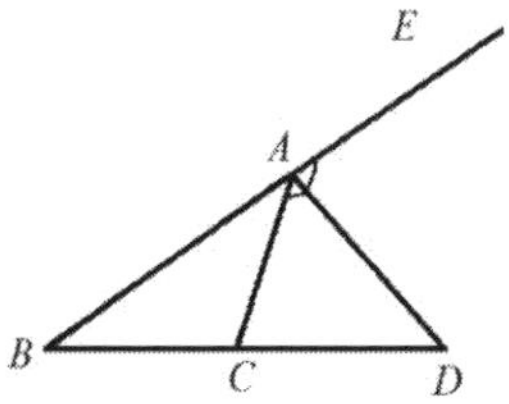

Proof:

Extend BA to E and connect DE such that $\angle CDA = \angle ADE$.

So ΔACD and ΔADE are congruent. Then $DE = CD$ and $AC = AE$.

AD is the angle bisector of triangle BDE. By the angle bisector Theorem 1a, $\dfrac{BD}{AB} = \dfrac{DE}{AE} = \dfrac{CD}{AC} \quad \Rightarrow \quad \dfrac{AB}{BD} = \dfrac{AC}{CD}$.

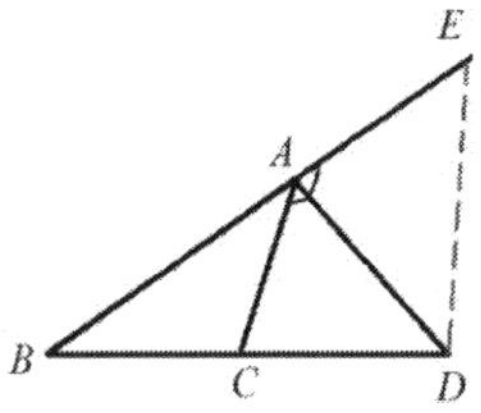

Theorem 2 (The angle bisector length formula):

$$AD^2 = AB \times AC - BD \times DC$$

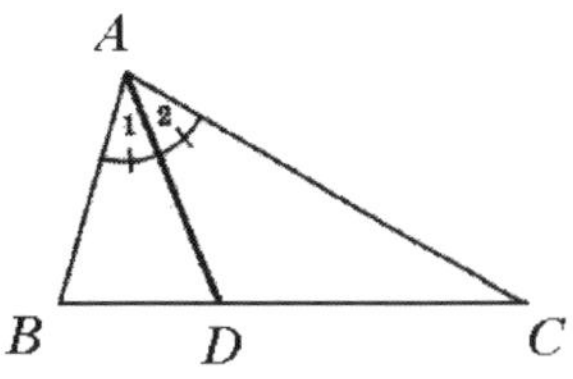

Proof:

Construct a circle that circumscribes the triangle as shown in the figure. Extend AD to meet the circle at E and connect BE.

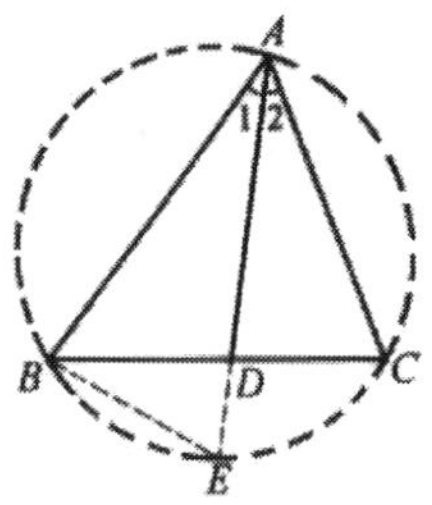

Since $\angle E = \angle C$, $\angle 1 = \angle 2$, $\Delta ABE \sim \Delta ADC$

$AB \cdot AC = AD \cdot AE$ (1)

$BD \cdot DC = AD \cdot DE$ (2)

(1) – (2):

$AB \cdot AC - BD \cdot CD = AD \cdot AE - AD \cdot DE = AD(AE - DE)$

$= AD \cdot AD = AD^2$

Therefore $AD^2 = AB \cdot AC - BD \cdot CD$.

Median

A median of a triangle is a segment from a vertex to the midpoint of the opposite side.

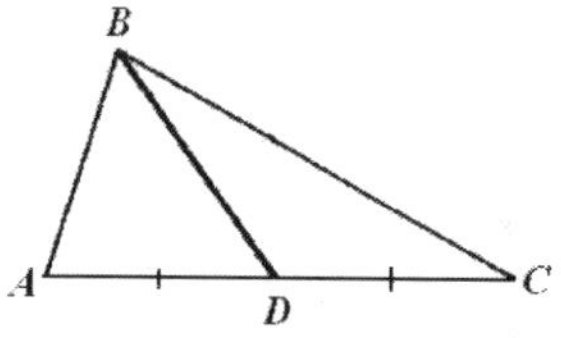

Median

Theorem 3: The three medians of a triangle meet in a point called the centroid. The centroid lies on each median so that the measure of the segment from the vertex to the centroid is two-thirds the measure of the median.

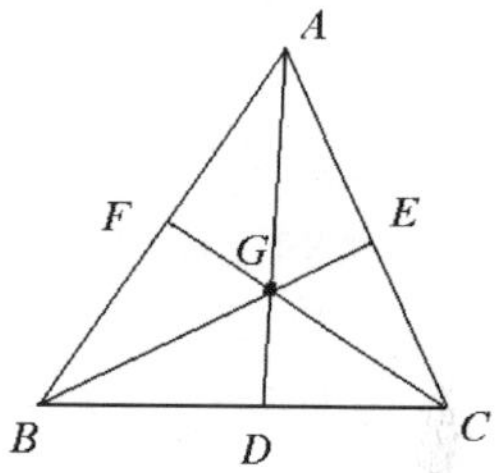

$AG = \dfrac{2}{3}AD$, $BG = \dfrac{2}{3}BE$, $CG = \dfrac{2}{3}CF$.

Proof:

Let E and F denote the midpoints of AC and AB, respectively.

Connect EF. $EF = \dfrac{1}{2}BC$ and $EF \parallel BC$.

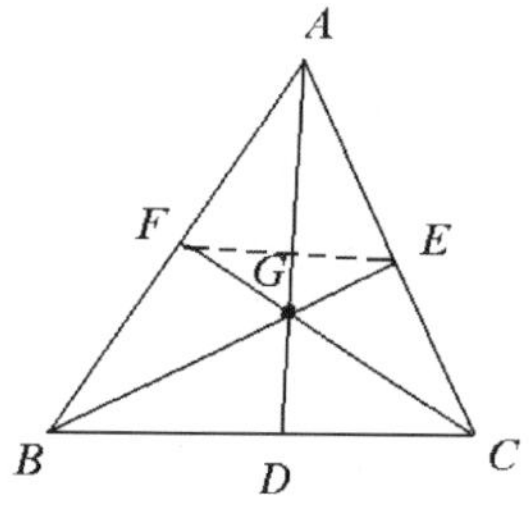

Since $\Delta GEF \sim \Delta GBC$, $\dfrac{GE}{GB} = \dfrac{EF}{BC}$.

Since $BC = 2EF$, $GB = 2GE$.

$BG = \dfrac{2}{3}BE$.

Similarly we can prove $AG = \frac{2}{3}AD$ and $CG = \frac{2}{3}CF$.

Theorem 4: Three medians divide the triangle ABC into six small triangles of equal areas.

$$S_{\Delta ADG} = S_{\Delta DCG} = S_{\Delta CFG} = S_{\Delta FBG} = S_{\Delta BEG} = S_{\Delta EAG} = \frac{1}{6}S_{\Delta ABC}$$

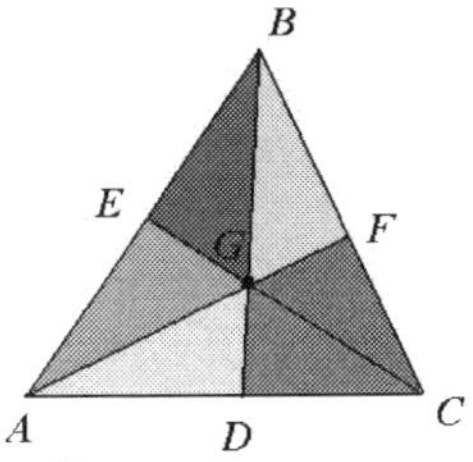

Theorem 5 (The median length formula):

$$(BD^2) + (BD^2) = (AB^2 - AD^2) + (BC^2 - CD^2)$$

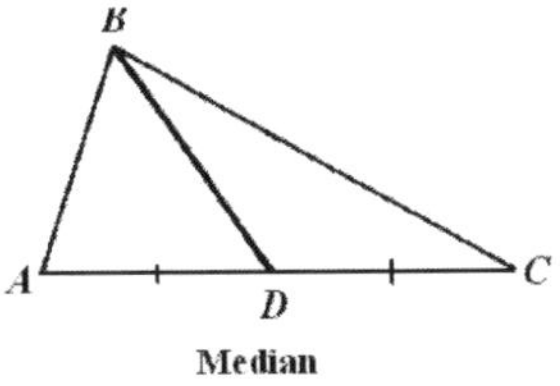

Proof:

In triangle ABC, let $AB = c$, $AC = b$, $BC = a$ and D be the midpoint of AC. Let m_b be the length of the median BD.

Extend BD to O such that $BD = DO$ and connect AO and CO. Since AC and BO bisect each other, they are two diagonals of a parallelogram, and $ABCO$ is a parallelogram.

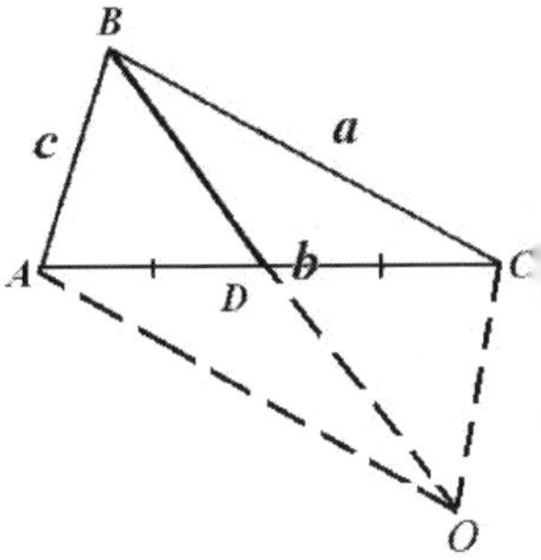

Therefore $2(AB^2 + BC^2) = AC^2 + BO^2 = 4(\frac{AC}{2})^2 + 4(\frac{BO}{2})^2$

$$= 4(\frac{AC}{2})^2 + 4BD^2$$

So $AB^2 + BC^2 = 2[BD^2 + (\frac{AC}{2})^2] \Rightarrow c^2 + a^2 = 2[m_b^2 + (\frac{b}{2})^2]$

$$\Rightarrow \quad m_b = \frac{1}{2}\sqrt{2a^2 + 2c^2 - b^2}.$$

Note that this is the formula to calculate the median of a triangle if three sides are known.

Similarly, we can have: $m_a = \frac{1}{2}\sqrt{2b^2 + 2c^2 - a^2}$ and $m_c = \frac{1}{2}\sqrt{2a^2 + 2b^2 - c^2}$.

Theorem 6: ΔABC is a right triangle ($\angle C = 90°$). D is any point on BC, and E is any point on AC.

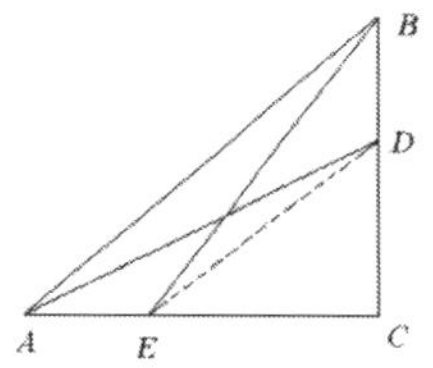

Then $AD^2 + BE^2 = AB^2 + DE^2$

Theorem 7: As shown in the figure, triangle ABC has the vertices $A(x_1, y_1)$, $B(x_2, y_2)$, and $C(x_3, y_3)$. Show that the coordinates of G, the centroid (the point where three medians meet) are ($\frac{x_1+x_2+x_3}{3}, \frac{y_1+y_2+y_3}{3}$).

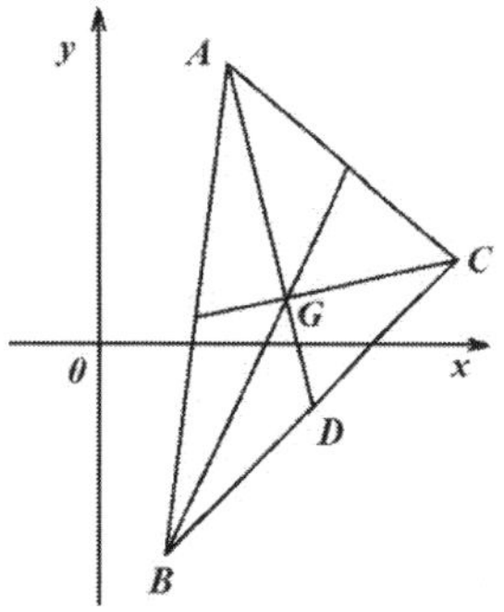

Proof:
Let the coordinates of G be $G(x, y)$.
Call the midpoint of BC point D.
By the midpoint formula, we can get the coordinates of D:
$\left(\frac{x_2+x_2}{2}, \frac{y_2+y_2}{2}\right)$.

Since G is the centroid of the triangle ABC, we know that $AG : GD = 2 : 1$.
In other words, $\lambda = \frac{AG}{GD} = 2$.

Using the formula $x = \frac{x_1+\lambda x_2}{1+\lambda}$ and $y = \frac{y_1+\lambda y_2}{1+\lambda}$, we can find the coordinates of G:

$$x = \frac{x_1 + 2\cdot\frac{x_2+x_3}{2}}{1+2} = \frac{x_1+x_2+x_3}{3}, \text{ and } y = \frac{y_1 + 2\cdot\frac{y_2+y_3}{2}}{1+2} = \frac{y_1+y_2+y_3}{3}.$$

EXAMPLES

Example 1. (NYML) 234 is the inch-length of the altitude to base AC of isosceles triangle ABC. If the inch-length of the median to BC is 195, find the number of square inches in the area of triangular region ABC.

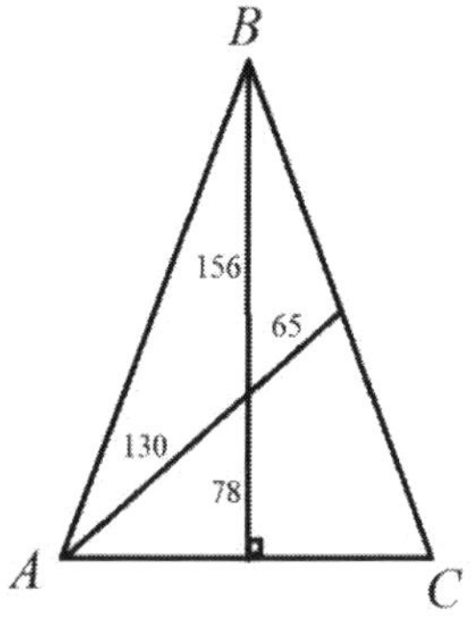

Solution: 24336.
Method 1 (official solution):
In figure at right, since the altitude is also a median, a right triangle whose hypotenuse has length 130 and one of whose legs has length 78 is formed near the base. This is a 3-4-5 right triangle, and $AC = 2(104) = 208$, making the area of triangle ABC equal to 24336.

Method 2 (our solution):
AF, CE, and BD are three medians. They meet at G.

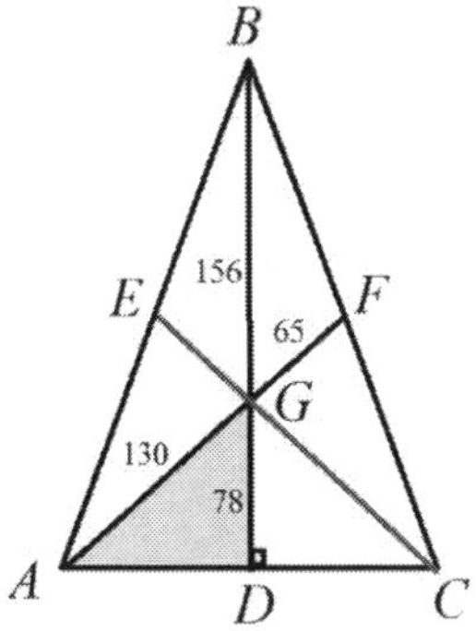

$$GD = \frac{1}{3}BD = \frac{1}{3}\times 234 = 78.\ \ AG = \frac{2}{3}AF = \frac{2}{3}\times 195 = 130.$$

Triangle ADG is a 3–4–5 right triangle (3×26, 4×26, 5×26) and $AD = 104$.

$$S_{\Delta ADG} = \frac{78\times 104}{2} = 4056$$

$$S_{\Delta ABC} = 6S_{\Delta ADG} = 6\times 4056 = 24336.$$

Example 2. (AMC) Medians BD and CE of a triangle ABC are perpendicular, $BD = 8$, and $CE = 12$. Find the area of triangle ABC.

Solution: 64.
Method 1 (official Solution):

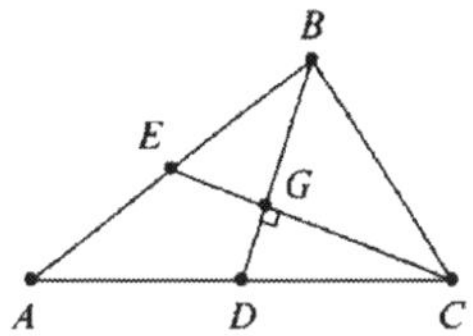

Let the medians meet at point G. $CG = (2/3)CE = 8$ and the area of triangle BCD is $(1/2)BD \cdot CG = (1/2) \cdot 8 \cdot 8 = 32$. Since BD is a median, triangles ABD and DBC have the same area. Hence the area of the triangle is 64.

Method 2: (our Solution): Connect AG and extend it to meet BC at F.

$DG = \frac{1}{3}BD = \frac{1}{3} \times 8 = \frac{8}{3}$, and $CG = \frac{2}{3}CE = \frac{2}{3} \times 12 = 8$

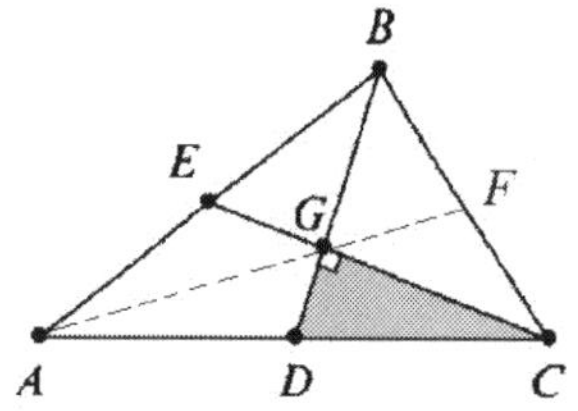

$$S_{\Delta CDG} = \frac{1}{2}DG \times CG = \frac{1}{2} \times \frac{8}{3} \times 8 = \frac{32}{3}$$

We know that

$$S_{\Delta CDG} = \frac{1}{6}S_{\Delta ABC} = \frac{32}{3}$$

Multiplying both sides by 6, $S_{\Delta ABC} = 6S_{\Delta CDG} = 6 \times \frac{32}{3} = 64$

Example 3. (ARML) In triangle ABC, median $BM = 29$. A perpendicular from C to ray BM meets BM at R. If $CR = 4$, compute the area of triangle ABC.

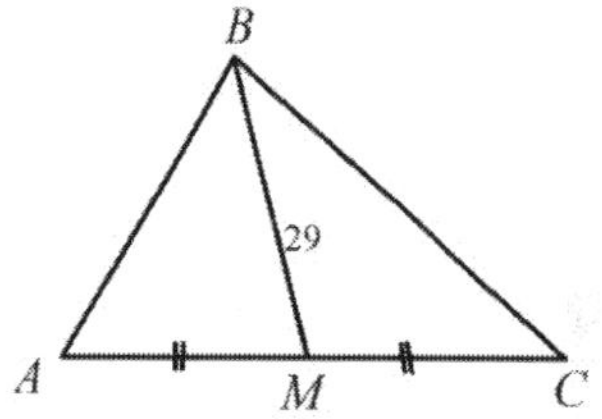

Solution: 116.

Method 1 (official solution):

Area of BMC = (1/2)(4)(29); area of ABC = (2)(area of BMC) = 116.

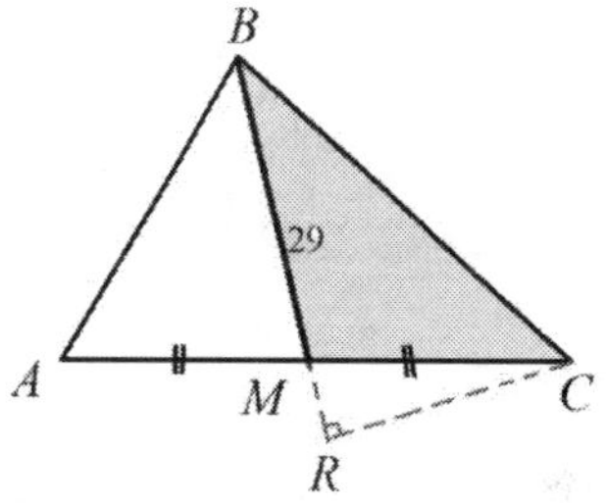

Method 2 (our solution):

$$S_{\Delta MBC} = \frac{BM \times CR}{2} = \frac{29 \times 4}{2} = 58$$

$$S_{\Delta ABC} = S_{\Delta MBC} + S_{\Delta MBA} == 2S_{\Delta MBC} = 2 \times 58 = 116.$$

Example 4. In ΔABC, CD and AE are medians, $FC \,//\, AB$, H is a point between B and D such that points F, E, and H lie in a straight line. The area of $\Delta AEH = 22$ and the area of ΔCEF is 14. Compute the area of ΔABC.

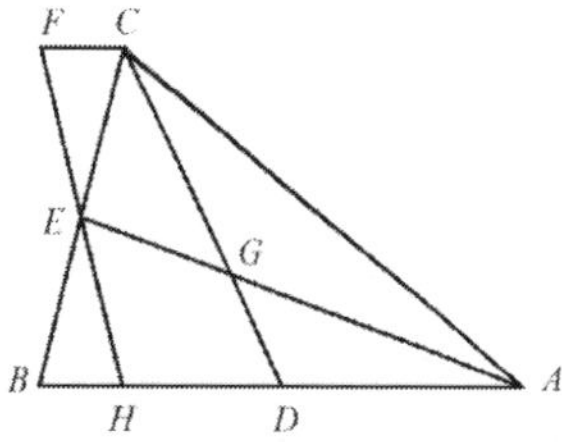

Solution: 72.

Since $FC \parallel AB$, $\angle FCE = \angle EBH$, $\angle FEC = \angle HEB$ by the vertical angle theorem, and since E is the midpoint of CB, $EC = EB$. Thus, $\Delta ECF = \Delta EBH \to$ the area of ΔECF equals the area of ΔEBH. Thus the area of $\Delta ABE = 14 + 22 = 36$ which also equals the area of ΔACE. Since the area of ΔABE is half the area of ΔABC because CD is a median, the area of ΔABC is 72.

Example 5. (ARML) In triangle *ABC*, angle bisectors *AD* and *BE* intersect at *P*. If $a = 3$, $b = 5$, $C = 7$, $BP = x$, and $PE = y$, compute the ratio $x : y$, where x and y are relatively prime integers.

Solution: 2 : 1.

Method 1 (official solution):

Let $AE = r$. Then $r : (5 - r) = 7 : 3$, so $r = 3\ 1/2$. Now in triangle *ABE*, $x : y = 7 : r = 2 : 1$ or 2.

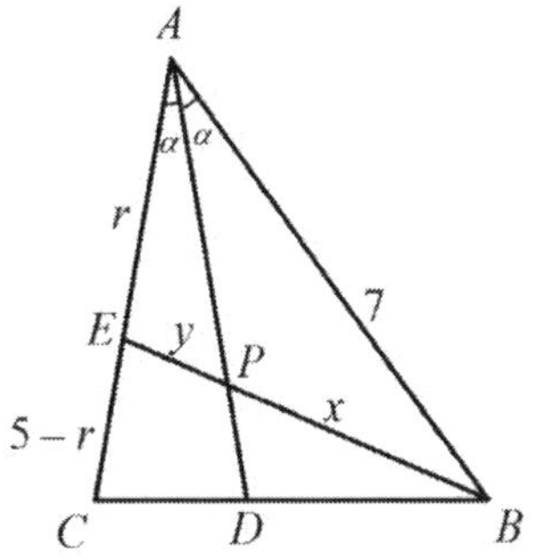

Method 2 (our solution):

$$\frac{S_{\Delta AEP}}{S_{\Delta ABP}} = \frac{\frac{1}{2}AE \times AP \sin\alpha}{\frac{1}{2}AB \times AP \sin\alpha} = \frac{AE}{AB} = \frac{r}{7} = \frac{y}{x} \quad \Rightarrow \quad \frac{x}{y} = \frac{7}{r} \quad (1)$$

Since *BE* is the angle bisector of $\angle B$, by the angle bisector theorem, $\frac{7}{r} = \frac{3}{5-r} \quad \Rightarrow \quad \frac{7}{r} = \frac{3}{5-r} = \frac{7+3}{r+5-r} = \frac{10}{5} = 2$

$$\Rightarrow \quad r = \frac{7}{2}.$$

Substituting the value of r into (1): $\frac{x}{y} = \frac{7}{r} = \frac{7}{\frac{7}{2}} = \frac{2}{1}$.

Method 3 (our solution):

Since we want to find *BP*: *PE*, we need to find the masses of *B* and *E*.

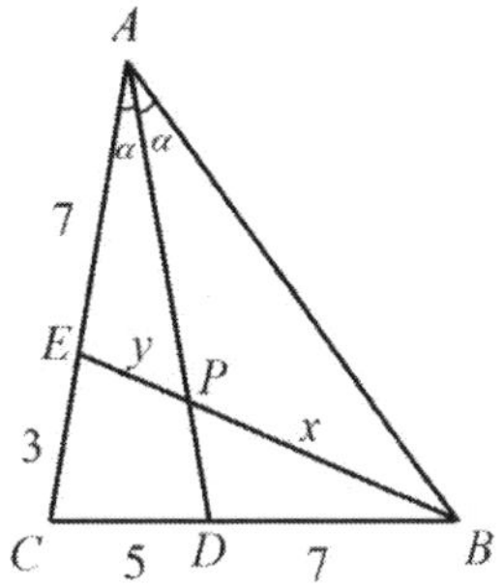

By the Angle bisector theorem, we have

$\frac{CE}{AE} = \frac{3}{7}$, and $\frac{BD}{CD} = \frac{7}{5}$.

Then we label the lengths of each line segment as shown.

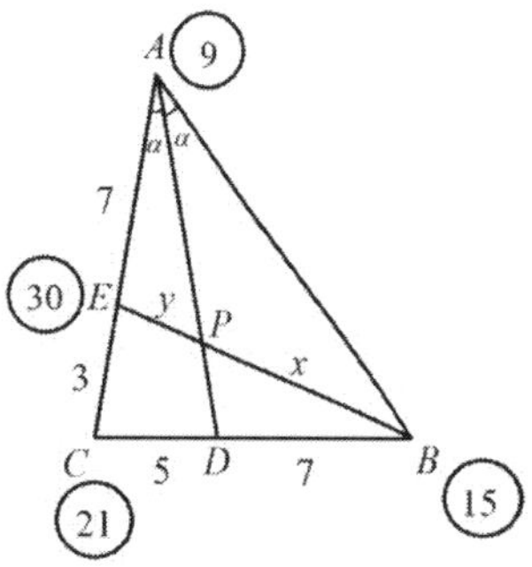

Let the masses in each point be m_A, m_B, m_C, and m_E, respectively. We need to find m_B and m_E.

We assign a mass of 15 to point *B*.

We look at the side *BC*.

$m_B \times 7 = m_C \times 5 \qquad \Rightarrow \qquad m_C = 21$.

Now we determine m_A.

We look at the side *AC*. The center of mass of *AC* is on *E*.

$m_C \times 3 = m_A \times 7 \qquad \Rightarrow \qquad m_A = 9$

$m_E = m_A + m_C = 9 + 21 = 30$.

The last step is to find the answer:

$m_B \times BP = m_E \times PE \quad \Rightarrow \quad \frac{x}{y} = \frac{30}{15} = 2$.

Example 6. In triangle *ABD*, *BC* is the angle bisector of $\angle B$. *AB* = 5, *AC* = 3, *BC* = 7. Find the length of *CD*.

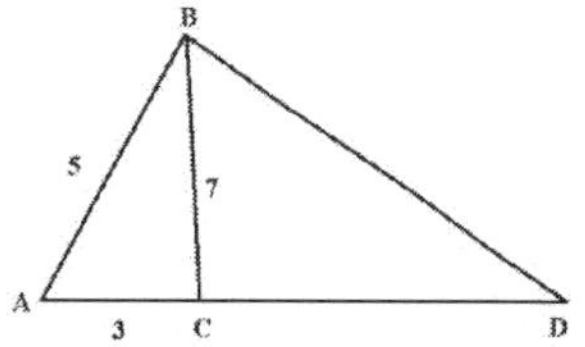

Solution: 147/16.

By the angle bisector theorem, we have:

$$\frac{AB}{AC} = \frac{BD}{CD} \qquad (1)$$

$$BC^2 = AB \times BD - AC \times CD \qquad (2)$$

$$\left.\begin{aligned} \frac{5}{3} &= \frac{BD}{CD} \\ 7^2 &= 5 \times BD - 3CD \end{aligned}\right\}$$ Solve for *CD*, *CD* = 147/16.

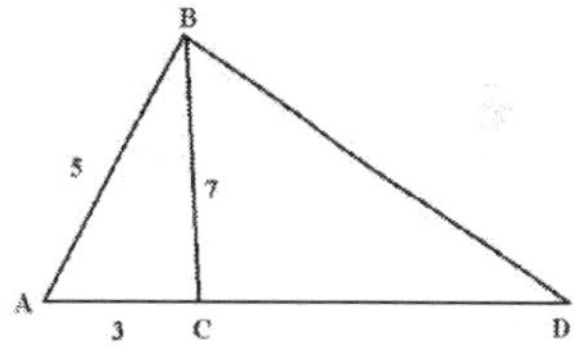

Example 7. (AMC) In ΔABC, we have *AB* = 1 and *AC* = 2. Side *BC* and the median from *A* to *BC* have the same length. What is *BC*?

Solution: $\sqrt{2}$.

By the median length formula:

$$(AD^2+DC^2)+(AD^2+BD^2)=AB^2+AC^2$$
$$(2m)^2+m^2+(2m)^2+m^2=1^2+2^2$$
$$10m^2=5 \quad \Rightarrow \quad m^2=\frac{1}{2} \quad \Rightarrow \quad m=\frac{\sqrt{2}}{2}$$
$$BC=2m=2\times\frac{\sqrt{2}}{2}=\sqrt{2}.$$

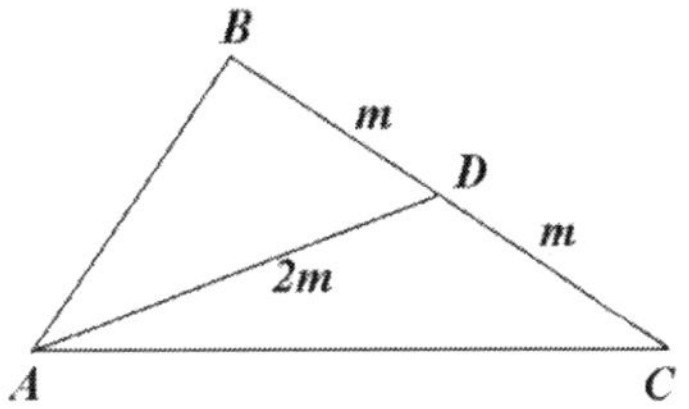

(Note: This is Problem 23 in 2002 AMC 12 B. There are two official solutions given by AMC, with one using the law of cosine and one using the coordinate system. We provided a third solution that has not been published elsewhere).

Example 8. (ARML) Triangle ABC is inscribed in a circle and BP bisects angle ABC. If $AB = 6$, $BC = 8$, and $AC = 7$, compute BP.

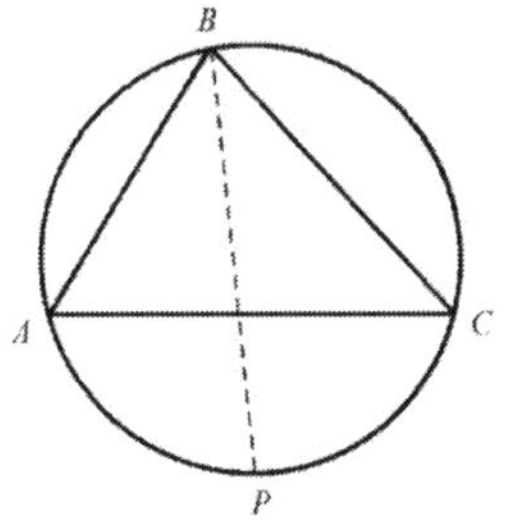

Solution: 8.
Method 1 (official solution):
Let AC and BP intersect at Q, and let $AQ = p$, CQ $= q$, $BQ = t$, and $PQ = x$. Utilizing two "angle-bisector" theorems and one theorem about chords intersecting in a circle, we have
(1) $p : q = 6 : 8$ implies $p = 6k$, $q = 8k$. Thus $14k = 7$, so $k = 1/2$. Therefore $p = 3$ and $q = 4$.
(2) $t^2 = 6 \times 8 - p \times q$. Therefore $t^2 = 36$, so $t = 6$.

(3) $tx = pq$, so $6x = 12$, making $x = 2$, and thus $BP = 8$.

Method 2 (our solution):
Connect CP and AP. Since PB bisects $\angle ABC$, $CP = AP$.
By the angle bisector theorem, $\frac{BA}{AQ}=\frac{BC}{CQ}=\frac{BA+BC}{AQ+CQ}=\frac{6+8}{7}=2 \Rightarrow$

$AQ = 3$.

Triangle ABQ is similar to triangle PBC. So we have $\frac{AB}{PB}=\frac{AQ}{PC}=\frac{BQ}{8}$ $\Rightarrow$

$\frac{6}{PB}=\frac{3}{PC}$ $\Rightarrow$ $PB=2PC=2x$.

Triangle ABQ is similar to triangle PCQ. So we have $PQ=\frac{1}{2}PC=\frac{1}{2}x$.

We also have $PQ\times QB=AQ\times CQ$ $\Rightarrow$ $\frac{1}{2}x\times\frac{3}{2}x=3\times 4$ $\Rightarrow$

$x=4 \Rightarrow$ $2x = 8$.

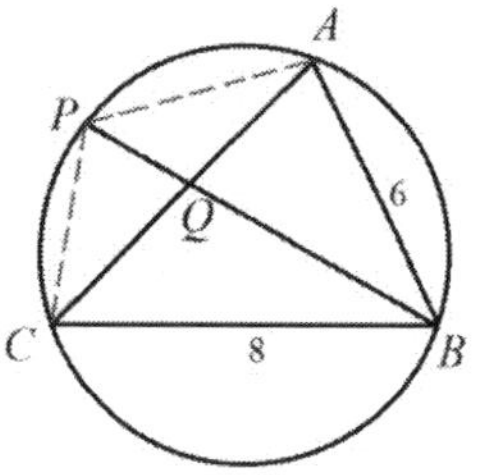

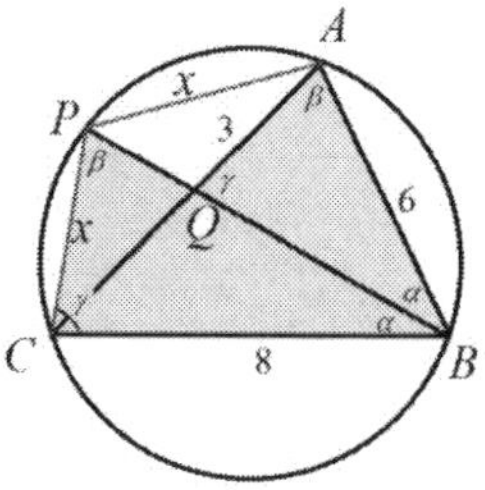

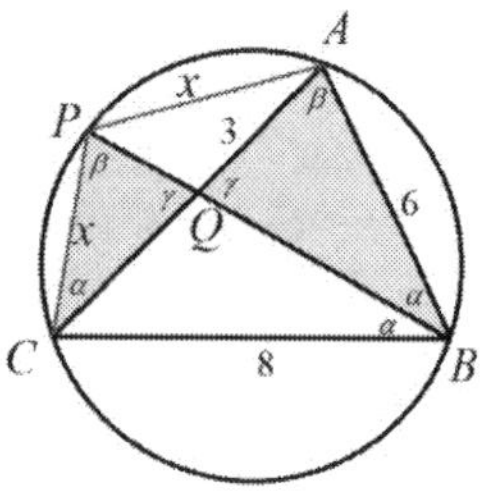

Example 9. (1992 ARML) Points *P, Q*, and *R* are the midpoints of the medians of triangle *ABC*. If the area of triangle *ABC* is 1,024, compute the area of triangle *PQR*.

Solution: 64.

Method 1 (official solution):

Let *P* and *Q* be the midpoints of medians *AD* and *BE* respectively, and let the medians intersect at *O*. Letting $OD = 2x$, we have $AO = 4x$, $AP = 3x$, so $PO = x$. Since *PQ* is parallel to *AB*, triangles *PQO* and *ABO* are similar, with ratio of similitude 1 : 4. Thus the area of *PQO* == (1/16) the area of *ABC*. Similarly, we see that the area of *PQR* = (1/16) the area of *ABC* = (1/16) (1024) = 64.

Method 2 (our solution):

Let the centroid be *O*. Let $AD = 6x$. Then $AP = 3x$, $AO = 4x$, $OD = 2x$,

So $PO = AO - AP = 4x - 3x = x$.

We know that triangle *ABC* and triangle *PQR* are similar. So the ratio of their areas is

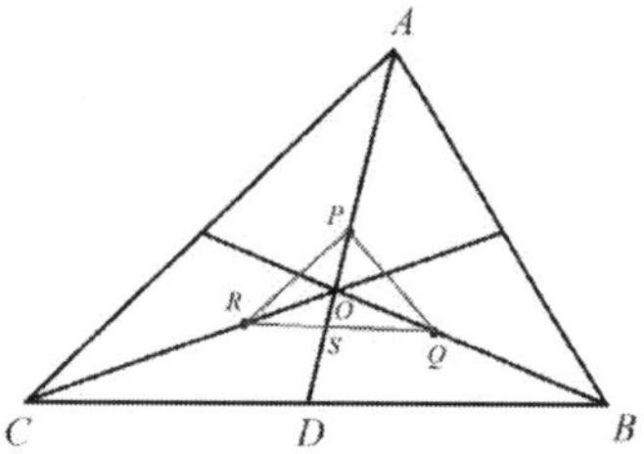

$$\frac{S_{\Delta PQR}}{S_{\Delta ABC}} = (\frac{PO}{AO})^2 = (\frac{x}{4x})^2 = \frac{1}{16} \qquad \Rightarrow$$

$$S_{\Delta PQR} = \frac{1}{16} S_{\Delta ABC} = \frac{1}{16} \times 1024 = 64$$

Example 10. (NYML) In acute triangle *ABC, AH* and *AM* are respectively an altitude and a median. The bisector of $\angle A$ cuts *BC* in *D*. The inch lengths of *AB*, *AC*, and *MD* are respectively 11, 8, and 1. Find the inch length of *MH*.

Solution: 2.25.

Method 1 (official solution):

(See figure to right.) As *AD* is the bisector of $\angle A$, $CD : DB = 8 : 11$. Let $CD = 8a$ and $DB = 11a$ for some number *a*. As CM = *MB*. $CM = MB = 9.5a$ (or $19a/2$). Now $DM = 1.5a$. It is given that $DM = 1$. Hence. $1.5a = 1$ so $a = 2/3$. Then $CD = 16/3$ and $DB = 22/3$. Let $x = HD$. Then $8^2 - (16/3 - x)^2 = AH^2 = 11^2 - (22/3 + x)^2$. The x^2 term falls out leaving a linear equation and thus $HM = 1 + x = 2.25$.

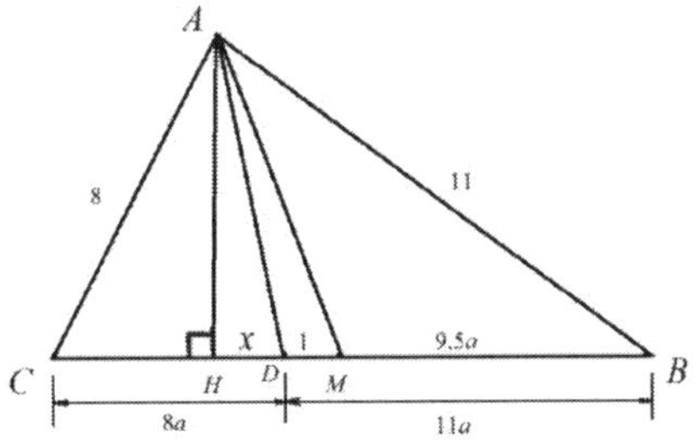

Method 2 (our solution):

As *AD* is the bisector of $\angle A$, $CD : DB = 8 : 11$. Let $CD = 8a$ and $DB = 11a$ for some number *a*. As CM = *MB*. $CM = MB = 9.5a$ (or $19a/2$). Now $DM = 1.5a$. It is given that $DM = 1$. Hence. $1.5a = 1$ so $a = 2/3$. Then $CD = 16/3$ and $BD = 22/3$.

$$AD^2 = AB \cdot AC - BD \cdot CD$$

$$= 8 \times 11 - \frac{16}{3} \times \frac{22}{3} = \frac{440}{9}.$$

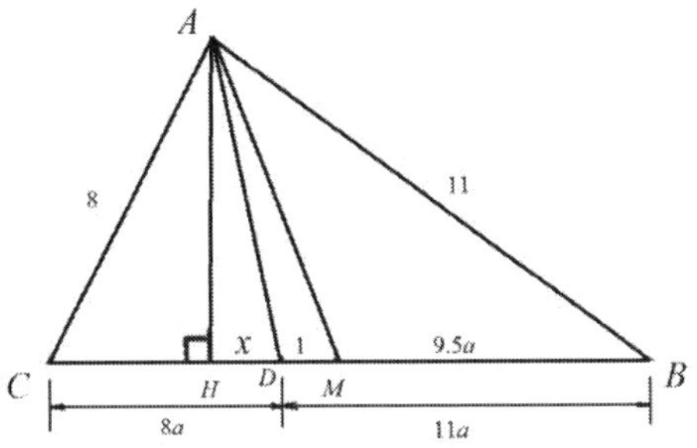

Let $x = HD$. Then $(440/9) - x^2 = AH^2 = 8^2 - (16/3 - x)^2$. Solving we get $x = 5/4$. $HM = 1 + x = 9/4 = 2.25$.

Example 11. (NYML) In triangle *RST* the inch-lengths of *RS, ST*, and *RT* are, respectively, 16. 24, and 20. If *SB* and *SM* are, respectively, the angle-bisector and the median from S, the number of square inches in the area of triangle BSM is $k\sqrt{7}$. Find the value of k.

Solution: 6.

Method 1 (official solution):

(See adjacent figure.) Let $x = RD$ where SD is the altitude from S. Then $SD^2 = 16^2 - x^2 = 24^2 - (20 - x)^2$.

Solving for x we get $x = 2$. Angle bisector SB divides the side it is drawn to in the ratio of the included sides; let $p = DB$. Then $\frac{16}{24} = \frac{2+p}{18-p}$

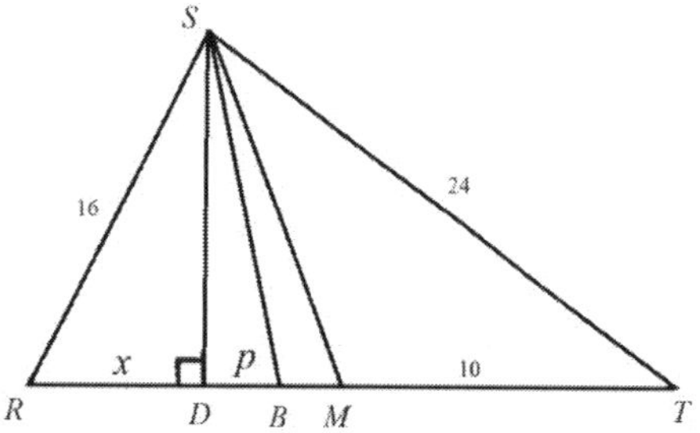

$\Rightarrow \quad p = 6$.

Area of ΔSBM = Area of $\Delta SDM - \Delta SDB = (6\sqrt{7} \times 8)/2 - (6\sqrt{7} \times 6)/2 = 6\sqrt{7} = k\sqrt{7}$. So $k = 6$.

Method 2 (our solution):

By the angle bisector theorem, $\frac{16}{RB} = \frac{24}{TB} \quad \Rightarrow \frac{2}{RB} = \frac{3}{TB} = \frac{5}{RB+TB} = \frac{5}{20} = \frac{1}{4}$.

So $TB = 12$. We also know that $TM = 10$.

So $BM = TB - TM = 12 - 10 = 2$.

Triangle RST is a $16 - 20 - 24$ triangle with the area of (Heron Formula):

$$A = \sqrt{s(s-a)(s-b)(s-c)} = \sqrt{30(30-16)(30-20)(30-24)} = 60\sqrt{7},$$

where $s = \frac{1}{2}(16+20+24) = 30$.

$$\frac{S_{\Delta BSM}}{S_{\Delta RST}} = \frac{BM}{RT} = \frac{2}{20} = \frac{1}{10} \quad \Rightarrow \quad S_{\Delta BSM} = \frac{1}{10} \times S_{\Delta RST} = 6\sqrt{7} = k\sqrt{7}.$$ So $k = 6$.

Example 12. (2009 Tie break ARML) In ΔABC, D is on AC so that BD is the angle bisector of $\angle B$. Point E is on AB and CE intersects BD at P. Quadrilateral $BCDE$ is cyclic, $BP = 12$ and $PE = 4$. Compute the ratio $\frac{AC}{AE}$.

Solution: 3.

Method 1 (official solution):

Let ω denote the circle that circumscribes quadrilateral *BCDE*. Draw in line segment *DE*. Note that $\angle DPE$ and $\angle CPB$ are congruent, and $\angle DEC$ and $\angle DBC$ are congruent, since they cut off the same arc of ω. Therefore, ΔBCP and ΔEDP are similar. Thus $\frac{BC}{DE}=\frac{BP}{EP}=\frac{12}{4}=3$.

Because $\angle BCE$ and $\angle BDE$ cut off the same arc of ω, these angles are congruent. Let α be the measure of these angles. Similarly, $\angle DCE$ and $\angle DBE$ cut off the same arc of ω. Let β be the measure of these angles.

Since *BD* is an angle bisector, $m\angle CBD = \beta$.

Note that $m\angle ADE = 180° - m\angle BDE - m\angle BDC$. It follows that

$m\angle ADE = 180° - m\angle BDE - (180° - m\angle CBD - m\angle BCD)$

$\Rightarrow m\angle ADE = 180° - m\angle BDE - (180° - m\angle CBD - m\angle BCE - m\angle DCE)$

$\Rightarrow m\angle ADE = 180° - \alpha - (180° - \beta - \alpha - \beta)$

$\Rightarrow m\angle ADE = 2\beta = m\angle CBD$.

Thus $\angle ADE$ is congruent to $\angle CBD$, and it follows that ΔADE is similar to ΔABC. Hence $BC/DE = AC/AE$, and by substituting in given values, we have $AC/AE = 3$.

Method 2 (our solution):

Triangle *ACE* is similar to triangle *ABD*.

$$\frac{AC}{AB}=\frac{AE}{AD} \quad\Rightarrow\quad \frac{AC}{AE}=\frac{AB}{AD} \qquad (1)$$

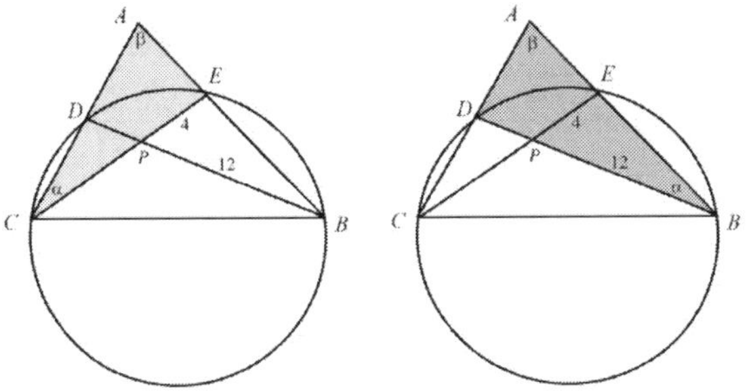

Connect *DE*. As shown in the figure, $CD = DE$.

Since BD is the angle bisector of $\angle B$, by the angle bisector theorem,

$$\frac{AB}{AD} = \frac{BC}{CD} \quad \Rightarrow \quad \frac{AB}{AD} = \frac{BC}{DE} \qquad (2)$$

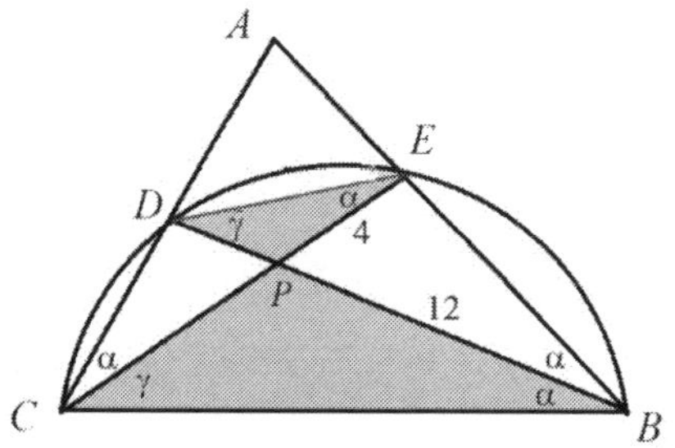

We also know that triangle BCP is similar to triangle EDP.

$$\frac{BC}{DE} = \frac{BP}{EP} = \frac{12}{4} = 3.$$

So $\frac{AB}{AD} = \frac{BC}{DE} = 3$ and $\frac{AC}{AE} = \frac{AB}{AD} = 3$.

Example 13. (2012 ARML) In triangle ABC, $AB = BC$. A trisector of $\angle B$ intersects AC at D. If AB, AC, and BD are integers and $AB - BD = 7$, compute AC.

Solution: 146.
Method 1 (official solution):
Let E be the point where the other trisector of $\angle B$ intersects side AC. Let $AB = BC = a$, and let $BD = BE = d$. Draw X on BC so that $BX = d$. Then $CX = 7$.

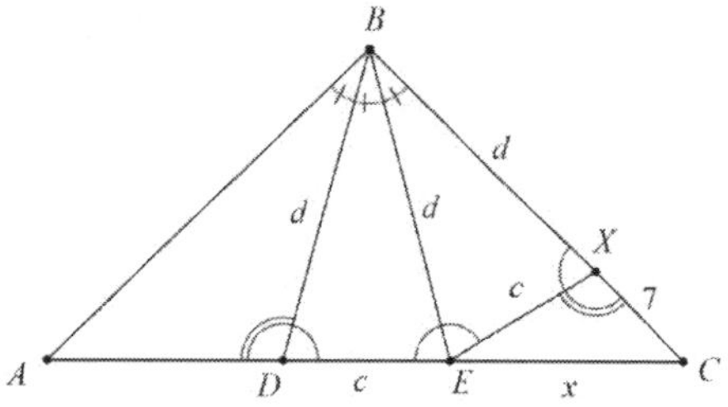

The placement of point X guarantees that $\Delta BEX \cong \Delta BDE$ by Side-Angle-Side. Therefore $\angle BXE \cong \angle BEX \cong \angle BDE$, and so $\angle CXE \cong \angle ADB \cong \angle CEB$. By Angle-Angle, $\Delta CEX \sim \Delta CBE$. Let $EX = c$ and $EC = x$. Then comparing ratios of corresponding sides yields

$$\frac{c}{d}=\frac{7}{x}=\frac{x}{d+7}$$

Using the right proportion, $x^2 = 7(d + 7)$. Because d is an integer, x^2 is an integer, so either x is an integer or irrational. The following argument shows that x cannot be irrational. Applying the Angle Bisector Theorem to ΔBCD yields $DE = c = \frac{d}{d+7}\cdot x$. Then $AC = 2x + c = x(2+\frac{d}{d+7})$. Because the expression $(2+\frac{d}{d+7})$ is rational, AC will not be an integer if x is irrational.

Hence x is an integer, and because x^2 is divisible by 7, x must also be divisible by 7. Let $x = 7k$ so that $d = ck$.
Rewrite the original proportion using $7k$ for x and ck for d:

$$\frac{c}{d}=\frac{x}{d+7}$$

$$\frac{c}{ck}=\frac{7x}{ck+7}$$

$$7k^2=ck+7$$

$$7k=c+\frac{7}{k}$$

Because the left side of this last equation represents an integer, $7/k$ must be an integer, so either $k = 1$ or $k = 7$. The value $k = 1$ gives the extraneous solution $c = 0$. So $k = 7$, from which $c = 48$. Then $d = 336$ and $AC = 2x + c = 2 \times 49 + 48 = 146$.

Method 2 (our solution):
Let E be the point where the other trisector of $\angle B$ intersects side AC. Let $BD = BE = d$. Draw X on BC so that $BX = d$. Then $CX = 7$. Let $\angle ABD = \angle DBE = \angle EBC = \alpha$. Let $\angle A = \angle C = \gamma$.
$\Delta BEX \cong \Delta BDE$ by Side-Angle-Side. So $DE = EX = c$. $\angle CEX = \alpha$. $\angle CXE = \angle ADB = \beta$.

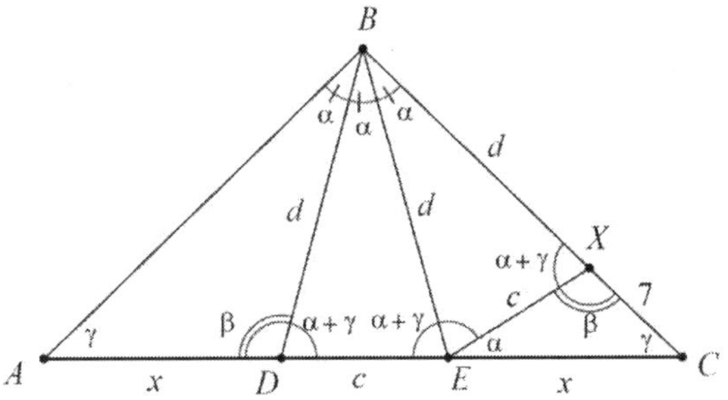

By Angle-Angle, $\Delta CEX \sim \Delta CBE$. Let $EX = c$ and $EC = x$.

$$\frac{7}{x}=\frac{c}{d}=\frac{x}{d+7} \quad \Rightarrow \quad \frac{7}{x}=\frac{c+2x}{d+2(d+7)}=\frac{AC}{3d+14} \quad \Rightarrow$$

$$AC=\frac{7(3d+14)}{x} \qquad (1)$$

By the angle bisector theorem, in triangle BCD, $\frac{d}{c}=\frac{d+7}{x}$ (2)

By the angle bisector length formula, in triangle BCD, $d^2=(d+7)d-cx$ (3)

Solving (2) and (3) by eliminating x: $7d=x^2-49$ (4)

Substituting (4) into (1): $AC=\frac{3\times 7d+14\times 7}{x}=\frac{3(x^2-49)+14\times 7}{x}$ or

$$AC=\frac{3x^2-3\times 49+14\times 7}{x}=3x-\frac{49}{x}.$$

Since AC is an positive integer, x can only be 7 or 49.

If $x = 7$, $AC=3\times 7-\frac{49}{7}=21-7=14$. From the figure, c will be zero and this is not possible.

If $x = 49$, $AC=3\times 49-\frac{49}{49}=147-1=146$. From the figure, c will be 48 and this is possible. So the answer is 146.

Example 14. (NYML) Two sides of a triangle lie along the x- and y-axes. Compute the area of the triangle if its medians meet at (4,2).

Solution: 36.

Method 1 (official solution):

Let the centroid of the triangle [intersection of the medians] be $G(4, 2)$, and the vertices be $A(a, 0)$, $B(0, b)$, and $O(0,0)$. Let two medians be AM and BN. Noting that a vertical line through G would be parallel to OM, that line would cut MA and OA proportionally. Since $MG = (1/3)(MA)$, then we have $4 = (1/3)(OA)$, so $OA = a = 12$. Similarly considering

a horizontal line through G, we find that $2 = (1/3)(OB)$, so $OB = b = 6$. The area of triangle $OAB = (1/2)ab = 36$.

Method 2 (official solution):
It can be shown that the coordinates of the centroid of any triangle are the "averages" of the coordinates of its vertices [considering abscissas and ordinates separately]. Then $a/3 = 4$ and $b/3 = 2$ imply $a = 12$, $b = 6$, and the area of this right triangle is $(1/2)ab = 36$.

Method 3 (our solution):
Let the centroid of the triangle [intersection of the medians] be $G(4, 2)$, and the vertices be $A(a, 0), B(0, b)$, and $O(0,0)$. Let two medians be AM and BN. The coordinates of N are $(a/2, 0)$.

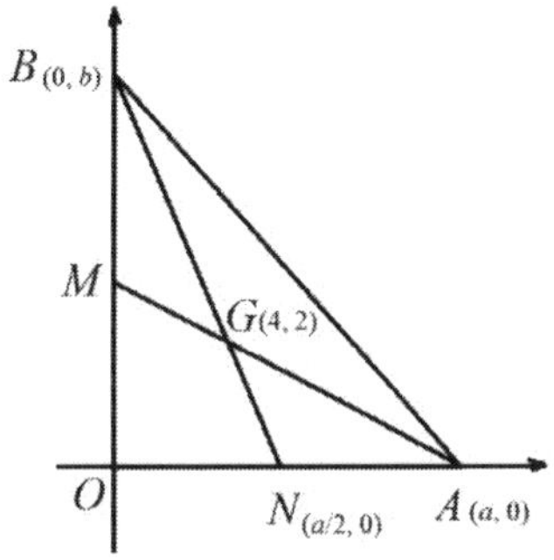

We know that $\lambda = BG/GN = 2/1$, then:

$$x = \frac{x_1 + \lambda x_2}{1+\lambda} \Rightarrow \quad 4 = \frac{0 + 2\times\frac{a}{2}}{1+2} \Rightarrow \quad a = 12$$

$$y = \frac{y_1 + \lambda y_2}{1+\lambda} \Rightarrow \quad 2 = \frac{b + 2\times 0}{1+2} \Rightarrow \quad b = 6$$

The area of triangle $OAB = (1/2)ab = 36$.

Example 15. In ΔABC, $\angle C = 90°$. $CD \perp BA$. BE is the angle bisector of $\angle B$ and meets CD at O and AC at E. Draw $OF // AB$ such that OF meets AC at F. Find AF if $CE = 2016$.

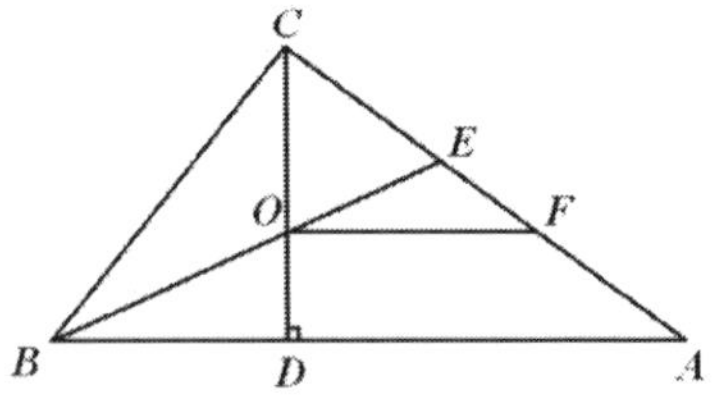

Solution: 2016.

Since $OF // AB$, $\frac{CO}{OD} = \frac{CF}{FA}$.

BO is the angle bisector of $\angle CBD$, so the angle bisector theorem tells us that:
$\frac{CO}{OD} = \frac{BC}{BD}$.

Therefore $\frac{CF}{FA} = \frac{BC}{BD}$ (1)

We know that $CF = AC - FA$. Substituting this into (1), we get:

$$\frac{AC-FA}{FA}=\frac{BC}{BD} \quad \Rightarrow \quad \frac{AC}{AF}-1=\frac{BC}{BD} \quad \Rightarrow \quad \frac{AC}{AF}=\frac{BC}{BD}+1 \qquad (2)$$

Since BE is the angle bisector of $\angle ABC$, the angle bisector theorem tells us that:

$$\frac{AE}{CE}=\frac{AB}{BC} \qquad (3)$$

We also know that $AE = AC - CE$, so substituting in $AC - CE$ for AE into (3), we get:

$$\frac{AC-CE}{CE}=\frac{AB}{BC} \quad \Rightarrow \quad \frac{AC}{CE}-1=\frac{AB}{BC} \quad \Rightarrow \quad \frac{AC}{CE}=\frac{AB}{BC}+1 \qquad (4)$$

We also know that $BC^2 = BD \cdot BA$ or $\dfrac{AB}{BC}=\dfrac{BC}{BD}$ (5)

From (2), (4), (5), we have $\dfrac{AC}{AF}=\dfrac{AC}{CE}$ $\Rightarrow CE = AF = 2016$.

PROBLEMS

Problem 1. (AMC) Let line AC be perpendicular to line CE. Connect A to the midpoint D of CE, and connect E to the midpoint B of AC. If AD and EB intersect in point F, and $BC = CD = 15$ inches, find the area of triangle DFE in square inches.

Problem 2. 1989 (NYML) The altitude to the hypotenuse of a right triangle cuts it into segments of lengths p and q, $p < q$. If that altitude is 1/4 the hypotenuse, then p/q will equal $a - b\sqrt{3}$. Compute the ordered pair of positive integers (a, b).

Problem 3. (ARML) In triangle ABC, median $BM = 25$. A perpendicular from A to ray BM meets BM at R. If $AR = 6$, compute the area of triangle ABC.

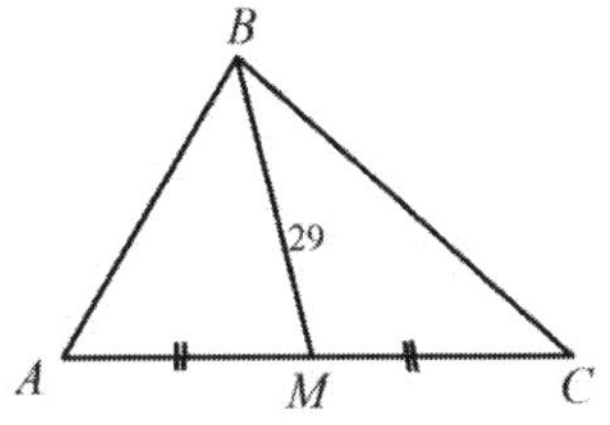

Problem 4. (ARML) In ΔCBA, CD and AE are medians, $FC \parallel AB$, FEH, CGD, and AGE. The area of $FCGE = 7$ and the area of $EGDH$ is 11. Compute the area of ΔCBA.

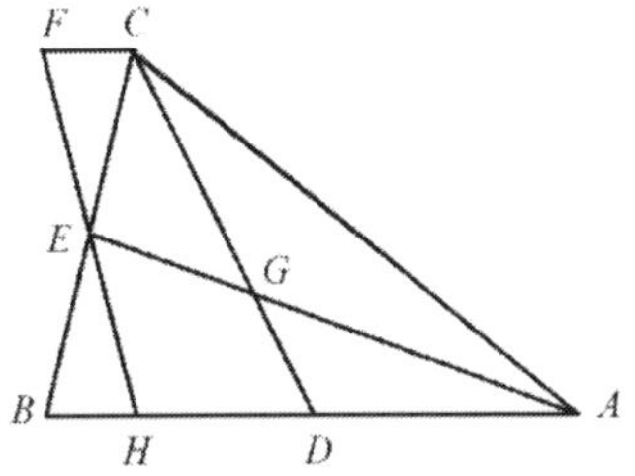

Problem 5. (ARML) In triangle ABC, points D and E are on AB and AC, and angle bisector AT intersects DE at F [as shown in the diagram]. If $AD = 1$, $DB = 3$, $AE = 2$, and $EC = 4$, compute the ratio $AF:AT$.

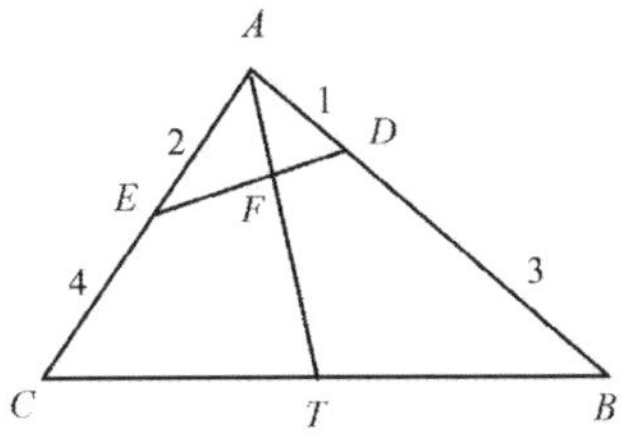

Problem 6. (NC Math Contest) Two sides of a triangle have lengths 25 and 20, and the median to the third side has length 19.5. Find the length of the third side.
a. 22.5 b. 23 c. 23.5 d. 24 e. 24.5

Problem 7. In square *ABCD*, *AC* and *BD* meet at *O*, the angle bisector of $\angle CAB$ meets *BD* at *F*, and meets *BC* at *G*. Find the ratio of *OF* to *CG*.

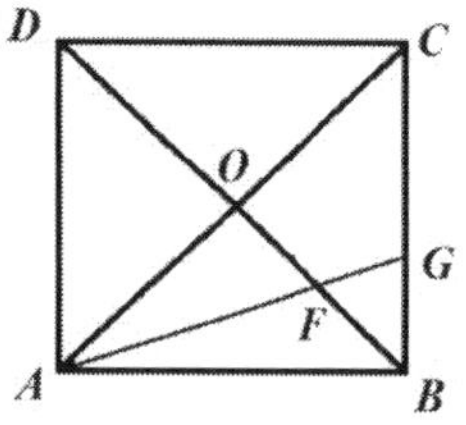

Problem 8. (ARML "An isosceles triangle has a median equal to 15 and an altitude equal to 24." This information determines exactly two triangles. Compute the area of either one of these triangles. [Only give *one* answer.]

Problem 9. (AMC) In the adjoining figure triangle *ABC* is such that $AB = 4$ and $AC = 8$. If *M* is the midpoint of *BC* and $AM = 3$, what is the length of *BC*?

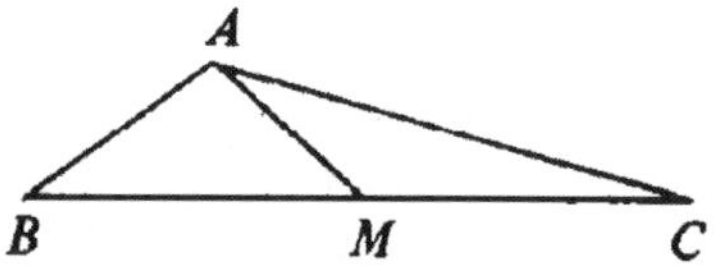

(A) $2\sqrt{26}$ (B) $2\sqrt{31}$ (C) 9 (D) $4 + 2\sqrt{13}$
(E) not enough information given to solve the problem

Problem 10. In acute triangle *ABC, AH* and *AM* are respectively an altitude and a median. The bisector of $\angle A$ cuts *BC* in *D*. The inch lengths of *AB*, *AC*, and *MD* are respectively 11, 8, and 1. Find the inch length of *AD*.

Problem 11. In acute triangle *ABC, AH* and *AM* are respectively an altitude and a median. The bisector of $\angle A$ cuts *BC* in *D*. The inch lengths of *AB*, *AC*, and *MD* are respectively 11, 8, and 1. Find the inch length of *AM*.

Problem 12. The lengths of the three sides of a triangle are consecutive positive integers. The largest angle of the triangle is two times of the smallest angle. What is the largest side of the triangle?

Problem 13. (NC Math Contest Geometry) A triangle has sides of length 11, 13, and 16 inches. How long is the median to the side of length 16 inches?

Problem 14. In ΔABC, median AD is perpendicular to median BE. Find AB if $BC = 6$ and $AC = 8$.

Problem 15. Find the measure of a side of a triangle if the other two sides and the bisector of the included angle have measures 12, 15, and 10, respectively.

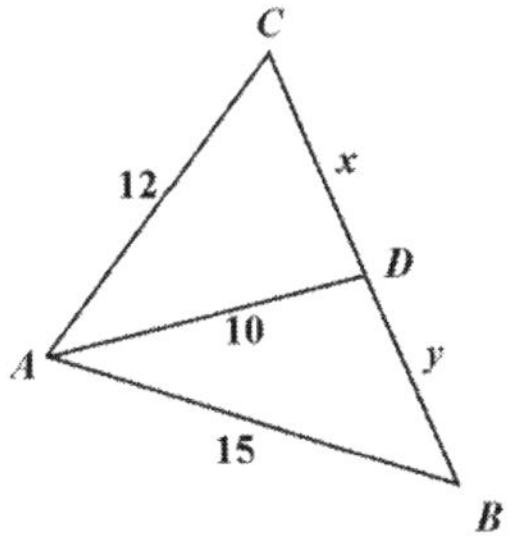

Problem 16. In a right triangle, the bisector of the right angle divides the hypotenuse into segments that measure 3 and 4. Find the measure of the angle bisector of the larger acute angle of the right triangle.

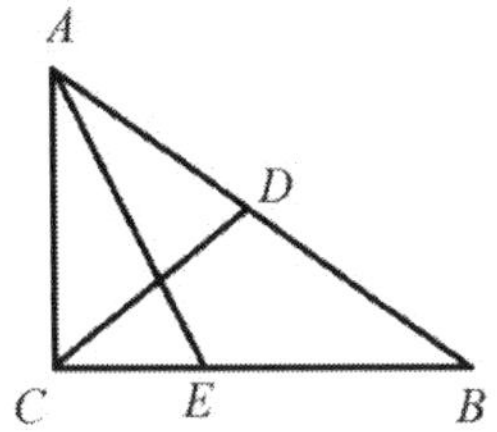

Problem 17. In a 30−60−90 right triangle, if the measure of the hypotenuse is 4, find the distance from the vertex of the right angle to the point of intersection of the angle bisectors.

Problem 18. (North Carolina Math Contest Geometry) Consider the ΔABC where CD bisects $\angle ACB$. If $\angle ACD = \angle CBD$ and $AD = a$ and $CD=b$, determine AC.

a) $\sqrt{a^2+ab}$ b) $\sqrt{a^2+b^2}$ c) $\sqrt{a^2+ab+b^2}$ d) $2\sqrt{ab}$ e) $\sqrt{(a-b)^2+a^2}$

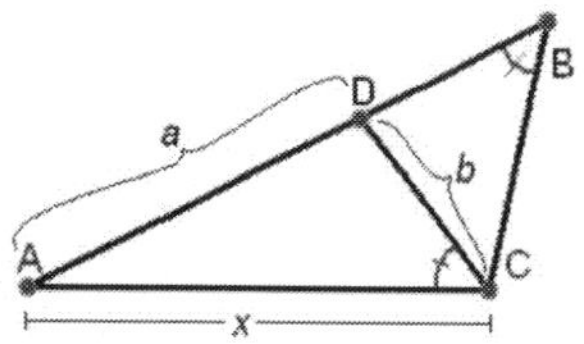

Problem 19. In isosceles ΔABC ($AB = AC$), the median BE divides the perimeter into the ratio of 5:3. If the perimeter of the triangle is 24 cm, find the length BC.

Problem 20. The vertices of triangle ABC are $A(4, 1)$, $B(7, 5)$, and $C(-4, 7)$. Find the equation of the angle bisector of $\angle A$.

SOLUTIONS

Problem 1. Solution: 75.

Method 1 (official solution):

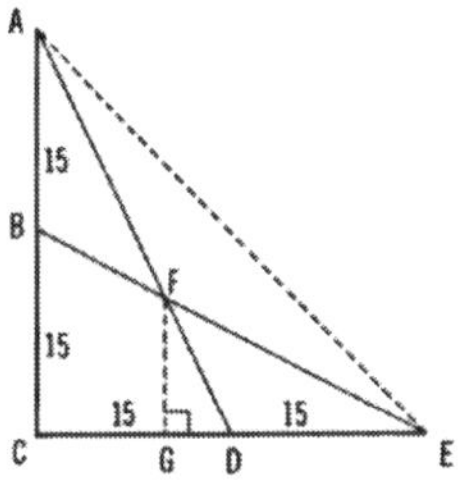

Draw AE and the altitude FG to the base DE of triangle DEF. Since F is the intersection point of the medians of a triangle ACE,

$$FD = \frac{1}{3}AD.$$

$$\therefore\ FG = \frac{1}{3}AC = \frac{1}{3}\cdot 30 = 10.$$

$$\therefore\ \text{area}(\Delta DEF) = \frac{1}{2}\cdot 15\cdot 10 = 75.$$

The three medians of a triangle divide the triangle into six triangles of equal area. Therefore, $\text{Area}(\Delta FDE) = 75$.

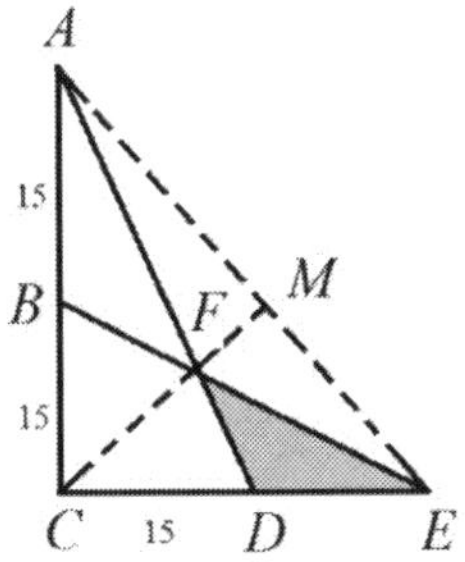

Method 2 (our solution):

Connect AE. Then connect CF and extend it to meet AE at M. F is the centroid and triangle ACE is divided into six smaller triangles with the same area.

The area of $(\Delta ACD) = \frac{1}{2}\cdot 30\cdot 15 = 225$. The area of $(\Delta FDE) = \frac{225}{3} = 75$.

Problem 2. Solution: $7 - 4\sqrt{3}$.

Method 1:

There is no loss of generality if we let the altitude be 1; then the hypotenuse is 4, the median to the hypotenuse is 2, and the distance between the feet of the altitude and median will be $\sqrt{3}$. Since each half of the hypotenuse is 2, we have $p/q = (2 - \sqrt{3})/(2 + \sqrt{3}) = 7 - 4\sqrt{3}$, so $(a, b) = (7, 4)$.

Method 2:

Altitude $= \sqrt{pq} = (p + q)/4$. Squaring both sides, clearing fractions and simplifying, then dividing through by q^2, produces a quadratic in p/q. Replacing p/q by x produces $x^2 - 14x + 1 = 0$, so $x = 7 - 4\sqrt{3}$.

Problem 3. Solution: 100.

Method 1:
Area of *BMC* = (1/2)(4)(29); area of *ABC* = (2)(area of *BMC*) = 116.

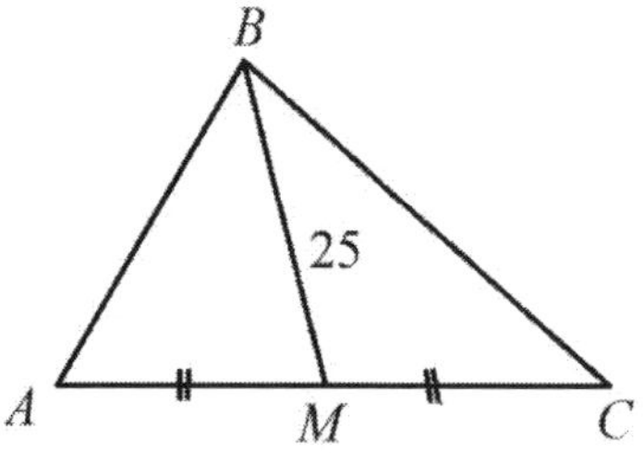

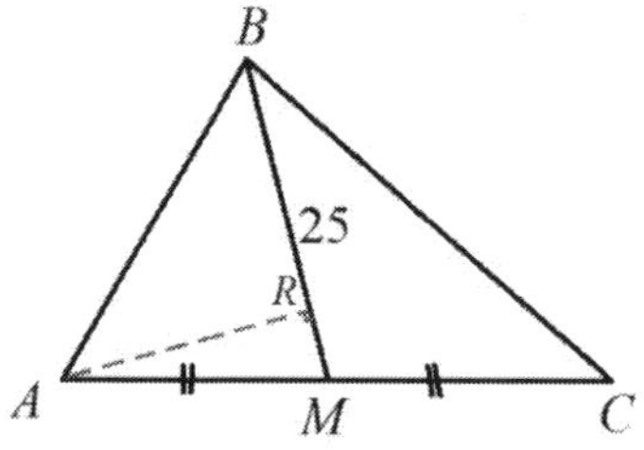

Method 2:

$$S_{\Delta MBC} = \frac{BM \times CR}{2} = \frac{25 \times 4}{2} = 50$$

$$S_{\Delta ABC} = S_{\Delta MBC} + S_{\Delta MBA} == 2S_{\Delta MBC} = 2 \times 50 = 100.$$

Problem 4. Solution: 36.
Since $FC \parallel AB$, $\angle FCE = \angle EBH$, $\angle FEC = \angle HEB$ by the vertical angle theorem, and since *E* is the midpoint of CB, $EC = EB$. Thus, $\Delta\ ECF = \Delta EBH \rightarrow$ the area of ΔECF equals the area of ΔEBH. Thus the area of *FCGE* plus the area of *EGDH* which equals 18 also equals the area of ΔCBD. Since the area of ΔCBD is half the area of ΔCBA because *CD* is a median, the area of ΔCBA is 36.

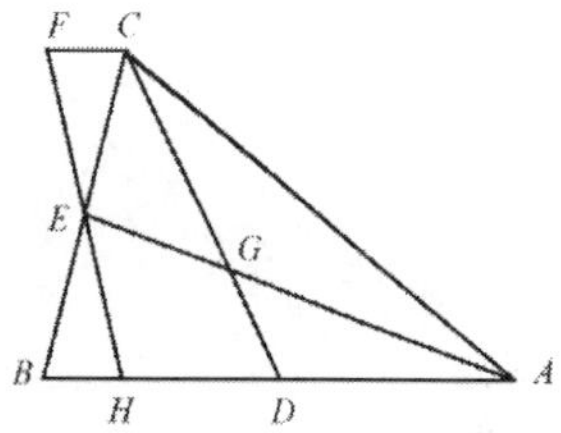

Problem 5. Solution: $\frac{5}{18}$.

Method 1 (official solution):
We will solve this in general. Let *AD* == *a*, *AB* == *b*, *AE* == *c*, *AC* = *d*, *AF* == *x*, *AT* = *y*, and angle *BAT* = angle *CAT* = 8.

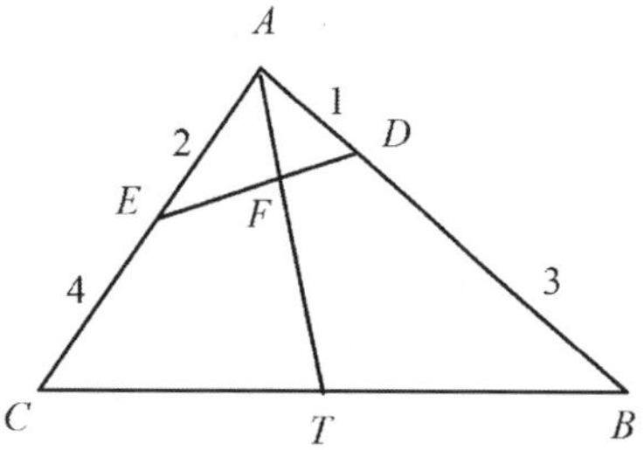

Using K for area, we have $K_{DAE} / K_{BAC} = (K_{DAF} + K_{EAF}) / (K_{BAT} + K_{CAT})$, which implies $\frac{1}{2}ac\sin 2\theta / \frac{1}{2}bd\sin 2\theta$

$$= (\frac{1}{2}ax\sin\theta + \frac{1}{2}cx\sin\theta)/(\frac{1}{2}by\sin\theta + \frac{1}{2}dy\sin\theta).$$

Therefore we have $ac/bd == x(a + c)/y(b + d)$, so $x/y = ac(b + d)/bd(a + c)$ [nice formula!]. Thus $AF/AT == 5/18$ or 5 : 18. Note that $x : y$ is *not* determined by simply giving the *ratios* of $a : b$ and $c : d$! [e.g. using $a = 1$, $b == 4$, compare the results of $c = 2$, $d == 6$ with $c = 1$, $d = 3$.]

Method 2 (our solution):

By the Angle bisector theorem, we have

$$\frac{CT}{BT} = \frac{6}{4} = \frac{3}{2}$$

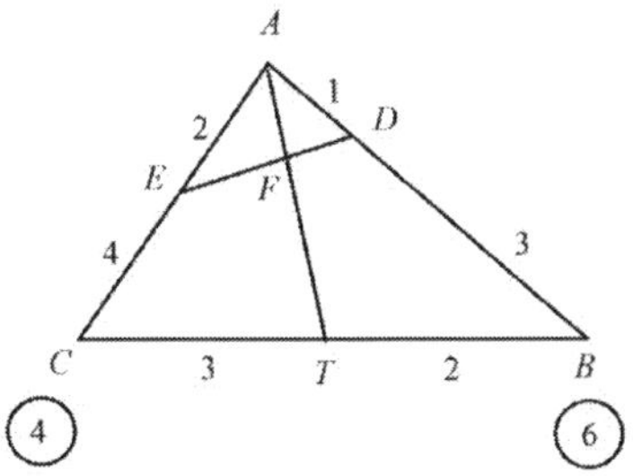

(1) We label the lengths of each line segment as shown. Let the masses in each point be m_A, m_B, m_C, and m_T, respectively. We need to find m_A and m_T.

(2) We assign a mass of 4 to point C.

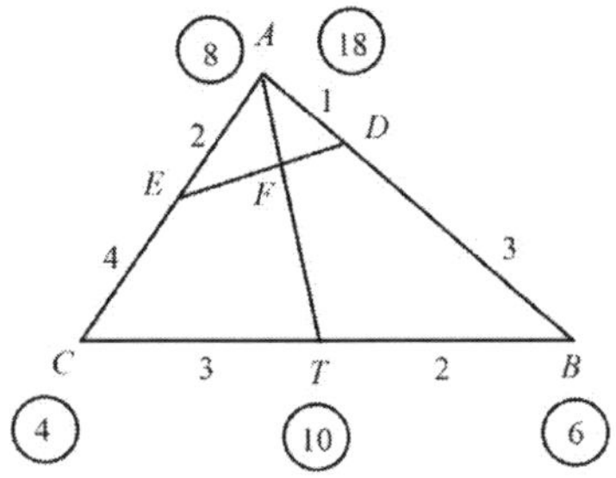

We look at the side BC.

$m_C \times 3 = m_B \times 2 \qquad \Rightarrow \qquad m_C = 6$.

$m_T = m_C + m_B = 4 + 6 = 10$.

Now we determine m_A by splitting masses.

We look at the side AC. The center of mass of AC is on E.

$m_{A_{AC}} \times 2 = m_C \times 4 \qquad \Rightarrow \qquad m_{A_{AC}} = 8$.

We look at the side AB. The center of mass of AB is on D.

$m_{A_{AB}} \times 1 = m_B \times 3 \qquad \Rightarrow \qquad m_{A_{AB}} = 18$.

Thus $m_A = m_{A_{AB}} + m_{A_{AC}} = 18 + 8 = 26$.

The last step is to find the answer:

$$m_A \times AF = m_T \times FT \quad \Rightarrow \quad \frac{FT}{AF} = \frac{26}{10} = \frac{13}{5} \quad \Rightarrow \quad \frac{AT - AF}{AF} = \frac{13}{5}$$

$$\Rightarrow \quad \frac{AT}{AF} - 1 = \frac{13}{5} \quad \Rightarrow \quad \frac{AT}{AF} = \frac{18}{5} \Rightarrow \quad \frac{AF}{AT} = \frac{5}{18}.$$

Problem 6. Solution: (b).

Method 1 (official solution):

Let the angle opposite to the side of length 25 be θ and the length of the third side be x.

The law of cosines tells us

$25^2 = 20^2 + 4x^2 - 80x\cos\theta$and $19.5^2 = 20^2 + x^2 - 40x\cos\theta$.

Multiplying the second equation by negative two and adding the two equations gives

$25^2 - 2 \times 19.5^2 = -20^2 + 2x^2$.

Solving for x, we get $x = 11.5$. Hence the third side is 23.

Method 2 (our solution):

Let the length of the third side be $2x$.

By Theorem 5 (The median length formula):

$$(19.5^2) + (19.5^2) = (20^2 - x^2) + (25^2 - x^2) \quad \Rightarrow \quad 760.5 = 1025 - 2x^2 \quad \Rightarrow$$

$$2x^2 = 1025 - 760.5 = 264.5 \quad \Rightarrow \quad x^2 = 1025 - 760.5 = 132.25 \quad \Rightarrow$$

$$(x - 11.5)(x + 11.5) = 0 \quad \Rightarrow \quad x = 11.5$$

The length of the third side is $2x = 2 \times 11.5 = 23$.

Problem 7. Solution: $\frac{1}{2}$.

Assume that $AB = 1$. The diagonal of the square then equals $AC = \sqrt{2}$.

$$\frac{AB}{BF} = \frac{AO}{OF} \text{ (Angle bisector theorem).} \quad \frac{1}{y} = \frac{\frac{\sqrt{2}}{2}}{\frac{\sqrt{2}}{2} - y}$$

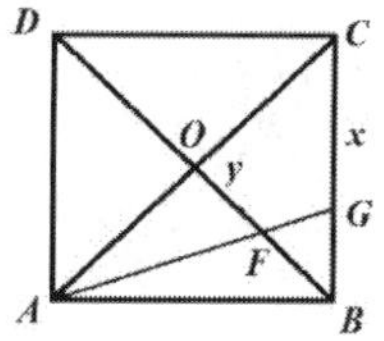

$\frac{AB}{GB}=\frac{AC}{CG}$ (Angle bisector theorem). $\frac{1}{1-x}=\frac{\sqrt{2}}{x}$

Solve for $\frac{y}{x}$, $\frac{y}{x}=\frac{1}{2}$.

Problem 8. Solution: 144 or 300.

Method 1 (official solution):
Note that this median and altitude cannot come from the same vertex. Let the triangle be *ABC,* with *AB* == *AC.*

Case 1: Let the altitude be *AH,* and medians *BQ* and *CR* meet at *P.* Since *AH* must also be a median, *PH* == 8 and *CP* == 10. Then *CH* == 6 and the area of *ABC* is (24)(12)/2 == 144.

Case 2: Let the median be *AM,* let an altitude be *BS,* and let *CM* == *x*. Then, since *AM* must also be an altitude, we have $AC=\sqrt{x^2+225}$. Using two approaches to the area of triangle *ABC,* we have $24\sqrt{x^2+225}=15(2x)$, so *x* == 20, and the area of triangle *ABC* = 300. Either answer is acceptable.

Method 2 (our solution):
Note that this median and altitude cannot come from the same vertex. Let the triangle be *ABC,* with *AB* = *AC.*

Case 1: Let the altitude be *AE,* and medians *CD* and *CR* meet at *F.*

Draw $DG \perp BC$ at *G*. So $DG=\frac{1}{2}AE=12$.

Triangle *CDG* is a 9 – 12 – 15 right triangle.
So *CG* = 9. Note that *CE* = *EB, EG* = *GB*. Thus *GB* = 3 and *BC* = 9 + 3 = 12. the area of *ABC* is (24)(12)/2 == 144.

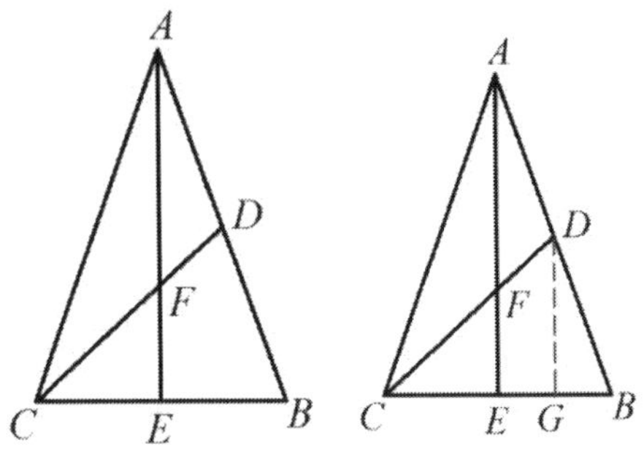

Case 2: Let the median be *AE,* let an altitude be *CD,*

$AE^2 = AB^2 - BE^2 \quad \Rightarrow \quad AE^2 = AB^2 - (\frac{BC}{2})^2$ (1)

We also know that $S_{\Delta ABC} = \frac{BC \times AE}{2} = \frac{AB \times CD}{2} \quad \Rightarrow \quad \frac{BC \times 15}{2} = \frac{AB \times 24}{2}$

$\Rightarrow \quad AB = \frac{15BC}{24}$ (2)

Substituting (2) into (1): $15^2 = (\frac{15BC}{24})^2 - (\frac{BC}{2})^2$

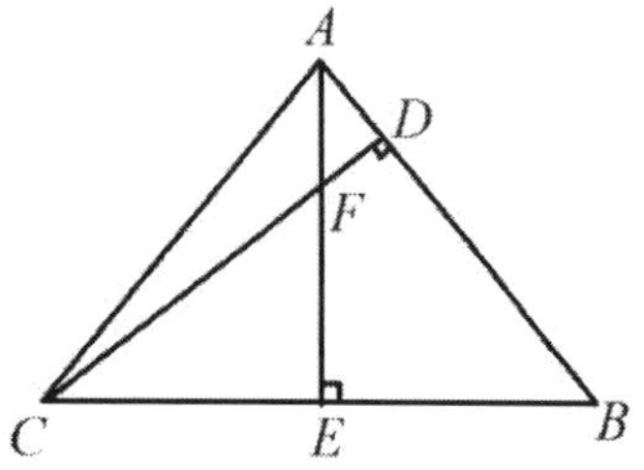

$\Rightarrow (\frac{15BC}{24} - \frac{BC}{2})(\frac{15BC}{24} + \frac{BC}{2}) = 225$

$\Rightarrow \quad \frac{BC}{8} \times \frac{27BC}{24} = 225 \quad \Rightarrow \quad BC = 40$

$S_{\Delta ABC} = \frac{BC \times AE}{2} = \frac{40 \times 15}{2} = 300$.

Problem 9. Solution: (B).

Method 1(official solution):

In the adjoining figure, let h be the length of altitude AN drawn to BC, let $x = BM$, and let $y = NM$. Then

$h^2 + (x+y)^2 = 64, \quad h^2 + y^2 = 9,$
$h^2 + (x-y)^2 = 16.$

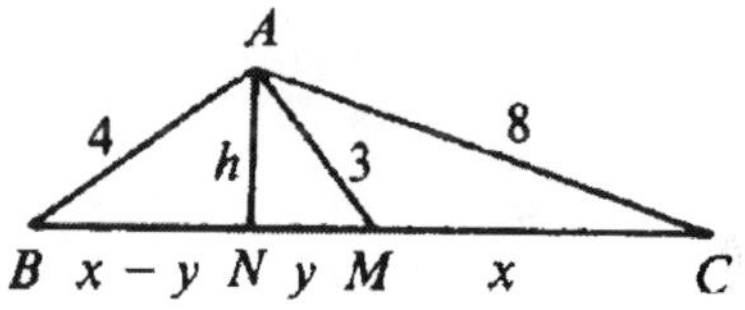

Subtracting twice the second equation from the sum of the first and third equations yields $2x^2 = 62$. Thus $x = \sqrt{31}$ and $BC = 2\sqrt{31}$.

Method 2 (our solution):
By the Theorem 5 (The median length formula):
$AM^2 + AM^2 = (AB^2 - BM^2) + (AC^2 - CM^2)$

$$2\times 3^2 = 4^2 - BM^2 + 8^2 - BM^2 \quad \Rightarrow \quad 2BM^2 = 8^2 + 4^2 - 18 = 62 \quad \Rightarrow \quad BM^2 = 31$$

$$\Rightarrow \quad BM = \sqrt{31} \quad \Rightarrow \quad BC = 2BM = 2\sqrt{31}.$$

Problem 10. Solution: $\dfrac{2\sqrt{110}}{3}$.

As AD is the bisector of $\angle A$, $CD : DB = 8 : 11$. Let $CD = 8a$ and $BD = 11a$ for some number a. As $CM = MB$. $CM = MB = 9.5a$ (or $19a/2$). Now $DM = 1.5a$. It is given that $DM = 1$. Hence. $1.5a = 1$ so $a = 2/3$. Then $CD = 16/3$ and $BD = 22/3$.

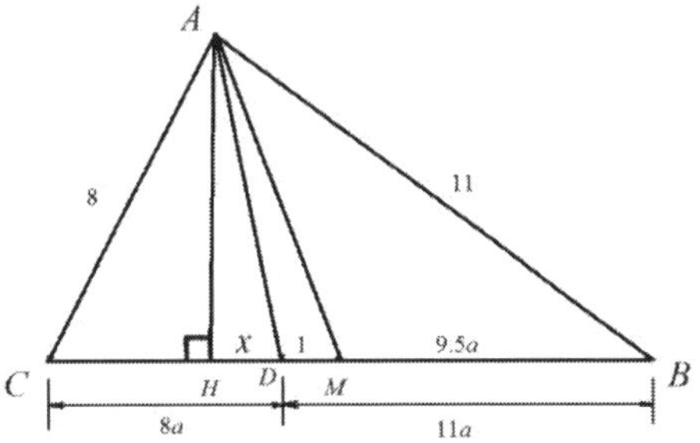

$$AD^2 = AB\cdot AC - BD\cdot CD$$

$$= 8\times 11 - \frac{16}{3}\times\frac{22}{3} = \frac{440}{9}.$$

$$AD = \frac{2\sqrt{110}}{3}.$$

Problem 11. Solution: $AM = \dfrac{\sqrt{943}}{3}$.

As AD is the bisector of $\angle A$, $CD : DB = 8 : 11$. Let $CD = 8a$ and $BD = 11a$ for some number a. As $CM = MB$. $CM = MB = 9.5a$ (or $19a/2$). Now $DM = 1.5a$. It is given that $DM = 1$. Hence. $1.5a = 1$ so $a = 2/3$. Then $BM = CM = 19/3$.

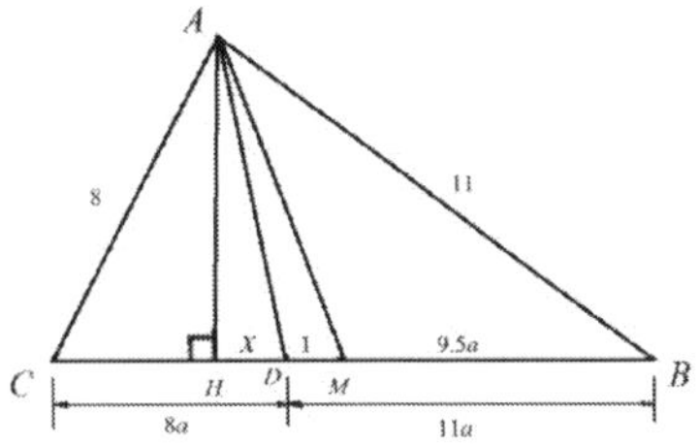

$$(AM^2) + (AM^2) = (AB^2 - BM^2) + (AC^2 - CM^2)$$

$$= 11^2 - (\frac{19}{3})^2 + 8^2 - (\frac{19}{3})^2 = \frac{943}{9}.$$

$$AM = \frac{\sqrt{943}}{3}.$$

Problem 12. Solution: 6.

Method 1: Let $\angle A$ be the largest angle and $\angle B$ be the smallest angle.

Draw the angle bisector of $\angle A$ to meet BC at D. We are given from the problem that $\angle A$ is twice $\angle B$.

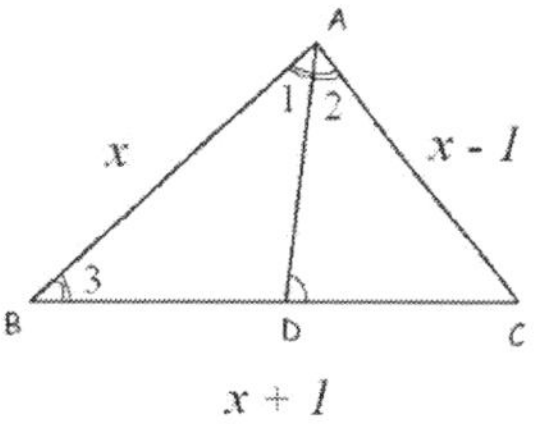

We know that $\angle 2 = \angle 3$, $\angle ADC = \angle 1 + \angle 3 = \angle A$, and so $\Delta\, CAD \sim \Delta\, CBA$.

It follows that $\dfrac{CD}{AC} = \dfrac{AC}{BC}$

$$\Rightarrow \qquad CD = \frac{AC^2}{BC} \qquad (1)$$

According to the angle bisector theorem,

$$\frac{AB}{BD} = \frac{AC}{CD} \qquad \Rightarrow \qquad \frac{CD}{BC - CD} = \frac{AC}{AB}$$

Separate CD to one side and we get $CD = \dfrac{AC \times BC}{AB + AC}$ (2)

Substitute (2) into (1) yields

$$\frac{AC^2}{BC} = \frac{AC \times BC}{AB + AC} \qquad \Rightarrow \qquad \frac{AC}{BC} = \frac{BC}{AB + AC}$$

$$\Rightarrow \qquad \frac{x-1}{x+1} = \frac{x+1}{2x-1} \qquad \Rightarrow \qquad x^2 - 5x = 0 \qquad \Rightarrow \qquad x = 5$$

The largest side is $x + 1 = 6$.

Method 2:

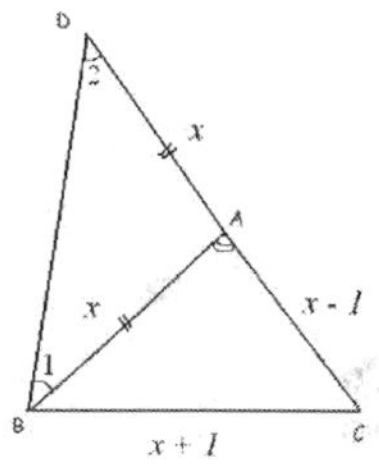

Extend CA to D such that $AD = AB$. Then $\angle 1 = \angle 2$ and $\angle CAB = 2\angle 2$.

We are given that $\angle CAB = 2\angle ABC$, so $\angle 2 = \angle ABC$ and $\Delta ABC \sim \Delta BDC$.

$$\frac{x-1}{x+1} = \frac{x+1}{x-1+x} \qquad \Rightarrow \qquad (x-1)(2x-1) = (x+1)^2$$

$$\Rightarrow \qquad x^2 - 5x = 0 \qquad \Rightarrow \qquad x = 5 \;\Rightarrow\; \qquad x + 1 = 6.$$

Method 3:

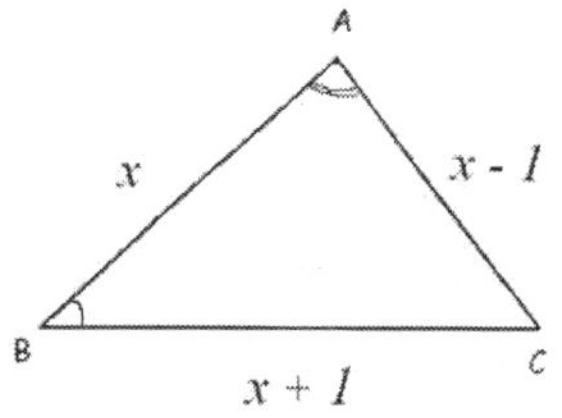

We have the following theorem: In ΔABC, if $\angle A = 2\angle B$, then $a^2 = b^2 + bc$

$a = (x \quad 1)$, $b = (x - 1)$, and $c = x$

$(x+1)^2 = (x-1)^2 + (x-1)x \quad \Rightarrow \quad x^2 - 5x = 0 \Rightarrow \quad x = 5 \quad \Rightarrow$
$x + 1 = 6.$

Problem 13. Solution: 9 in.
Method 1 (official solution):
Let x be the length of the median. By Heron's Theorem the area of the triangle is $\sqrt{20(9)(7)(4)} = 6\sqrt{140}.$

The area of the triangle with sides 11, 8, and x will then have the area of $3\sqrt{140}$.

Applying Heron's theorem again to the triangle with sides 11, 8, and x, $\left(\dfrac{19+x}{2}\right)\times \left(\dfrac{19-x}{2}\right)\times\left(\dfrac{x+3}{2}\right)\times\left(\dfrac{x-3}{2}\right) = 1260.$

Hence $(361 - x^2)(x^2 - 9) = 20160 \Rightarrow -x^4 + 370x^2 - 3249 = 20160 \Rightarrow$
$x^4 - 370x^2 - 23409 = 0$.
Factoring gives $(x^2 - 81)(x^2 - 289) = 0.$
Solving for x, we have two solutions: 9 and 17. The length of the median of the triangle cannot be 17, so the length is 9 in.

Method 2 (our solution):
Let x be the length of the median.
By the median length formula: $(BD^2) + (BD^2) = (AB^2 - AD^2) + (BC^2 - CD^2)$, we have

$(x^2) + (x^2) = (11^2 - 8^2) + (13^2 - 8^2) \Rightarrow$
$2x^2 = 3(11+8) + 5(13+8) = 3\times 19 + 5\times 21 = 3(19+35) = 3\times 54$.
$x^2 = 3\times 27 = 9^2 \qquad \Rightarrow \qquad x = 9$.

Problem 14 Solution: $2\sqrt{5}$.

Method 1: Let $AD = 3x$. Since G is the intersection of two medians of triangle ABC, and by the definition of Theorem 3 that states that the measure of the segment from the vertex to the centroid is two-thirds the measure of the median, $AG = 2x$ and $DG = x$.

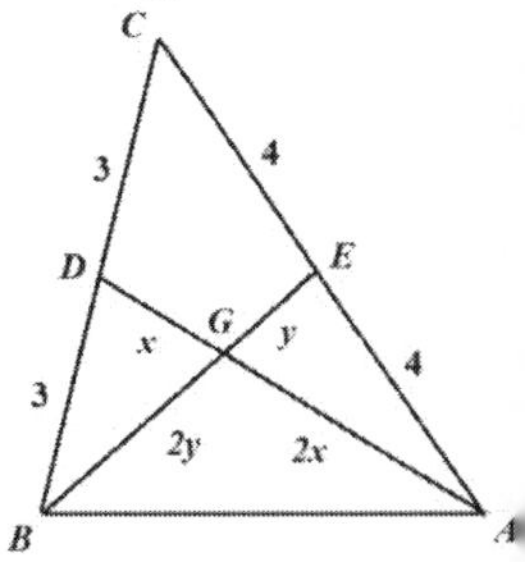

Let $BE = 3y$. Similarly, $BG = 2y$ and $GE = y$.
Applying the Pythagorean Theorem to ΔDGB yields
$x^2 + (2y)^2 = 9$;

Applying the Pythagorean Theorem to ΔEGA gives us
$y^2 + (2x)^2 = 16$.
Adding the two equations results in $5x^2 + 5y^2 = 25$; therefore, $x^2 + y^2 = 5$.
Since AD is perpendicular to median BE, from right triangle ΔBGA,
$(2y)^2 + (2x)^2 = (AB)^2 \Rightarrow \quad 4y^2 + 4x^2 = (AB)^2$.

Substituting in 5 for $x^2 + y^2$, we get that $4x^2 + 4y^2 = 20$.
$(AB)^2 = 20$, and $AB = 2\sqrt{5}$.
Method 2:

$$BC^2 + CA^2 = 5AB^2 \quad \Rightarrow \quad AB = 2\sqrt{5}.$$

Problem 15. Solution: 18.
As shown in the figure, AD is the angle bisector of $\angle BAC$.
By the angle bisector length formula, we have

$$AD^2 = AB \times AC - BD \times DC \Rightarrow 10^2 = 15 \times 12 - xy \qquad (1)$$

By the angle bisector theorem, we have

$$\frac{AB}{y} = \frac{AC}{x} \Rightarrow \frac{15}{y} = \frac{12}{x} \qquad (2)$$

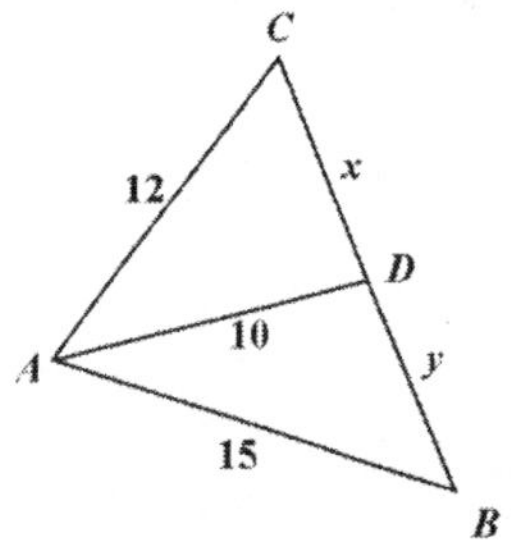

Solving (1) and (2) for x and y, we get $x = 8$ and $y = 10$, so $BC = x + y = 18$.

Problem 16. Solution: $\frac{21\sqrt{5}}{10}$.

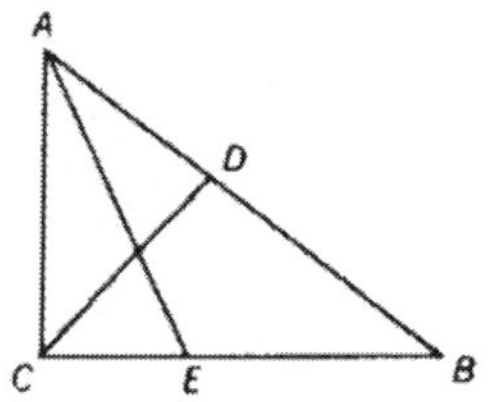

In right ΔABC, with right angle at C and angle bisector CD, $AD = 3$ while $DB = 4$.

Since $AC/CB = AD/DB$, $AC = 3x$, and $CB = 4x$.

Applying the Pythagorean Theorem to ΔABC gives us
$(3x)^2 + (4x)^2 = 7^2$, and $x = 7/5$.

Thus, $AC = 21/5$ and $CB = 28/5$.
Since AE is the angle bisector of angle A, $AC/AB = CE/EB$.
Substituting in the values that we calculated for AC and CB, we get

$$\frac{\frac{21}{5}}{7} = \frac{CE}{\frac{28}{5} - CE}.$$

Thus $CE = 21/10$ and $EB = 7/2$.
Applying the Pythagorean Theorem to ΔACE:
$(AE)^2 = (AC)^2 + (CE)^2$.

Therefore, $AE = \dfrac{21\sqrt{5}}{10}$.

Problem 17. Solution: $\sqrt{6} - \sqrt{2}$.

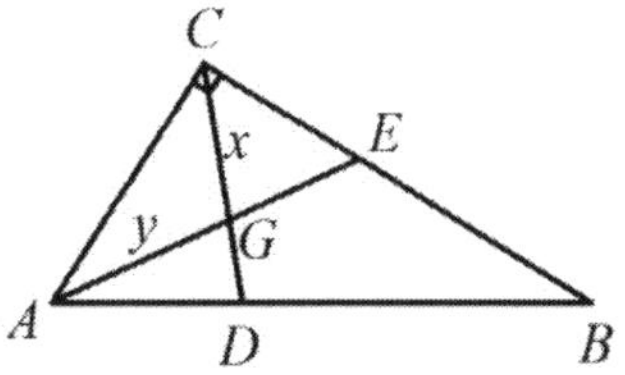

In ΔABC, if $AB = 4$, then $AC = 2$.

In ΔACE, since $\angle CAE = 30$, $CE = \dfrac{2}{\sqrt{3}}$ (1)

and $AE = \dfrac{4}{\sqrt{3}}$

CD is the angle bisector of angle C, so in ΔACE,
$AC/CE = AG/GE$. (2)

If we let $AG = y$, equation (2) gives us $GE = \dfrac{y}{\sqrt{3}}$.

Since $AG + GE = AE$, $y + \dfrac{y}{\sqrt{3}} = \dfrac{4}{\sqrt{3}}$ and $y = \dfrac{4}{1+\sqrt{3}} = 2\sqrt{3} - 2$

Thus, $AG = 2\sqrt{3} - 2$ (3)

and $GE = 2 - \dfrac{2\sqrt{3}}{3}$ (4)

We know that $(CG)^2 = (AC)(CE) - (AG)(GE)$. (5)

Substituting (1), (3), and (4) into (5), we get
$(CG)^2 = 8 - 4\sqrt{3}$.

Therefore, $CG = \sqrt{8-4\sqrt{3}} = \sqrt{6}-\sqrt{2}$.

Problem 18. Solution: (A).

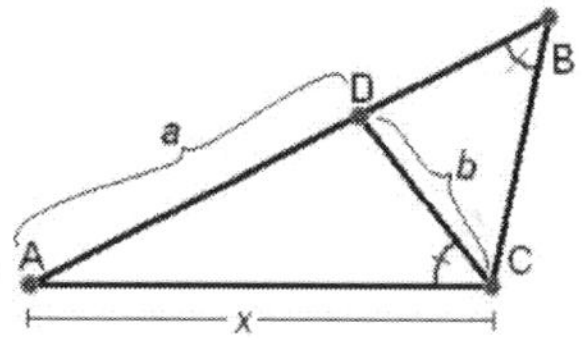

Let $BC = y$.

By the angle bisector theorem, we have

$$\frac{x}{a} = \frac{y}{b} \quad \Rightarrow \quad ay = bx \qquad (1)$$

By the angle bisector length formula, we have

$$b^2 = xy - ab \quad \Rightarrow \quad xy = ab + b^2 \qquad (2)$$

$$(2) \div (1): \ \frac{x}{a} = \frac{b^2+ab}{bx} \quad \Rightarrow \quad x^2 = a(b+a) \quad \Rightarrow \quad x = \sqrt{a(b+a)}.$$

Problem 19. Solution: 4.

Let $AB = 2x$ and $BC = y$.

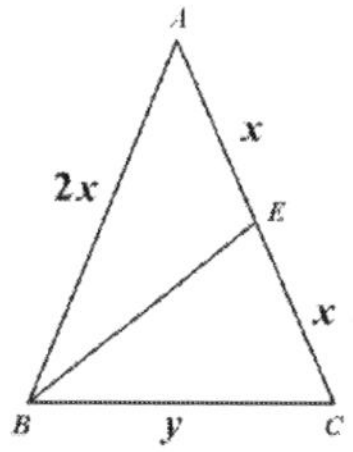

$$\begin{cases} \dfrac{3x}{x+y} = \dfrac{5}{3} \\ 4x+y=24 \end{cases} \Rightarrow \begin{cases} x=5 \\ y=4 \end{cases}$$

$$\begin{cases} \dfrac{3x}{x+y} = \dfrac{3}{5} \\ 4x+y=24. \end{cases} \Rightarrow \begin{cases} x=3, \\ y=12. \end{cases}$$

Since $y = 12$ is half of the perimeter, we can discard this answer.

The answer is then $y = 4$.

Problem 20. Solution: $7x+y-29=0$.

Let $p(x, y)$ be a point on the angle bisector AD.

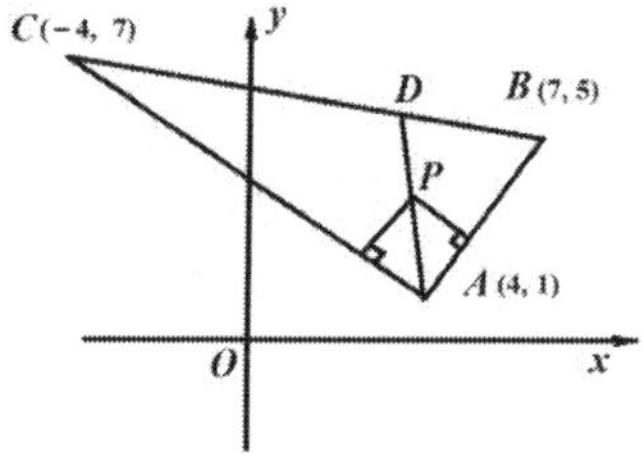

Method 1:

The distance from point p to AC is the same as the distance from p to AB.

The equation for line AB is:

$$y-1 = \frac{4}{3}(x-4) \text{ or } 4x-3y-13=0.$$

The equation for AC is:

$y-1=-\frac{4}{3}(x-4)$ or $3x+4y-16=0$.

$\therefore \frac{|4x-3y-13|}{\sqrt{4^2+(-3)^2}}=\frac{|3x+4y-16|}{\sqrt{3^2+4^2}}$

$4x-3y-13=\pm(3x+4y-16)$

$x-7y+3=0$ or $7x+y-29=0$.

We can easily see that $x-7y+3=0$ is the equation of the angle bisector of the exterior angle of $\angle A$, so the equation of the angle bisector of $\angle A$ is then $7x+y-29=0$.

Method 2:

By the angle bisector theorem,

$$\frac{BD}{DC}=\frac{AB}{AC}=\frac{\sqrt{(4-7)^2+(1-5)^2}}{\sqrt{(4+4)^2+(1-7)^2}}=\frac{\sqrt{3^2+4^2}}{\sqrt{8^2+6^2}}=\frac{5}{10}=\frac{1}{2}$$

So $\lambda=\frac{BD}{DC}=\frac{1}{2}$.

Then,

$$D_x=\frac{x_1+\lambda x_2}{1+\lambda}=\frac{7+\frac{1}{2}\cdot(-4)}{1+\frac{1}{2}}=\frac{10}{3}, \text{ and } D_y=\frac{y_1+\lambda y_2}{1+\lambda}=\frac{5+\frac{1}{2}\cdot 7}{1+\frac{1}{2}}=\frac{17}{3}$$

The equation is:

$$\frac{y-y_1}{x-x_1}=\frac{y_2-y_1}{x_2-x_1} \quad\Rightarrow\quad \frac{y-1}{x-4}=\frac{\frac{17}{3}-1}{\frac{10}{3}-4}=-7$$

$\Rightarrow \quad y-1=-7x-28$

$\Rightarrow \quad 7x+y-29=0$.

BASIC KNOWLEDGE

1. Definition

If a and x are positive real numbers and $a \neq 1$, then real number y is the logarithm to the base a of x. This can be written as

$$y = \log_a x \qquad (1.1)$$

if and only if

$$x = a^y \qquad (1.2)$$

A quick way to convert the logarithm to the exponent:

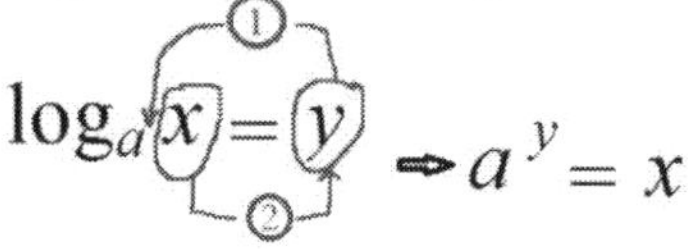

Notes:

(1) The logarithm base 10 is called the **common logarithm.** $\log x$ always refers to log base 10, i.e., $\log x = \log_{10} x$.

(2) The logarithm base e is called the **natural logarithm**. $\ln x = \log_e x$.

(3) $\log_{10} x$ is always written as $\log x$.

(4) Zero and negative numbers have no logarithm expressions. The following expressions are undefined: $\log_a 0$, $\log_a(-3)$, or $\log_{-10} x$.

The graphs of logarithmic functions $f(x) = \log_a x$ all have an x-intercept of 1, and are increasing when $a > 1$ and decreasing when $a < 1$.

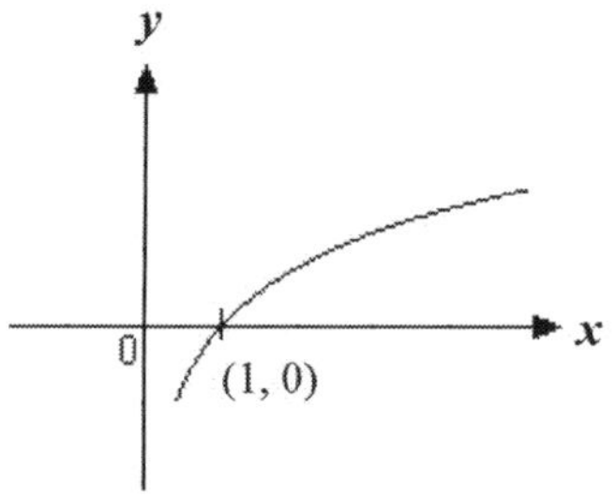

$y = \log_a x\ (a > 1)$

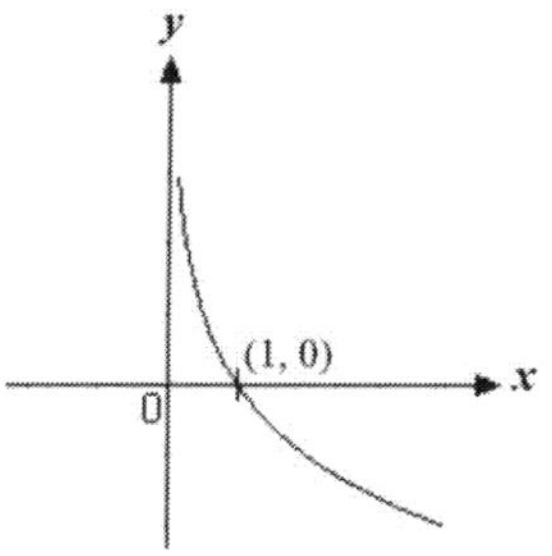

$y = \log_a x\ (a < 1)$

2. Properties of Logarithms:

If a, b, and x are positive real numbers, $a \neq 1$, $b \neq 1$, and r is any real number, we have

$$\log_a 1 = 0 \tag{2.1}$$

$$\log_a a = 1 \tag{2.2}$$

$$a^{\log_a x} = x \tag{2.3}$$

$$\log_a a^r = r \tag{2.4}$$

$$\log_a b \log_b c = \log_a c \tag{2.5}$$

3. The Laws of Logarithms:

Law 1: the Product Identity

For any positive real numbers a, x and y:

$$\log_a xy = \log_a x + \log_a y \tag{3.1}$$

Proof :

Let $m = \log_a x$ and $n = \log_a y$.

The exponential form of the equations is $a^m = x$ and $a^n = y$.

Multiplying these two equations, we get $a^m a^n = xy \Rightarrow a^{m+n} = xy$

Transforming the exponential form to the logarithmic form, we have $\log_a xy = m + n$.

Since $m = \log_a x$ and $n = \log_a y$, $\log_a xy = \log_a x + \log_a y$.

Law 2: the Quotient Identity

For any positive real numbers a, x and y:

$$\log_a\left(\frac{x}{y}\right) = \log_a x - \log_a y \tag{3.2}$$

Proof:

Let $m = \log_a x$ and $n = \log_a y$.

The exponential form of the equations is $a^m = x$ and $a^n = y$

Dividing these two equations, we get $a^m / a^n = x/y \Rightarrow a^{m-n} = x/y$

Use the definition of the logarithm, we get $\log_a(\frac{x}{y}) = m - n$.

Since $m = \log_a x$ and $n = \log_a y$, $\log_a(\frac{x}{y}) = \log_a x - \log_a y$.

Note: Both x and y in the expressions $\log_a xy$ and $\log_a(\frac{x}{y})$ can be negative.

However, in the expressions $\log_a x + \log_a y$ or $\log_a x - \log_a y$, neither of them can be negative.

Law 3: the Power Identity

Formula 1: For any positive real numbers a, x, y, and real number r:

$$\log_a x^r = r \log_a x \tag{3.3}$$

Proof:

Since $x = a^{\log_a x}$, $\log_a x^r = \log_a (a^{\log_a x})^r \rightarrow \log_a x^r = (r \log_a x)\log_a a$.

Recall that $\log_a a = 1$. Substituting this value into the equation, we have

$\log_a x^r = r \log_a x$.

Note: In the expression $\log_a x^r$, x can be negative if r is even. However, x must be positive in the expression $r \log_a x$.

Formula 2: $\log_{a^m} b^n = \frac{n}{m} \log_a b \;\; (a, b > 0, a \neq 1)$ (3.4)

Proof:

Let $\log_{a^m} b^n = c$.

The exponential form of the equations is $(a^m)^c = b^n$.

Taking the logarithm of both sides yields $c \log_a a^m = n \log_a b$ or $cm = n \log_a b$.

$$c = \frac{n}{m}\log_a b \quad \Rightarrow \quad \log_{a^m} b^n = \frac{n}{m}\log_a b.$$

4. Change-of-Base Theorem:

Formula 1: $\log_a x = \dfrac{\log_b x}{\log_b a}$ $\quad (a > 0, a \neq 1, b > 0, b \neq 1, x > 0) \quad$ (4.1)

Proof:
Let $y = \log_a x$. The exponential form of this equation is $a^y = x$.
Taking the logarithm on both sides, we get $\log_b a^y = \log_b x \Rightarrow \quad y\log_b a = \log_b x$
Dividing both sides by $\log_b b$, we obtain $y = \dfrac{\log_b x}{\log_b a} \Rightarrow \quad \log_a x = \dfrac{\log_b x}{\log_b a}$.

Formula 2: $\log_a N = \log_{a^m} N^m, \quad m \neq 0$ $\quad$ (4.2)

Proof:

$$\log_a N = \frac{\log_b N}{\log_b a} = \frac{m\log_b N}{m\log_b a} = \frac{\log_b N^m}{\log_b a^m} = \log_{a^m} N^m.$$

Formula 3: $\log_a N = \dfrac{1}{\log_N a}, \quad N \neq 1$ $\quad$ (4.3)

Proof:

$$\log_a N = \frac{\log_N N}{\log_N a} = \frac{1}{\log_N a}.$$

Formula 4: $\log_a N = -\log_a \dfrac{1}{N}$ $\quad$ (4.4)

Proof:

$$\log_a N = \log_a (\frac{1}{N})^{-1} = -\log_a \frac{1}{N}$$

Formula 5: $\log_a N = -\log_{\frac{1}{a}} N$ (4.5)

Proof:

$\log_a N = \log_{a^{-1}} N^{-1} = -\log_{\frac{1}{a}} N$

Formula 6: $\log_a N = m\log_{a^m} N,\ m \neq 0$ (4.6)

Proof:

$\log_a N = \log_{a^m} N^m = m\log_{a^m} N$

Formula 7: $\dfrac{\log_a M}{\log_a N} = \dfrac{\log_b M}{\log_b N}$ $(a > 0, a \neq 1, b > 0, b \neq 1, M, N > 0, N \neq 1)$ (4.7)

Proof :

By the Change-of-Base Theorem, we have $\dfrac{\log_a M}{\log_a N} = \log_N M$, and

$\dfrac{\log_b M}{\log_b N} = \log_N M$.

Therefore $\dfrac{\log_a M}{\log_a N} = \dfrac{\log_b M}{\log_b N}$.

Formula 8: $\log_a \sqrt[n]{N} = \dfrac{1}{n}\log_a N$, N is integer greater than 1. (4.8)

Formula 9: $b^{\log_a c} = c^{\log_a b}$ $((a > 0, a \neq 1, b, c \in R^+)$ (4.9)

Proof :

Taking the log a on both sides, we get $(\log_a c)(\log_a b) = (\log_a b)(\log_a c)$, which is true.

5. Solving Logarithm Equations

If x, y and $a \neq 1$ are positive real numbers, $x = y$ if and only if $\log_a x = \log_a y$. Similarly $x^a = y^a$ if and only if $x = y$.

6. Some Basic Constants:

$\log 2 \approx 0.3010$ $\log 3 \approx 0.4771$ $\log 5 \approx 0.6989$

EXAMPLES

1. Properties and Laws

Example 1. (ARML) Let $B = 3$. Compute $(B^{\log 4})\,(B^{\log 25})$.

Solution: 9.
Method 1 (official solution):
$B^{(\log 4) + (\log 25)} = B^{\log 100} = B^2 = 9$.

Method 2 (our solution):
$(B^{\log 4}) = x \quad \Rightarrow \quad \log 4 \times \log B = \log x$ (1)
$(B^{\log 25}) = y \quad \Rightarrow \quad \log 25 \times \log B = \log y$ (2)
(1) + (2): $\log 3 \times (\log 4 + \log 25) = \log x + \log y \Rightarrow \log 3 \times \log (4 \times 25) = \log xy$
$\Rightarrow \quad \log 3 \times \log 100 = \log xy \quad \Rightarrow \quad 2\log 3 = \log xy \quad \Rightarrow$
$\log 3^2 = \log xy \Rightarrow \quad xy = 3^2 = 9$.

Example 2. (NYSML) If $a = \log 9$ and $b = \log 16$, compute $4^{a/b} + 3^{b/a}$.

Solution: 7.
Method 1 (official solution):
From $\dfrac{a}{b} = \dfrac{\log 9}{\log 16} = \dfrac{2\log 3}{2\log 4} = \log_4 3$

We get $4^{\frac{a}{b}} = 4^{\log_4 3} = 3$. Similarly, $3^{\frac{b}{a}} = 4$. The sum is 7.

Method 2 (our solution):
Let $4^{a/b} = x$ (1)
and $3^{b/a} = y$ (2)

Taking the log of each side, base 4, on (1) produces$\Rightarrow$ $\dfrac{a}{b} = \log_4 x$ (3)

Taking the log of each side, base 3, on (2) produces$\Rightarrow$ $\dfrac{b}{a} = \log_3 y$ (4)

Since $\dfrac{a}{b} = \dfrac{\log 9}{\log 16} = \dfrac{2\log 3}{2\log 4} = \log_4 3$ and $\dfrac{b}{a} = \log_3 4$,

(3) becomes $\log_4 x = \log_4 3 \quad \Rightarrow \quad x = 3$.
(4) becomes $\log_3 y = \log_3 4 \quad \Rightarrow \quad y = 4$. The sum is 7.

Example 3. Which pairs are the same?

(A) $y = \log x^2$, $y = 2\log x$. (B) $y = \log x$, $y = \log \frac{x^2}{x}$.

(C) $y = 10^{\log x}$, $y = x$. (D) $y = \log(x^2 - 1)$, $y = \log(x+1) + \log(x-1)$.

Solution: (B).

The domain is the same $(0, +\infty)$ for $y = \log x$, or $y = \log \frac{x^2}{x}$.

For $x \in (0, +\infty)$, $\frac{x^2}{x} = x$. Therefore, $y = \log x$ and $y = \log \frac{x^2}{x}$ are the same.

Example 4. (1992 ARML) Let $K = 11$. If $\log_n 2 = K$, and $n > 1$, compute $\log_4 n$.

Solution: 1/22.
Method 1 (official solution):
$\log_4 n = (\log n)/(\log 4) = (\log n)/(2\log 2) = 1/[2(\log 2)/(\log n)] = 1/(2K) = 1/22$.

Method 2 (our solution):
By **Formula 3,** $\log_n 2 = K \quad \Rightarrow \quad \log_2 n = 1/K$
By **Formula 2,** $\log_2 n = 1/K \Rightarrow \log_{2^2} n^2 = 1/K \quad \Rightarrow \quad \log_4 n^2 = 1/K$
By **Formula 1,** $\log_4 n^2 = 1/K \quad \Rightarrow \quad 2\log_4 n = 1/K \Rightarrow \quad \log_4 n = 1/(2K) = 1/22$.

Example 5. (NYSML) Compute the numerical value of $(5^{\log 2})(2^{\log 3})(2^{\log 6})(5^{\log 9})$.

Solution: 18.
Method 1 (official solution):
$(5^{\log 2+\log 9})(2^{\log 3+\log 6}) = (5^{\log 18})(2^{\log 18}) = 10^{\log 18} = 18$.

Method 2 (our solution):

$(5^{\log 2}) = a \quad \Rightarrow \quad (\log 2)(\log 5) = \log a \quad (1)$

$(2^{\log 3}) = b \quad \Rightarrow \quad (\log 3)(\log 2) = \log b \quad (2)$

$(2^{\log 6}) = c \quad \Rightarrow \quad (\log 6)(\log 2) = \log c \quad (3)$

$(5^{\log 9}) = d \quad \Rightarrow \quad (\log 9)(\log 5) = \log d \quad (4)$

(1) + (4): $(\log 5)(\log 2 + \log 9) = \log ad \Rightarrow \quad (\log 5)(\log 18) = \log ad \quad (5)$

(2) + (3): $(\log 2)(\log 6 + \log 3) = \log bc \Rightarrow \quad (\log 2)(\log 18) = \log bc \quad (6)$

(5) + (6): $(\log 18)(\log 5 + \log 2) = \log abcd \Rightarrow \log 18 = \log abcd \Rightarrow$

$abcd = 18$.

2. Change-of-Base Theorem

Example 6. (1999 ARML) If $\frac{\log_b a}{\log_c a} = \frac{19}{99}$, then $\frac{b}{c} = c^k$. Compute k.

Solution: $\frac{80}{19}$.

Method 1 (official solution):

Set $\log_b a = 19t$ and $\log_c a = 99t$, giving $a = b^{19t}$ and $a = c^{99t} \quad \Rightarrow b^{19t} = c^{99t}$

$\Rightarrow b^{19} = c^{99}$. Thus, $\frac{b^{19}}{c^{19}} = c^{80} \Rightarrow \quad \frac{b}{c} = c^{80/19}$. Thus $k = \frac{80}{19}$.

Method 2 (our solution):

By **Change-of-Base Theorem**, $\frac{\log_b a}{\log_c a} = \frac{19}{99} \Rightarrow \quad \frac{\frac{\log a}{\log b}}{\frac{\log a}{\log c}} = \frac{19}{99} \Rightarrow \frac{\log c}{\log b} = \frac{19}{99} \Rightarrow$

$\frac{\log b}{\log c} = \frac{99}{19} \Rightarrow \log_c b = \frac{99}{19} \Rightarrow b = c^{\frac{99}{19}} \Rightarrow \quad \frac{b}{c} = c^{\frac{80}{19}}$. Thus $k = \frac{80}{19}$.

Example 7. (1989 ARML) Let $n = 2$, compute the positive number x such that $x^{\log_{19} 89} = 89^n$.

Solution: 361.

Method 1 (official solution):
Taking the log of each side, base 19, produces $(\log_{19}89)(\log_{19}x) = 2 \cdot \log_{19}89$, so $\log_{19}x = 2$. This implies $x = 19^2 = 361$.

Method 2 (our solution):
Taking the log of each side, base 10, produces $(\log_{19}89)(\log x) = 2 \cdot \log 89$ (1)
Using change-of base formula to left hand side of (1): $\frac{\log 89}{\log 19} \cdot \log x = 2\log 89$

$\Rightarrow \quad \frac{1}{\log 19} \cdot \log x = 2 \quad \Rightarrow \quad \log x = 2\log 19 \quad \Rightarrow \quad \log x = \log 19^2$

$\Rightarrow x = 19^2 = 361$.

Example 8. (AIME) Determine the value of ab if $\log_8 a + \log_4 b^2 = 5$ and $\log_8 b + \log_4 a^2 = 7$.

Solution: 512.
Method 1:
Adding the two given equations, we get: $\log_8 ab + \log_4 a^2b^2 = 12$
By the Change-of-Base formula, we can change the two logarithms from base 8 and 4, respectively into base 2: $\frac{\log_2 ab}{3} + \log_2 ab = 12$.

So $\frac{4}{3}\log_2 ab = 12$, $\log_2 ab = 9$ and $ab = 2^9 = 512$.

Method 2:
$\log_8 a + \log_8 b + \log_4 a^2 + \log_2 b^2 = \log_8 ab + \log_4 a^2b^2 = 12$

$= \log_{2^3}(\sqrt[3]{ab})^3 + \log_{2^2}(ab)^2 = \log_2 \sqrt[3]{ab} + \log_2 ab = \log_2 (ab)^{\frac{4}{3}}$

Therefore $\log_2 (ab)^{\frac{4}{3}} = 12 \quad \Rightarrow \quad (ab)^{\frac{4}{3}} = 2^{12} \quad \Rightarrow ab = 2^9 = 512$.

3. Solving Logarithm Equations

Example 9. Compute the number of real values of x for which the following equation is true: $(\log x)^{(4+\log x)} = 1$.

Solution: 2.
Case 1: $(\log x) = 1$.
If $(\log x) = 1$, then $x = 10$.

Case 2: $4 + \log x = 0$ and $\log x \neq 0$ $(x \neq 1)$
$4 + \log x = 0 \Rightarrow \log x = -4 \Rightarrow x = 10^{-4}$ is a solution.

Case 3: $\log x = -1$ and $4 + \log x$ is even.
$\log x = -1 \Rightarrow x = 10^{-1}$. $4 + \log x = 4 - 1 = 3$ is not even.
Therefore the solutions are $x = 10$, $x = -10^{-4}$.

Example 10. (1990 ARML) Compute the integer k, $k > 2$, for which $\log(k-2)! + \log(k-1)! + 2 = 2\log k!$.

Solution: 5.
Method 1 (official solution):
We have $2 = \log(k!)^2 - \log(k-2)! - \log(k-1)! = \log[k!k!/(k-2)!(k-1)!]$ which implies that $\log 100 = \log k^2(k-1)$, so $k^2(k-1) = 100 = 5 \times 5 \times 4$ and hence $k = 5$.

Method 2 (our solution):
$\log(k-2)! + \log(k-1)! = \log(k-2) + \log(k-3) + \ldots + \log(k-1) + \log(k-2) + \log(k-3) + \ldots = \log(k-1) + 2\log(k-2) + 2\log(k-3) + \ldots\ldots$ (1)

$2\log k! = 2\log k + 2\log(k-1) + 2\log(k-2) + 2\log(k-3) + \ldots..$ (2)

Substituting (1) and (2) into the original equation:
$\log(k-2)! + \log(k-1)! + 2 = 2\log k! \Rightarrow 2 = 2\log k + \log(k-1)$
$\Rightarrow 2 = \log k^2 + \log(k-1) \Rightarrow 2 = \log k^2(k-1) \Rightarrow k^2(k-1) = 100$.

Since k is a positive integer, $k = 5$.

Example 11. (ARML) Let $K = 64$. If $\log_2 x + \log_4 x + \log_8 x = \log_K x^n$ for each $x > 0$, compute n.

Solution: 11.
Method 1 (official solution):

Since $\log_2 x + \log_4 x + \log_8 x = \log_2 x + \log_2 x^{\frac{1}{2}} + \log_2 x^{\frac{1}{3}} = \log_2 x^{1\frac{1}{6}} = \log_K x^n$, then $\frac{11}{6}\cdot\frac{\log x}{\log 2} = \frac{n\log x}{\log K} \Rightarrow n = \frac{11}{6}\cdot\frac{\log K}{\log 2}$. Since $K = 64 = 2^6$, then $\log_K = 6\log 2$, making $n = 11$.

Method 2 (our solution):

$$\log_2 x + \log_4 x + \log_8 x = \frac{\log x}{\log 2} + \frac{\log x}{\log 4}\cdot\frac{\log x}{\log 8} = \log x\left(\frac{1}{\log 2} + \frac{1}{\log 4} + \frac{1}{\log 8}\right)$$

$$= \log x\left(\frac{1}{\log 2} + \frac{1}{2\log 2} + \frac{1}{3\log 2}\right) = \frac{\log x}{\log 2}\left(\frac{1}{1} + \frac{1}{2} + \frac{1}{3}\right) = \frac{11}{6}\cdot\frac{\log x}{\log 2} = \frac{11}{6}\log_2 x.$$

$$\log_K x^n = n\log_{64} x = n\log_2 x^{\frac{1}{6}} = \frac{n}{6}\log_2 x.$$

So we have $\frac{11}{6}\log_2 x = \frac{n}{6}\log_2 x \quad \Rightarrow \quad \frac{11}{6} = \frac{n}{6} \quad \Rightarrow \quad n = 11.$

Example 12. (ARML) If $\log_8 a + \log_8 b = (\log_8 a)(\log_8 b)$ and $\log_a b = 3$, compute the value of a.

Solution: 11.
Method 1 (official solution):

$\log_a b = 3 \quad \Rightarrow \quad \frac{\log_8 b}{\log_8 a} = 3 \quad \Rightarrow \quad \log_8 b = 3\log_8 a$. Substituting into

$\log_8 a + \log_8 b = (\log_8 a)(\log_8 b)$ gives $4\log_8 a = 3(\log_8 a)^2$.

Since $\log_8 a \ne 0$, then $4 = 3\log_8 a \Rightarrow \log_8 a = \frac{4}{3}$ so $a = (2^3)^{4/3} = 16$.

Method 2 (our solution):

$\log_8 a + \log_8 b = (\log_8 a)(\log_8 b)$ $\Rightarrow$ $\dfrac{\log a}{\log 8} + \dfrac{\log b}{\log 8} = \dfrac{\log a}{\log 8} \cdot \dfrac{\log b}{\log 8}$ $\Rightarrow$

$(\log 8)(\log a + \log b) = (\log a)(\log b)$ (1)

We also know that $\log_a b = 3 \Rightarrow$ $\dfrac{\log b}{\log a} = 3$ $\Rightarrow$ $\log b = 3\log a$ (2)

Substituting (2) into (1): $(\log 8)(\log a + 3\log a) = (\log a)(3\log a)$ $\Rightarrow$

$(\log 8)(4\log a) = 3(\log a)^2$ $\Rightarrow$ $4(\log 8) = 3\log a$ $\Rightarrow$

$\dfrac{4}{3} = \dfrac{\log a}{\log 8}$ $\Rightarrow$ $\log_8 a = \dfrac{4}{3}$ so $a = (2^3)^{4/3} = 16$.

Example 13. (ARML) Compute the largest real value of b such that the solutions to the following equation are integers: $(\log_{2^{10}} x^{2b})^2 = \log_{2^{10}} x^4$.

Solution: $b = \sqrt{10}$.

Method 1 (from the book "Intermediate Algebra" by Art of Problem Solving):
We remove the exponents from the arguments, x^{2b} and x^4:

$(2b\log_{2^{10}} x)^2 = 4\log_{2^{10}} x$ (1)

Noting that $\log_{2^{10}} x = \log_2 x^{1/10} = \dfrac{1}{10}\log_2 x$, our expression becomes:

$(\dfrac{b}{5}\log_2 x)^2 = \dfrac{2}{5}\log_2 x$ (2)

Multiplying both sides of (2) by 25 gives us:

$b^2(\log_2 x)^2 = 10\log_2 x$ $\Rightarrow$ $(b^2\log_2 x - 10)\log_2 x = 0$.

We have $\log_2 x = 0$ or $b^2\log_2 x - 10 = 0$.

The first equation gives us $x = 1$ no matter what b is. The second equation gives us $x = 2^{10/b^2}$.

In order for x to be an integer, the expression $10/b^2$ must be a positive integer. The largest value is $b = \sqrt{10}$.

Note: We believe that equation (1) is correct only when $x > 0$. However, the original equation $(\log_{2^{10}} x^{2b})^2 = \log_{2^{10}} x^4$ is true for $x < 0$ as well.

Method 2 (official solution):

$$(\log_{2^{10}} x^{2b})^2 = 4\log_{2^{10}} x \qquad (1)$$

$$\Rightarrow \qquad 4b^2(\log_{2^{10}} x)^2 - 4\log_{2^{10}} x = 0 \qquad (2)$$

$(\log_{2^{10}} x)(b^2 \log_{2^{10}}(x) - 1) = 0$

If $\log_{2^{10}} x = 0$, then $x = 1$.

If $b^2 \log_{2^{10}} x - 1 = 0$, then $\log_{2^{10}} x = \frac{1}{b^2}$, giving $x = (2^{10})^{\frac{1}{b^2}} = 2^{\frac{10}{b^2}}$.

There are several values that b can hold so that x an integer. If $b = \pm 1$, the $x = 2^{10}$. If $b = \pm\frac{\sqrt{10}}{3}$, the $x = 2^9$. But the largest value of b such that the second solution an integer is $b = \sqrt{10}$, which gives us $x = 2$.

Note: We believe that both equations (1) and (2) are correct only if $x > 0$. The given equation is valid whether $x > 0$ or $x < 0$ but (2) and (3) will not be true if $x < 0$, so (2) and (3) are not equivalent to the given equation.

Method 3 (our solution):

The correct way should be the following:

$(\log_{2^{10}} x^{2b})^2 = \log_{2^{10}} x^4 \qquad \Rightarrow \qquad (b\log_{2^{10}} x^2)^2 = 2\log_{2^{10}} x^2$ (We should make sure that the argument is still positive even when $x < 0$).

Taking b^2 out, the equation becomes

$$b^2(\log_{2^{10}} x^2)^2 = 2\log_{2^{10}} x^2 \qquad \Rightarrow \qquad b^2(\log_{2^{10}} x^2)^2 - 2\log_{2^{10}} x^2 = 0$$

$$\Rightarrow \qquad (b^2 \log_{2^{10}} x^2 - 2)\log_{2^{10}} x^2 = 0.$$

This gives us $\log_{2^{10}} x^2 = 0$ or $b^2 \log_{2^{10}} x^2 - 2 = 0$.

The first equation results in $x^2 = 1$. Solving for x, we get $x = 1$ or $x = -1$. We can see that both values of x are the solutions to the given equation. Under these values of x, b can be any value. So there is no largest value of b possible.

Solving the second equation, we get $b^2 \log_{2^{10}} x^2 = 2$.

Since we want the largest value of b and we can assume that $b \neq 0$, we have

$$\log_{2^{10}} x^2 = \frac{2}{b^2} \qquad \Rightarrow \qquad x^2 = (2^{10})^{\frac{2}{b^2}} = 2^{\frac{20}{b^2}}$$

Therefore $x_1 = (2^{\frac{20}{b^2}})^{\frac{1}{2}} = 2^{\frac{10}{b^2}}$ or $\qquad x_2 = -(2^{\frac{20}{b^2}})^{\frac{1}{2}} = -2^{\frac{10}{b^2}}$.

In order for x to be an integer, the expression $10/b^2$ must be a positive integer. Since b is real number, there are many values that b can hold such that x is an integer for example, $b = \pm 1$, $b = \pm\sqrt{2}$, $b = \pm\sqrt{5}$, $b = \pm\frac{\sqrt{10}}{n}$, where n can be any positive integer. The largest such value is $b = \sqrt{10}$.

Example 14. (2004 ARML) Compute all values of b for which the following system has a solution (x, y) in real numbers:

$$\sqrt{xy} = b^b$$

$$\log_b\left(x^{\log_b y}\right) + \log_b\left(y^{\log_b x}\right) = 4b^4.$$

Solution: $0 < b \le \frac{1}{\sqrt{2}}$.

Method 1 (official solution):

Let $m = \log_b x$ and $n = \log_b y$. Take the $\log_b$ of both sides of the first equation to obtain

$$\log_b \sqrt{xy} = \log_b b^b \qquad \Rightarrow \qquad \frac{1}{2}(\log_b x + \log_b y) = b \Rightarrow \qquad m + n = 2b.$$

The second equation can be rewritten as $(\log_b y)(\log_b x) + (\log_b x)(\log_b x) = 4b^4$ $\Rightarrow mn = 2b^4$.

Thus, m and n are the roots of $z^2 - (m+n)z + mn = 0 \Rightarrow z^2 - 2bz + 2b^4 = 0$. For these roots to be real, then $(-2b)^2 - 4\cdot 1\cdot(2b^4) \ge 0 \Rightarrow 1 \ge 2b^2 \Rightarrow -\frac{1}{\sqrt{2}} \le b \le \frac{1}{\sqrt{2}}$.

Since $b > 0$, the solution set is $0 < b \le \frac{1}{\sqrt{2}}$.

Method 2 (our solution):
Let $m = \log_b x$ and $n = \log_b y$. Take the $\log_b$ of both sides of the first equation to obtain

$$\log_b \sqrt{xy} = \log_b b^b \quad \Rightarrow \quad \frac{1}{2}(\log_b x + \log_b y) = b \Rightarrow \quad m + n = 2b \quad (1)$$

The second equation can be rewritten as $(\log_b y)(\log_b x) + (\log_b x)(\log_b x) = 4b^4$

$\Rightarrow mn = 2b^4$ (2)

Squiring both sides of (1): $m^2 + 2mn + n^2 = 4b^2$ (3)

Rewrite (2) as $4\,mn = 8b^4$ (4)

(3) – (4): $(m-n)^2 = 4b^2 - 8b^4$ (5)

We know that the left hand side of equation (5) is a square number, so we have

$$4b^2 - 8b^4 \ge 0 \Rightarrow \quad 4b^2(1-2b^2) \ge 0 \quad \Rightarrow \quad 4b^2(2b^2-1) \le 0 \quad \Rightarrow$$
$$4b^2(\sqrt{2}b-1)(\sqrt{2}b+1) \le 0$$

We solve the above inequality:

$b \le -\dfrac{1}{\sqrt{2}}$ or $0 \le b \le \dfrac{1}{\sqrt{2}}$

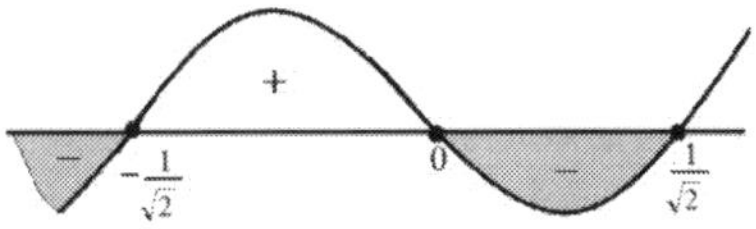

Since $b > 0$, the solution set is $0 < b \le \dfrac{1}{\sqrt{2}}$.

4. Logarithm Applications

Example 15. Find the maximum value of $\log|x| + \log|7-x|$ if $-1 \le x \le 2, x \ne 0$.

Solution: 1.

$$\log|x| + \log|7-x| = \log|7x - x^2| = \log\left|(x-\frac{7}{2})^2 - \frac{49}{4}\right|.$$

We know that $-1 \le x \le 2$, $-\dfrac{9}{2} \le x - \dfrac{7}{2} \le -\dfrac{3}{2}$, $\dfrac{9}{4} \le (x-\dfrac{7}{2})^2 \le \dfrac{81}{4}$.

$$-10 \le (x-\frac{7}{2})^2 - \frac{49}{4} \le 8.$$

$$\therefore \left|(x-\frac{7}{2})^2-\frac{49}{4}\right| \le 10.$$

Equality occurs when $x = 2$.

Therefore the greatest value of $\log|x| + \log|7-x|$ is log 10 = 1.

Example 16. (1984 ARML) Compute the maximum value of $\log x + \log y + \log z$ if x, y, and z are positive, and $x + 4y + 16z = 120$.

Solution: 3.

Method 1 (official solution):

By the A.M.– G.M. Inequality, $(x + 4y + 16z)/3 \ge \sqrt[3]{x \cdot 4y \cdot 16z}$ which implies that $40 \ge 4\sqrt[3]{xyz}$, so $xyz \le 1000$. Therefore $\log x + \log y + \log z = \log xyz \le \log 1000 = 3$.

Method 2 (our solution):

The maximum value of $\log x + \log y + \log z = \log xyz$ is obtained when xyz is maximized.

Since $x + 4y + 16z = 120$, the maximum value of xyz is obtained when $x = 4y = 16z$ or when $x = 40$, $y = 10$, and $z = 40/16 = 5/2$. The maximum value of xyz is $40 \times 10 \times 5/2 = 1000$. $\log 1000 = 3$.

Example 17. If $A_n = \log_{(n+1)}(n+2)$, where n is a positive integer, and $B_n = A_1 A_2 A_3 \cdots A_n$, find the value of B_{1022}.

Solution: 10.

Note that $A_n = \dfrac{\log(n+2)}{\log(n+1)}$.

$B_{1022} = A_1 A_2 A_3 \cdots A_{1022} =$

$$\frac{\log 3}{\log 2} \cdot \frac{\log 4}{\log 3} \cdot \frac{\log 5}{\log 4} \cdot \cdots \cdot \frac{\log 1023}{\log 1022} \cdot \frac{\log 1024}{\log 1023} = \cdot \frac{\log 1024}{\log 2} = 10.$$

Example 18. If $\log_{10} 14 = x$, $\log_{10} 15 = y$ and $\log_{10} 16 = z$, the smallest number in $S = \{\log_{10} 1, \log_{10} 2, \log_{10} 3, \ldots \log_{10} 100\}$ which cannot be written in the form $ax + by + cz + d$ for rational numbers a, b, c, and d is $\log_{10} n$. What is n?

Solution: 11.
The equation $\log_{10} n \neq a(\log_{10} 14) + b(\log_{10} 15) + c(\log_{10} 16) + d$

$\neq \log_{10}(14^a \cdot 15^b \cdot 16^c \cdot 10^d)$ can be rewritten as

$n \neq 14^a \cdot 15^b \cdot 16^c \cdot 10^d = 2^{a+4c+d} \cdot 3^b \cdot 5^{b+d} \cdot 7^a$

So n has no prime factors of 2, 3, 5, or 7.
The smallest value is 11.

Example 19. (1996 ARML) Let n be a positive integer. If the number of integers in the domain of $y = \log((1 - x)(x - n))$ equals $2n - 6$, compute n.

Solution: 4.
Method 1 (official solution):
The integers in the domain of the log function are 2, 3, ... $n - 1$, making a total of $n - 2$ integers. Thus, $n - 2 = 2n - 6$ yields $n = 4$.

Method 2 (our solution):
$(1 - x)(x - n) > 0 \qquad \Rightarrow \qquad (x - 1)(x - n) > 0$

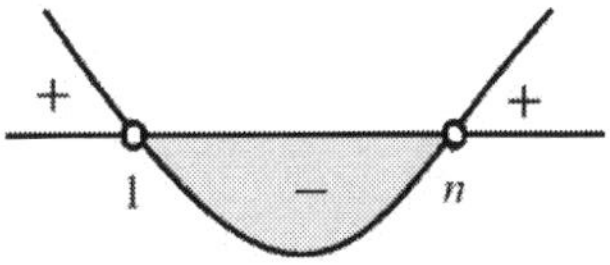

The solution is plotted as shown in the figure.
The number of integer solutions is $n - 1 - 1 = n - 2$.
Let $n - 2 = 2 - 6 \qquad \Rightarrow \qquad n = 4$.

Example 20. A triangle with sides $a \le b \le c$ is log-right if $\log(a^2) + \log(b^2) = \log(c^2)$. Compute the smallest possible value of c in a right triangle that is also log-right.

Solution: 2.
Method 1:
From $\log(a^2) + \log(b^2) = \log(c^2)$, we obtain $ab = c$. Substituting into $a^2 + b^2 = c^2$ yields $(ab)^2 = a^2 + b^2 \Rightarrow \qquad (ab)^2 - b^2 = a^2$.

Since $a \le b$, replacing b by a yields the following inequality: $a^2 a^2 - a^2 \le a^2$. Thus, $a^4 \le 2a^2 \Rightarrow a^2 \le 2a \Rightarrow \qquad a \le \sqrt{2}$. Thus, the largest value of a is $\sqrt{2}$. If $a = b = \sqrt{2}$, then $c = 2$ and both the Pythagorean Theorem and $\log(a^2) + \log(b^2) =$

$\log(c^2)$ are satisfied. Since $ab = c$, the greatest value of a will result in the smallest value of c.

Method 2:

By the Pythagorean Theorem: $a^2 + b^2 = c^2$ (1)

From $\log(a^2) + \log(b^2) = \log(c^2)$, we obtain $ab = c \Rightarrow 2ab = 2c$ (2)

(1) – (2): $a^2 - 2ab + b^2 = c^2 - 2c \Rightarrow (a - b)^2 = c^2 - 2c$ (3)

The left hand side of equation (3) is a square number, so we have $c^2 - 2c \geq 0$

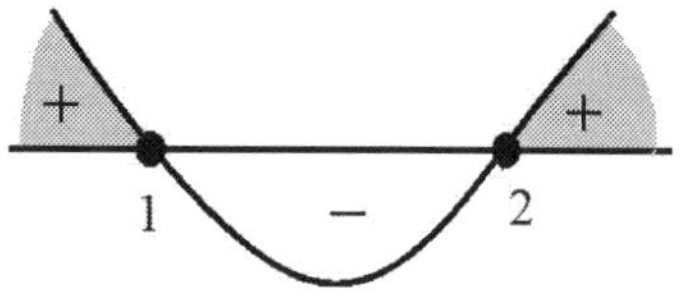

We solve the above inequality:
The smallest value of c is $c = 2$.

Example 21. Let $f(x) = ax + b$ where a and b are integers with $a > 0$. If the solution to $2^{f(x)} = 125$ is $x = \log_4 10$, compute the ordered pair (a, b).

Solution: (6, – 3).

Rewrite $2^{f(x)} = 125$ as $2^{ax+b} = 125$ or $2^{a\log_4 10 + b} = 125$.

Take the log of both sides of the above equation to obtain

$$(a\log_4 10 + b)\cdot\log 2 = \log 125 \quad\Rightarrow\quad \frac{a}{2}\log_2 10 + b = \frac{\log 125}{\log 2}$$

$$\Rightarrow \quad b = \log_2 5^3 - \log_2 10^{\frac{a}{2}} = \log_2 \frac{5^3}{10^{\frac{a}{2}}} \quad\Rightarrow\quad 2^b = \frac{5^3}{10^{\frac{a}{2}}} \quad\Rightarrow$$

$$2^b \cdot 10^{\frac{a}{2}} = 5^3 \quad\Rightarrow\quad 2^b \cdot 5^{\frac{a}{2}} \cdot 2^{\frac{a}{2}} = 5^3 \Rightarrow \quad 5^{\frac{a}{2}} \cdot 2^{b+\frac{a}{2}} = 5^3.$$

So we have $\frac{a}{2} = 3 \quad\Rightarrow\quad$ a = 6 and $b + \frac{a}{2} = 0 \quad\Rightarrow\quad b + \frac{6}{2} = 0 \Rightarrow b = -3$

.

Example 22. Suppose a, b, and c are positive real numbers such that $\log a + \log b + \log = 0$. Compute $\frac{1}{ab+a+1} + \frac{1}{bc+b+1} + \frac{1}{ca+c+1}$.

Solution: 1.

Since $\log a + \log b + \log = 0$, then $abc = 1$.

$$\frac{1}{ab+a+1}+\frac{1}{bc+b+1}+\frac{1}{ca+c+1}$$
$$=\frac{1}{ab+a+1}+\frac{a}{a(bc+b+1)}+\frac{ab}{ab(ca+c+1)}$$
$$=\frac{1}{ab+a+1}+\frac{a}{ab+a+1}+\frac{ab}{ab+a+1}$$
$$=\frac{1+a+ab}{ab+a+1}=1$$

Example 23. Suppose *a, b,* and *c* are positive real numbers such that $3^a=4^b=6^c$. Compute $\frac{-2ab+2bc+ac}{abc}$.

Solution: 0.

Let $m=3^a=4^b=6^c$. We have $a=\log_3 m$, $b=\log_4 m$, and $c=\log_6 m$.

$$\frac{-2ab+2bc+ac}{abc}=\frac{2}{a}+\frac{1}{b}-\frac{2}{c}=2\log_3 m+\log_4 m-2\log_6 m$$
$$=\log_m\frac{3^2\times 4}{6^2}=\log_m 1=0$$

Example 24. The domian of $f(x)=(\log_2\frac{x}{2})(\log_2\frac{x}{4})$ is the solution to the inequality $2(\log_{\frac{1}{2}}x)^2+7\log_{\frac{1}{2}}x+3\le 0$. Find the sum of the smallest and greatest possible values of *f*(*x*).

Solution: $\frac{7}{4}$.

Let $\log_{\frac{1}{2}}x$ be y. $2(\log_{\frac{1}{2}}x)^2+7\log_{\frac{1}{2}}x+3\le 0 \Rightarrow 2y^2+7y+3\le 0\Rightarrow$

$(2y+1)(y+3)\le 0$

The solution can be written as

$$-3\le\log_{\frac{1}{2}}x\le-\frac{1}{2}$$

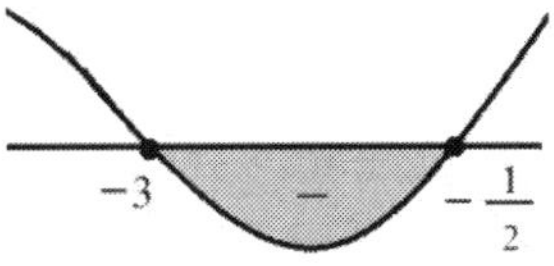

So $\sqrt{2} \le x \le 8$, $\frac{1}{2} \le \log_2 x \le 3$.

$f(x) = (\log_2 \frac{x}{2})(\log_2 \frac{x}{4}) = (\log_2 x - \log_2 2)(\log_2 x - \log_2 4)$

$= (\log_2 x - 1)(\log_2 x - 2) = (\log_2 x)^2 - 3\log_2 x + 3$

$= (\log_2 x - \frac{3}{2})^2 - \frac{1}{4}$

When $\log_2 x = \frac{3}{2}$, $f_{\min} = -\frac{1}{4}$.

When $\log_2 x = 3$, $f_{\max} = 2$. The sum is $2 - \frac{1}{4} = \frac{7}{4}$

Example 25. (AIME) Let *x*, *y* and *z* all exceed 1 and let *w* be a positive number such that $\log_x w = 24$, $\log_y w = 40$ and $\log_{xyz} w = 12$. Find $\log_z w$.

Solution: 60.

Method 1:

Changing the given logarithms into exponential forms, we get

$x^{24} = w$, $y^{40} = w$, $(xyz)^{12} = w$.

$$z^{12} = \frac{w}{x^{12}y^{12}} = \frac{w}{w^{\frac{1}{2}}w^{\frac{3}{10}}} = w^{\frac{1}{5}}.$$

Therefore $w = z^{60}$ and $\log_z w = 60$.

Method 2:

Let $\log_z w = t$. We then have $\log z = \frac{\log w}{t}$, $\log x = \frac{\log w}{24}$, and $\log y = \frac{\log w}{40}$.

$$\log_{xyz} w = \frac{\log w}{\log x + \log y + \log z} = \frac{\log w}{\frac{\log w}{24} + \frac{\log w}{40} + \frac{\log w}{t}} = 12$$

Or $\frac{1}{24} + \frac{1}{40} + \frac{1}{t} = \frac{1}{12}$. Solving for *t*, we get *t* = 60. Thus $\log_z w = 60$.

Method 3:

$\log_w z = \log_w \dfrac{zxy}{xy} = \log_w xyz - \log_w x - \log_w y = \dfrac{1}{12} - \dfrac{1}{24} - \dfrac{1}{40} = \dfrac{1}{60}$. $\therefore$ $\log_z w = 60$.

Method 4:

By (4.3), we have $\log_{xyz} w = 12 \qquad \Rightarrow \qquad \log_w xyz = \dfrac{1}{12}$ (1)

By (4.1): (1) becomes $\dfrac{\log x}{\log w} + \dfrac{\log y}{\log w} + \dfrac{\log z}{\log w} = \dfrac{1}{12} \quad \Rightarrow$

$$\frac{1}{\log_x w} + \frac{1}{\log_y w} + \frac{1}{\log_z w} = \frac{1}{12}$$

$$\frac{1}{\log_z w} = \frac{1}{12} - \frac{1}{24} - \frac{1}{40} = \frac{1}{60} \quad \Rightarrow \qquad \log_z w = 60 .$$

PROBLEMS

Problem 1. Compute $\log 2^{4^5} + \log 5^{2^{10}}$.

$2^{10}(\log 2 + \log 5) = 1024(\log 10) = 1024$

Problem 2: Simplify $(\log_4 3 + \log_8 3)(\log_3 2 + \log_9 2) - \log_2 \sqrt[4]{32}$.

Problem 3. Find the value of $x + y + z$ if $\log_2(\log_3 x) = \log_3(\log_4 y)$ $= \log_4(\log_2 z) = 1$.

Problem 4. (ARML) If a and b are positive integers with $a \neq b$, and $\frac{\log a}{\log b} = \frac{a}{b}$, compute the quantity $ab + 1$.

Problem 5. (AMC) If $\log_8 3 = p$ and $\log_3 5 = q$, then, in terms of p and q, $\log_{10} 5$ equals

(A) pq (B) $\frac{3p+q}{5}$ (C) $\frac{1+3pq}{p+q}$ (D) $\frac{3pq}{1+3pq}$

Problem 6. Compute the numerical value of $(25^{\log 5})(4^{\log 50})(4^{\log 2})(25^{\log 20})$.

Problem 7. Compute $\log((\sqrt[3]{5})^{\sqrt{18}}(\sqrt[2]{20})^{\sqrt{32}})$.

Problem 8. Find $\log_{10} 5$ in terms of p and q if $\log_8 3 = p$ and $\log_3 5 = q$,

Problem 9. If $\log_2 b - \log_2 a = 4$, and $b^2 + a^2 = Ma^2$. Compute M.

Problem 10. Compute the larger solution to $(\log x)^3 = \log x^4$.

Problem 11. (ARML) Compute all real values of x such that $\log_2(\log_2 x) = \log_4(\log_4 x)$.

Problem 12. (ARML) Given $\dfrac{\log(xy)}{\log(\dfrac{x}{y})}=\dfrac{1}{2}$, increasing y by 50% decreases x by a factor of k. Computer k.

Problem 13. Solve $x\log_{1-x}2=\log_{1-x}(2^x+x^2-1)$

Problem 14. (2008 ARML) The equation $\dfrac{\log_{12}(\log_8(\log_4 x))}{\log_5(\log_4(\log_y(\log_2 x)))}=0$ has a solution for x when $1<y<b$, $y\neq a$. Compute the ordered pair $(a,\ b)$ where b is as large as possible.

Problem 15. Find the value of y if

$$\begin{cases}\log_5(x^2+2x-2)=0, & (1)\\ 2\log_5(x+2)-\log_5 y+\dfrac{1}{2}=0. & (2)\end{cases}.$$

Problem 16. Find the product of α and β if they are two distinct roots of the equation $(\log 3x)(\log 5x)=k$.

Problem 17. Find $\log_{abcd}x$ if $\log_a x=m$, $\log_b x=n$, $\log_c x=p$, $\log_d x=q$. $x\neq 1$.

Problem 18. If a, b, c form a geometric sequence and $\log_c a$, $\log_b c$, $\log_a b$ form an arithmetic sequence, find the common difference of the arithmetic sequence.

Problem 19. If $A_n=\log_{(n+2)}(n+3)$, where n is a positive integer, and $B_n=A_1A_2A_3\cdots A_n$, find the value of B_{2184}.

Problem 20. Two of the vertices of a parallelogram $ABCD$ are $A(\log_{49} 7, 0)$ and $C(0, \log_{49} x)$ for $x > 1$. Add the coordinates of all four vertices. The result is 5. Compute x.

Problem 21. Given the points $A(\log 3, \log 5)$ and $B[\log(\log x^3), \log(\log(x^5)]$, compute the slop of the line containing points A and B.

Problem 22. (2000 ARML) If $a = 2016$, compute the numerical value of the infinite sum:

$$(\log_a 3)^0(\log_a 224^{2^0}) + (\log_a 3)^1(\log_a 224^{2^1}) + (\log_a 3)^2(\log_a 224^{2^2}) + \cdots$$

Problem 23. Compute base b if $\log_b(240) = 2 + \log_b 3 + \log_b 5$

Problem 24. (2007 ARML) Suppose a, b, and c are positive real numbers such that $a^2 + b^2 = c^2$ and $\log a + \log b = \log c$. Compute

$$\frac{((a+b)+c)((a+b)-c)((a-b)+c)((a-b)-c)}{c^2}.$$

Problem 25. Suppose a, b, and c are positive real numbers such that $\log a + \log b + \log = 0$. Compute $\dfrac{a}{ab+a+1} + \dfrac{b}{bc+b+1} + \dfrac{c}{ca+c+1}$.

Problem 26. (ARML) For integers x and y with $1 < x, y \le 100$, compute the number of ordered pairs (x, y) such that $\log_x y + \log_y x^2 = 3$.

Problem 27. Solve

$$\begin{cases} \log_2 x + \log_4 y + \log_4 z = 2 & (1) \\ \log_3 y + \log_9 z + \log_9 x = 2 & (2) \\ \log_4 z + \log_{16} x + \log_{16} y = 2 & (3). \end{cases}$$

Problem 28. Find the greatest value of $\log x + \log y$ if $2x + 5y = 20$.

SOLUTIONS

Problem 1. Solution: 1024.
This is $\log 2^{1024} + \log 5^{1024} = 1024(\log 2 + \log 5) = 1024 \cdot \log 10 = 1024$.

Problem 2: Solution: 0.

$$(\log_4 3 + \log_8 3)(\log_3 2 + \log_9 2) - \log_2 \sqrt[4]{32}$$

$$= (\frac{1}{2\log_3 2} + \frac{1}{3\log_3 2})(\log_3 2 + \frac{1}{2}\log_3 2) - \log_2 2^{\frac{5}{4}} = \frac{1}{2} + \frac{1}{3} + \frac{1}{4} + \frac{1}{6} - \frac{5}{4} = 0.$$

Problem 3. Solution: 89.
Since for any base $b \neq 0$, $\log_b N = 0$ only if $N = 1$, the given equations yield

$\log_3 x = 2 \quad \Rightarrow \quad x = 3^2$

$\log_4 y = 3 \quad \Rightarrow \quad y = 4^3$

$\log_2 z = 4 \quad \Rightarrow \quad z = 2^4$

Adding these results gives $x + y + z = 3^2 + 4^3 + 2^4 = 9 + 64 + 16 = 89$.

Problem 4. Solution: 9.
From $b \log a = a \log b$, we find that $a^b = b^a$. Clearly 2 and 4 satisfy this equation (and the problem implies that there is only one value for $ab + 1$) in either order, so $ab + 1 = 9$.

Problem 5. Solution: (D).
The exponential form of the given equations is $3 = 8^p = 2^{3p}$ and $5 = 3^p$.
$5 = (2^{3p})^q = 2^{3pq}$.

We are asked to find $\log_{10} 5 = x$, i.e. x such that $10^x = 5$. Since $5 = 2^{3pq}$, we have
$10^x = 2^{3pq}$.
$10^x = 2^x \cdot 5^x = 2^x \cdot 2^{3pqx} = 2^{x(1+3pq)}$.

It follows that $x(1 + 3pq) = 3pq$ and $x = \dfrac{3pq}{1+3pq}$.

Note: See problem 8 for two different solutions.

Problem 6. Solution: 10,000..

$(25^{\log 5+\log 20})(4^{\log 50+\log 2}) = (25^{\log 100})(4^{\log 100}) = 100^{\log 100} = 100^2 = 10{,}000$.

Problem 7. Solution: $2\sqrt{2}$.

We have $(\sqrt[3]{5})^{\sqrt{18}}(\sqrt[2]{20})^{\sqrt{32}}) = (\sqrt[3]{5})^{3\sqrt{2}}(\sqrt[4]{20})^{4\sqrt{2}}) = (5)^{\sqrt{2}}(20^{\sqrt{2}}) = 100^{\sqrt{2}} = 10^{2\sqrt{2}}$

then $\log 10^{2\sqrt{2}} = 2\sqrt{2}$.

Problem 8. Solution: $\dfrac{3pq}{1+3pq}$.

Method 1:

Using Change-of-Base Theorem (4.1):

$p = \log_8 3 = \dfrac{\log_{10} 3}{\log_{10} 8}$, and $q = \log_3 5 = \dfrac{\log_{10} 5}{log_{10} 3}$, we obtain $\log_{10} 3 = p\log_{10} 8$,

$\log_{10} 5 = q\log_{10} 3$, thus $\log_{10} 5 = pq\log_{10} 8 = pq\log_{10}(\dfrac{10}{5})^3 = 3pq(1-\log_{10} 5)$.

Soving this for $\log_{10} 5$ gives choice (D) as the answer.

Method 2:

We know that $\log_a b = \dfrac{1}{\log_b a}$ and can write

$p = \log_8 3 = \dfrac{1}{\log_3 8} = \dfrac{1}{\log_3 2^3} = \dfrac{1}{3\log_3 2}$,

so $\log_3 2 = \dfrac{1}{3p}$, and $\log_{10} 5 = \dfrac{\log_3 5}{\log_3 10} = \dfrac{q}{\log_3 2 + \log_3 5} = \dfrac{q}{\dfrac{1}{3p}+q} = \dfrac{3pq}{1+3pq}$.

Problem 9. Solution: 257.

$\log_2 b - \log_2 a = 4 \quad \Rightarrow \quad \log_2 \dfrac{b}{a} = 4 \quad \Rightarrow \quad \dfrac{b}{a} = 2^4 = 16 \quad \Rightarrow$

$b = 16a$

$b^2 + a^2 = Ma^2 \Rightarrow \quad (16a)^2 + a^2 = 16a^2 \quad \Rightarrow \quad M = 256 + 1 = 257$

Problem 10. Solution: 100.

$(\log x)^3 - 4\log x = 0 \Rightarrow \quad (\log x)(\log x)^2 - 4) = 0$
$\Rightarrow \quad (\log x)(\log x - 2)(\log x + 2) = 0$
$x = 1; x = 100, x = 10^{-2}$.
The answer is 100.

Problem 11. Solution: $\sqrt{2}$.
By the formula (4.6), we have $\log_2(\log_2 x) = 2\log_4(2\log_4 x) = \log_4(2\log_4 x)^2$.
Therefore $\log_4(2\log_4 x)^2 = \log_4(\log_4 x) \quad \Rightarrow \quad (2\log_4 x)^2 = \log_4 x \quad \Rightarrow$
$4(\log_4 x)^2 - \log_4 x = 0 \quad \Rightarrow (\log_4 x)(4\log_4 x - 1) = 0$
We have $\log_4 x = 0 \quad \Rightarrow \quad x = 4^0 = 1$ (extraneous).
Or $4\log_2 x - 1 = 0 \quad \Rightarrow \quad \log_4 x = \frac{1}{4} \quad \Rightarrow \quad x = 4^{1/4} = \sqrt{2}$.

Problem 12. Solution: 8/27.
Method 1 (official solution):

Step 1: $\log(xy) = \frac{1}{2}\log(\frac{x}{y}) = \log\sqrt{\frac{x}{y}}$ (1)

Step 2: $xy = \sqrt{\frac{x}{y}}$ (2)

Step 3: $\sqrt{x} = \frac{1}{y^{\frac{3}{2}}}$ (3)

Step 4: $x = \frac{1}{y^3}$ (4)

Increasing by 50% gives $\frac{1}{(\frac{3}{2}y)^3} = \left(\frac{8}{27}\cdot\frac{1}{y^3}\right) = \frac{8}{27}x$. Thus $k = \frac{8}{27}$.

Note: The given equation is valid for $x, y < 0$. From step 2 to step 3 in the official solution, they separated $\sqrt{\frac{x}{y}}$ to $\frac{\sqrt{x}}{\sqrt{y}}$, which is incorrect for the case $x, y < 0$.

The correct way should be: squaring both sides of (2): $(xy)^2 = \frac{x}{y} \quad \Rightarrow x = \frac{1}{y^3}$.

Method 2 (solution given by Intermediate Algebra from Art of Problem Solving): Multiplying both sides by 2 log (*x/y*), the equation becomes

$$2\log(xy) = \log\frac{x}{y} \qquad (1)$$

So $2\log x + 2\log y = \log x - \log y$ (2)

Rearranging this gives $\log x + 3\log y = 0$ (3)

Applying logarithm identities to the left sides gives

$\log x + 3\log y = \log x + \log y^3 = \log(xy^3)$, so $\log(xy^3) = 0$, which mean $xy^3 = 1$.

Hence if y increases by 50%, meaning that y is multiplied by 3/2, then x must be multiplied by a factor of $(2/3)^3 = 8/27$.

Note: The original equation is valid for $x, y < 0$ as well. But from equation (1) to equation (2), it was incorrectly assumed that $x, y > 0$. We cannot apply the product identity if $x, y < 0$.

Problem 13. Solution: – 1.

By **Law 3: the Power Identity,** $\log_a x^r = r \log_a x$, the given equation can be written as

$\log_{1-x} 2^x = \log_{1-x}(2^x + x^2 - 1)$

(1)

So $2^x = (2^x + x^2 - 1)$

$x^2 = 1 \qquad \Rightarrow \qquad x = 1$ or $x = -1$.

$x = 1$ is extraneous.

We obtained an extraneous solution because we missed something when using the law 3. Note that law 3 has three restrictions: $1 - x > 0$, $1 - x \neq 1$, and $2^x + x^2 - 1 > 0$ or $x < 1$. With these restrictions, we can rule out the extraneous solution $x = 1$.

Problem 14. Solution: (2, 16) .

The equation will have a solution for those values of x for which the numerator equals 0 and the denominator is defined but is not equal to 0.

i) The numerator is 0 if $\log_{12}(\log_8(\log_4 x)) = 0 \Rightarrow \log_8(\log_4 x) = 1 \Rightarrow \log_4 x = 8 \Rightarrow x = 4^8 = 2^{16}$.

ii) The denominator is not equal to 0 if $\log_5(\log_4(\log_y(\log_2 x))) \neq 0 \Rightarrow \log_4(\log_y(\log_2 x)) \neq 1 \Rightarrow \log_y(\log_2 2^{16}) \neq 4 \Rightarrow \log_y 16 \neq 4 \Rightarrow y \neq 2$. We are asked for a such that $y \neq a$. Clearly, $a = 2$.

iii) The denominator is defined if and only if $\log_4(\log_y(\log_2 x)) > 0 \Rightarrow \log_y(\log_2 2^{16}) > 1 \Rightarrow 16 > y$.
We are asked for solutions for x when $1 < y < b$ and b is as large as possible. Thus $b = 16$. Ans: (2, 16) .

Problem 15. Solution: $9\sqrt{5}$.
Simplifying (1), we get $x^2 + 2x - 2 = 1$. Solving this quadratic for x, we get $x = 1$, $x = -3$.
$x = -3$ is extraneous, since it yields a negative value that we must take the logarithm of when we substitute x into equation (2).

Simplifying (2), we get $\dfrac{\sqrt{5}(x+2)^2}{y} = 1$.

Substituting $x = 1$ into the above equation yields $y = \sqrt{5}(1+2)^2 = 9\sqrt{5}$.

Problem 16. Solution: $\dfrac{1}{15}$.
Since α and β are two distinct roots, we have

$$\log 3\alpha \cdot \log 5\alpha = k \qquad (1)$$

$$\log 3\beta \cdot \log 5\beta = k \qquad (2)$$

(1) – (2): $\log 3\alpha \cdot \log 5\alpha - \log 3\beta \cdot \log 5\beta = 0$.

$(\log 3 + \log \alpha)(\log 5 + \log \alpha) - (\log 3 + \log \beta)(\log 5 + \log \beta) = 0$.

$\log 15(\log \alpha - \log \beta) + (\log^2 \alpha - \log^2 \beta) = 0$.

$(\log \alpha - \log \beta)[(\log 15 + (\log \alpha + \log \beta)] = 0$

Since α ≠ β, and log α – log β ≠ 0, log 15 + (log α + log β) = 0 ⇒ log 15 = – log αβ

Therefore $\alpha\beta = \frac{1}{15}$.

Problem 17. Solution: $\frac{mnpq}{mnp+mpq+mnq+npq}$.

$$\log_{abcd} x = \frac{1}{\log_x abcd} = \frac{1}{\log_x a + \log_x b + \log_x c + \log_x d}$$

$$= \frac{1}{\frac{1}{\log_a x} + \frac{1}{\log_b x} + \frac{1}{\log_c x} + \frac{1}{\log_d x}} = \frac{1}{\frac{1}{m} + \frac{1}{n} + \frac{1}{p} + \frac{1}{q}} = \frac{mnpq}{mnp+mpq+mnq+npq}.$$

Problem 18. Solution: 3/2.

Let $\log_c a + d = \log_b c = \log_a b - d$.

$$\frac{\log a}{\log c} + d = \frac{\log c}{\log b} = \frac{\log b}{\log a} - d$$

$$\frac{\log a + d\log c}{\log c} = \frac{\log b - d\log a}{\log a} = \frac{\log c}{\log b}$$

$$\therefore \frac{\log a + d\log c + \log b - d\log a}{\log c + \log a} = \frac{\log c}{\log b}.$$

$$\frac{\log ab + d\log\frac{c}{a}}{\log ac} = \frac{\log c}{\log b} \qquad (1)$$

Substituting $b^2 = ac$ into (1) yields $\log ab + d\log\frac{c}{a} = 2\log c = \log c^2$.

Therefore $d = \frac{\log\frac{c^2}{ab}}{\log\frac{c}{a}} = \frac{\log\frac{c^2}{a\sqrt{ac}}}{\log\frac{c}{a}} = \frac{\log(\frac{c}{a})^{\frac{3}{2}}}{\log(\frac{c}{a})} = \frac{3}{2}$.

Problem 19. Solution: 7.

Note that $A_n = \dfrac{\log(n+3)}{\log(n+2)}$.

$$B_{1022} = A_1 A_2 A_3 \cdots A_{1022} = \frac{\log 4}{\log 3}\cdot\frac{\log 5}{\log 4}\cdot\cdots\cdot\frac{\log 2186}{\log 2185}\cdot\frac{\log 2187}{\log 2186} = \frac{\log 2187}{\log 3} = 7.$$

Problem 20. Solution: 2401.

For a parallelogram *ABCD*, the relationship between the vertices A (x_A, y_A), B (x_B, y_B), and C (x_C, y_C) are:

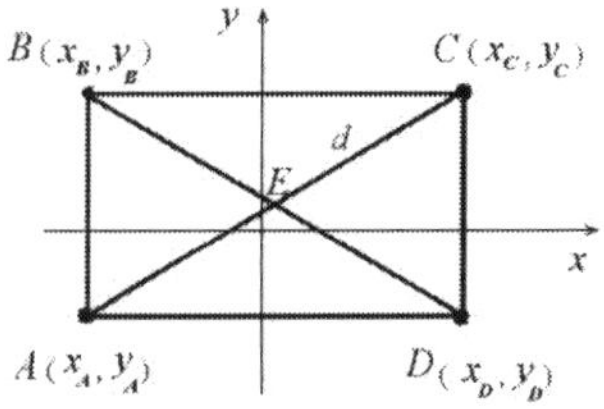

$x_B + x_D = x_A + x_C$

$y_B + y_D = y_A + y_C$

The sum of the coordinates of the vertices is clearly

$x_B + x_D + x_A + x_C + y_B + y_D + y_A + y_C$

$= 2(x_A + x_C) + 2(y_A + y_C)$

$= 2(\log_{49} 7 + 0) + 2(0 + \log_{49} x) = 2(\log_{49} 7 + \log_{49} x) = 2\log_{49}(7x)$

Thus, $2\log_{49}(7x) = 5 \Rightarrow \quad \log_{49}(7x) = \dfrac{5}{2} \Rightarrow \quad 7x = 49^{\frac{5}{2}} \Rightarrow \quad 7x = 7^5 \Rightarrow$

$x = 7^4 = 2401$.

Problem 21. Solution: 1.

Note that the domain of both $\log(\log x^3)$ and $\log(\log(x^5)$ consisting of all x for which

$\log x > 0 \Rightarrow x > 1$.

The slope of the line containing *AB* is

$$\frac{y_B - y_A}{x_B - x_A} = \frac{\log(\log(x^5)) - \log 5}{\log(\log(x^3)) - \log 3} = \frac{\log(\frac{\log(x^5)}{5})}{\log(\frac{\log(x^3)}{3})} = \frac{\log(\frac{5\log x}{5})}{\log(\frac{3\log x}{3})} = \frac{\log(\log x)}{\log(\log x)} = 1$$

Problem 22. Solution: 1.

$$1\cdot\log_a 224 + (\log 3)(2^1)(\log_a 224) + (\log_a 3)^2(2^2)(\log_a 224) + (\log_a 3)^3(2^3)(\log_a 224) + \cdots$$

$$= (\log_a 224)[1 + (\log_a 3)(2^1) + (\log_a 3)^2(2^2) + (\log_a 3)^3(2^3) + \cdots]$$

$= \log_a 224(\frac{1}{1-(\log_a 3)(2^1)}) = \log_a 224(\frac{1}{1-2\log_a 3}) = \log_a 224(\frac{1}{1-\log_a 3^2})$

$= \log_a 224(\frac{1}{\log_a a - \log_a 9}) = \frac{\log_a 224}{\log_a \frac{a}{9}} = \log_{\frac{a}{9}} 224$.

Since a = 2016, we have $\log_{\frac{a}{9}} 224 = \log_{224} 224 = 1$.

Problem 23. Solution: 4.

$\log_b(1240) = \log_b b^2 + \log_b 3 + \log_b 5 = \log_b(b^2 \cdot 3 \cdot 5) = \log_b(15b^2) \Rightarrow$

$\log_b(240) = \log_b(15b^2) \Rightarrow 240 = 15b^2 \Rightarrow b^2 = 16 \Rightarrow b = 4$

Problem 24. Solution: −4.

Method 1 (official solution):

$$\frac{((a+b)+c)((a+b)-c)((a-b)+c)((a-b)-c)}{c^2}$$

$$= \frac{((a+b)^2-c^2)((a-b)^2-c^2)}{c^2} = \frac{(2ab)(-2ab)}{c^2} \text{ since } a^2+b^2=c^2.$$

Since log a + log b = log c, then $ab = c$. Thus, $\frac{-4(ab)_2}{c^2} - 4$

Method 2 (our solution):

Since log a + log b = log c, then $ab = c$ (1)

$a^2 + b^2 = c^2$ (2)

(2) + 2 × (1): $(a+b)^2 = c^2 + 2c$ (3)

(2) − 2 × (1): $(a-b)^2 = c^2 - 2c$ (4)

$$\frac{((a+b)+c)((a+b)-c)((a-b)+c)((a-b)-c)}{c^2}$$

$$\frac{((a+b)^2-c^2)((a-b)^2-c^2)}{c^2} = \frac{(c^2+2c-c^2)(c^2-2c-c^2)}{c^2} = \frac{(2c)(-2c)}{c^2} = -4.$$

Problem 25. Solution: 1.

Since log a + log b + log = 0, then abc = 1.

$$\frac{a}{ab+a+1}+\frac{b}{bc+b+1}+\frac{c}{ca+c+1}$$
$$=\frac{a}{ab+a+1}+\frac{ab}{a(bc+b+1)}+\frac{c}{ca+c+abc}$$
$$=\frac{a}{ab+a+1}+\frac{ab}{a(bc+b+1)}+\frac{c}{ca+c+abc}$$
$$=\frac{a}{ab+a+1}+\frac{ab}{abc+ab+a}+\frac{1}{a+1+ab}$$
$$=\frac{a}{ab+a+1}+\frac{ab}{1+ab+a}+\frac{1}{ca+c+1}$$
$$=\frac{a+ab+1}{ab+a+1}=1$$

Problem 26. Solution: 108.
Method 1 (official solution):

$$\log_x y+\log_y x^2=3 \quad\Rightarrow\quad \log_x y+2\log_y x=3 \quad\Rightarrow\quad \log_x y+\frac{2}{\log_x y}=3$$
$$\Rightarrow\quad (\log_x y)^2+2=3\log_x y \quad\Rightarrow\quad (\log_x y)^2-3\log_x y+2=0$$
$$\Rightarrow\quad (\log_x y-1)(\log_x y-2)=0.$$

Thus $\log_x y-1=0$ or $\log_x y-2=0$.
The solutions to the first equation are the 99 ordered pairs from (2, 2) to (100, 100); the solutions to the second equation are the 9 ordered pairs (2, 4), (3, 9), (4, 16),…,(10, 100).
Thus there are 99 + 9 = 108 ordered pairs of solutions.

Method 2 (our solution):
Using the change of base formula,

$$\frac{\log y}{\log x}+\frac{2\log x}{\log y}=3 \quad\Rightarrow\quad (\log y)^2+2(\log x)^2=3(\log y)(\log y)\Rightarrow$$
$$(\log y-2\log x)(\log y-\log y)=0.$$

We have

$$\log y-\log x=0 \quad\Rightarrow\quad \log y=\log x \quad\Rightarrow\quad y=x \qquad (1)$$

or $\log y - 2\log x = 0 \Rightarrow \quad \log y = 2\log x \Rightarrow \quad y = x^2$ (2)

The solutions to the first equation are the 99 ordered pairs from (2, 2) to (100, 100); the solutions to the second equation are the 9 ordered pairs (2, 4), (3, 9), (4, 16),…,(10, 100).
Thus there are 99 + 9 = 108 ordered pairs of solutions.

Problem 27. Solution: $x = \frac{2}{3}$, $y = \frac{27}{8}$, $z = \frac{32}{3}$.

We know that $x > 0$, $y > 0$, and $z > 0$.
Use the Change-of-Base formula, we can change the bases to 2, 3, and 4 in (1), (2), and (3), respectively:

$$\begin{cases} \log_2 x + \frac{1}{2}\log_2 y + \frac{1}{2}\log_2 z = \log_2 4, \\ \log_3 y + \frac{1}{2}\log_3 z + \frac{1}{2}\log_3 x = \log_3 9 \\ \log_4 z + \frac{1}{2}\log_4 x + \frac{1}{2}\log_4 y = \log_4 16. \end{cases} \Rightarrow \begin{cases} x\sqrt{yz} = 4 & (4), \\ y\sqrt{zx} = 9 & (5), \\ z\sqrt{xy} = 16 & (6). \end{cases}$$

Multiplication of all three equations together gives $(xyz)^2 = 24^2$.
Since $x > 0$, $y > 0$, $z > 0$, $xyz = 24$ (7)
Square both sides of (4): $x^2yz = 16$ (8)

Dividing equation (8) by equation (7), we get $x = \frac{2}{3}$.

Similarly, we can obtain the values of y and z: $y = \frac{27}{8}$ and $z = \frac{32}{3}$.

Plugging these values back into the given equation, we can check and see that the values $x = \frac{2}{3}$, $y = \frac{27}{8}$, $z = \frac{32}{3}$ are the solutions.

Problem 28. Solution: 1.

We know that $x > 0$, $y > 0$, so $\log x + \log y = \log (xy)$. $\log x + \log y$ will be the greatest if xy is the greatest.
From *AM-GM* inequality, we have

$$20 = 2x + 5y \geq 2\sqrt{2x \cdot 5y} = 2\sqrt{10xy}$$

Simplifying this inequality gives us $xy \leq 10$, and so the greatest value of xy is 10 (when $x = 5$ and $y = 2$). Thus, the greatest value of log (xy) is 1 and the greatest value of log x + log y is 1.

BASIC KNOWLEDGE

1. Floor Function:

(1.1). Definition: $y = \lfloor x \rfloor$

(i). $\lfloor x \rfloor$ is an integer. (ii). $\lfloor x \rfloor \le x$, and (iii). $x < \lfloor x \rfloor + 1$.

$\lfloor x \rfloor$ is called the floor function. Whenever we see this notation, we take the greatest integer value not greater than *x*. It is also called Gaussian Function since it was introduced by Carl Friedrich Gauss in 1808 (using the square bracket notation [*x*]). The expressions $\lfloor x \rfloor$ and [*x*] are the same.

Example 1. Find the values of the following expressions:
(a) $\lfloor 3.14 \rfloor$. (b) $\lfloor 4.5 \rfloor$. (c) $\lfloor -0.5 \rfloor$.

Solutions:
(a) $\lfloor 3.14 \rfloor = 3$ (b) $\lfloor 4.5 \rfloor = 4$ (b) $\lfloor -0.5 \rfloor = -1$ (not 0).

(1.2). Graph:

$\lfloor x \rfloor$ is a piecewise constant function, with discontinuities at the integers. The domain of this function is all real numbers and the range is all positive integers.

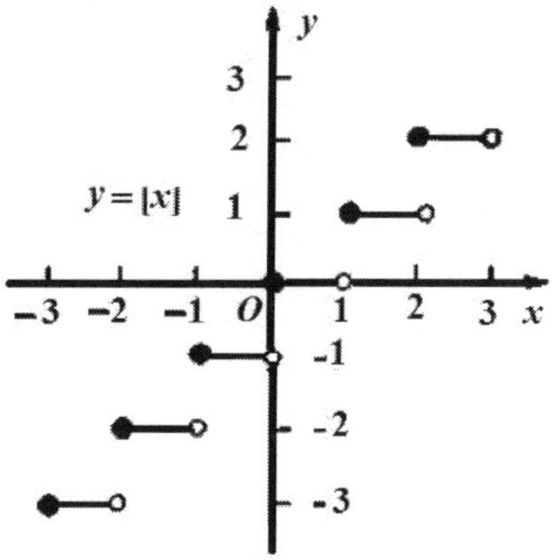

2. The fractional part of a floor function:

(2.1). Definition:

$\{x\} = x - \lfloor x \rfloor$

$\{x\}$ is called the decimal part of x. For all x, $0 \le \{x\} < 1$.

$\{-1.2\} = -1.2 - \lfloor -1.2 \rfloor = 0.8$.

(2.2). Graph:

$\{x\}$ is a piecewise constant function, with discontinuities at the integers. The domain is all real numbers and the range is [0, 1). The function's period is 1.

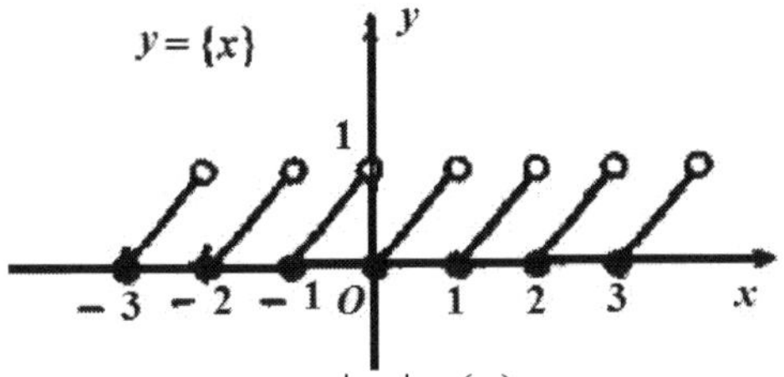

Any real number can be written as $x = \lfloor x \rfloor + \{x\}$.

3 Ceiling function:

$y = \lceil x \rceil$, $\lceil x \rceil$ is called the ceiling function. Whenever we see this notation, we take the smallest integer value not less than x.

When x is integer, $\lfloor x \rfloor = x = \lceil x \rceil$.
When x is not integer, $\lceil x \rceil = \lfloor x \rfloor + 1$.

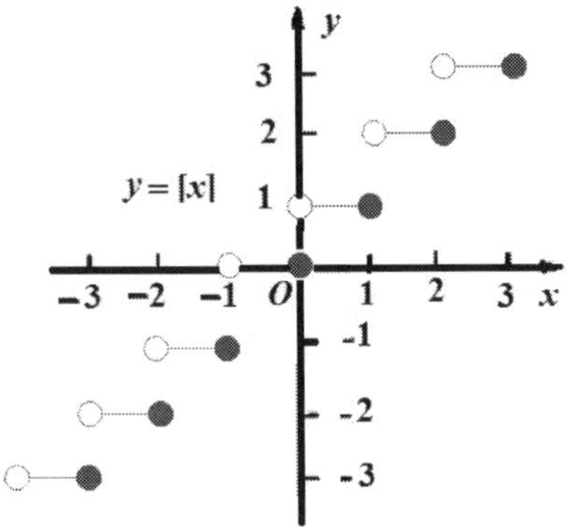

Example 2: Find the values of the following expressions: $\lceil \pi \rceil$, $\lceil 1.414 \rceil$, and $\lceil -1.414 \rceil$.

Solution:
$\lceil \pi \rceil = 4$, $\lceil 1.414 \rceil = 2$, $\lceil -1.414 \rceil = -1$.

$\lceil x \rceil$ is a piecewise constant functions, with discontinuities at the integers.

4. Properties of floor functions:

(1). $x - 1 < [x] \le x < [x] + 1$
(2). When $x \le y$, $\lfloor x \rfloor \le \lfloor y \rfloor$.

Proof:
By definition, we know that $[x] \le x$. Since $x \le y$, $[x] \le y$.
Taking the integer parts of each side of $[x] \le y$, we get $\lfloor \lfloor x \rfloor \rfloor \le \lfloor y \rfloor$.

Since $\lfloor x \rfloor$ is an integer, $\lfloor \lfloor x \rfloor \rfloor = \lfloor x \rfloor$. Therefore $\lfloor x \rfloor \le \lfloor y \rfloor$.

(3). $[x + m] = m + [x]$, when m is a positive integer..

Proof:
Method 1:
By definition, we know that $[x] \le x < [x] + 1$

Adding m to both sides: $[x] + m \le x + m < [x] + m + 1$

Taking the integer parts of both sides: $\lfloor m + \lfloor x \rfloor \rfloor \le \lfloor m + x \rfloor < \lfloor \lfloor x \rfloor + m + 1 \rfloor$

We know that m is an integer, so $\lfloor m + \lfloor x \rfloor \rfloor = \lfloor m \rfloor + \lfloor x \rfloor = m + \lfloor x \rfloor$, and $\lfloor \lfloor x \rfloor + m + 1 \rfloor = m + \lfloor x \rfloor + 1$.
Since $m + \lfloor x \rfloor$ and $m + \lfloor x \rfloor + 1$ are two consecutive integers, $m + \lfloor x \rfloor = \lfloor m + x \rfloor$.
(for example, if $2 \le n < 3$ and n is integer, we can conclude that n must be 2).

Method 2:
By definition, we have
$x+n=[x]+\{x\}+n=[x]+n+\{x\}$.
$x+n=[x]+n+\{x\}$ (1)
We know that n is integer, so $0\le\{x\}<1$.

Taking the integer part of (1), we get $[x+n]=[x]+n$.

(4) If $[x]=[y]=n$, then $x = n + a, y = n + b$ $0 \le a, b < 1$.

(5) For any real number x and y, $[x]+[y]\le[x+y]$.

Proof :
Taking the integer parts of each side of $[x]+[y]\le x+y$, we get
$[[x]+[y]]\le[x+y]$.

Since $[x]+[y]$ is an integer, $[[x]+[y]]$ = $[x]+[y]\le[x+y]$.

Generally,
$[x_1]+[x_2]+\cdots+[x_n]\le[x_1+x_2+\cdots+x_n]$

$2[x]\le[2x], 3[x]\le[3x],\cdots, \quad n[x]\le[nx]$

(6). If $x_1\ge 0,\ x_2\ge 0,$ then $[x_1\cdot x_2]\ge[x_1]\cdot[x_2]$.

Proof:
We are given that $x_1\ge 0,\ x_2\ge 0$. Thus, $0\le[x_1]\le x_1,\ 0\le[x_2]\ge x_2$.
$[x_1]\cdot[x_2]\le x_1x_2$,
$[x_1]\cdot[x_2]\le[x_2x_2]$.

(7) $[-x]=\begin{cases}-[x] & x\in z\\ -[x]-1 & x\notin z\end{cases}$

$$\{-x\}=\begin{cases}-\{x\}=0 & x\in z\\ 1-\{x\} & x\notin z\end{cases}$$

(8) $\left[\frac{[x]}{n}\right]=\left[\frac{x}{n}\right]$ for $n\in N$.

Proof:

Let $\left[\frac{[x]}{n}\right]=m$. By definition, $m\le\frac{[x]}{n}<m+1$. Multiplying by n yields $mn\le[x]<n(m+1)$.

Since mn and $n(m+1)$ are integers, $mn\le x<n(m+1)$.

Therefore $m\le\frac{x}{n}<m+1 \quad\Rightarrow\quad m=\left[\frac{x}{n}\right]=\left[\frac{[x]}{n}\right]$.

(9) For any natural numbers m and n, there must exist nonnegative integers q and r such that $n = mq + r$, where $0\le r<m$.

Proof:

Let m be a positive integer. Multiplying each term of the following inequalities by m,

$$\left[\frac{n}{m}\right]\le\frac{n}{m}<\left[\frac{n}{m}\right]+1$$

we get:

$$m\left[\frac{n}{m}\right]\le n<m\left[\frac{n}{m}\right]+m \quad\Rightarrow\quad 0\le n-m\left[\frac{n}{m}\right]<m.$$

Let $q=\left[\frac{n}{m}\right]$, $r = n - mq$, we get $n = mq + r$.

Example 3. Compute $\left\lfloor\sqrt{4n^2+3n+1}\right\rfloor$ for positive integer n.

Solution: $2n$.

We know that $2n < \sqrt{4n^2+3n+1} < \sqrt{4n^2+4n+1} = \sqrt{(2n+1)^2} = 2n+1$.

$2n \le \lfloor \sqrt{4n^2+3n+1} \rfloor < 2n+1$.

Since there is no any positive integer between $2n$ and $2n+1$, $\lfloor \sqrt{4n^2+3n+1} \rfloor = 2n$.

Example 4. Compute $\lfloor \sqrt{n^2-10n+31} \rfloor$ when $n = 20162016$. The brackets represent the Greatest Integer Function.

Solution: 20,162,011.

For larger n, $\sqrt{n^2-10n+31} = \sqrt{(n-5)^2+6}$ is fractionally more than $(n-5)$; therefore the answer is 20,162,011. In fact, this is true for $n \ge 7$.

Example 5. Let $[x]$ denote the largest integer less than or equal to the real number x, and $\{x\} = x - [x]$ is called the fractional part of x.

For, $z = \dfrac{\{\sqrt{5}\}^2 - 2\{\sqrt{3}\}^2}{\{\sqrt{5}\} - 2\{\sqrt{3}\}}$, find $[z]$.

Solution: -2.

Observe: $\{\sqrt{5}\} = \sqrt{5}-1$ and $\{\sqrt{3}\} = \sqrt{3}-1$.

Hence $z = \dfrac{\{\sqrt{5}\}^2 - 2\{\sqrt{3}\}^2}{\{\sqrt{5}\} - 2\{\sqrt{3}\}} = \dfrac{(\sqrt{5}-1)^2 - 2(\sqrt{3}-1)^2}{\sqrt{5}-1-2(\sqrt{3}-1)}$

$= \dfrac{5+1-2\sqrt{5}-2(3+1-2\sqrt{3})}{\sqrt{3}-1-2\sqrt{2}+2}$

$= \dfrac{4\sqrt{3}-2\sqrt{5}-2}{-2\sqrt{3}+\sqrt{5}+1} = -2$.

Therefore, $[z] = [-2] = -2$.

Example 6. For each real number x, let $\lfloor x \rfloor$ denote the greatest integer that does not exceed x. For how many positive integers n is it true that $n < 1000$ and that $\lfloor \log_2 n \rfloor$ is a positive odd integer?

Solution: 658.

We see that $\lfloor \log_2 n \rfloor = k \quad \Leftrightarrow \quad 2^k \le n < 2^{k+1}$,

When $2 = 2^1 \le n < 2^2 = 4$, or $n = 2, 3$, $\lfloor \log_2 2 \rfloor = 1$, $\lfloor \log_2 3 \rfloor = 1$.

When $4 = 2^2 \le n < 2^3 = 8$, or $n = 4, 5, 6, 7$, $k = \lfloor \log_2 n \rfloor = 2$.

When $8 = 2^3 \le n < 2^4 = 16$, or $n = 8, 9, 10, 11, 12, 13, 14, 15$, $k = \lfloor \log_2 n \rfloor = 3$.

When $16 = 2^4 \le n < 2^5 = 32$, or $n = 16, 17, \ldots, 31$, $k = \lfloor \log_2 n \rfloor = 4$.

When $32 = 2^5 \le n < 2^6 = 64$, or $n = 32, 33, 34, \ldots, 61$, $k = \lfloor \log_2 n \rfloor = 5$.

When $64 = 2^6 \le n < 2^7 = 128$, or $n = 64, 65, 66, \ldots, 127$, $k = \lfloor \log_2 n \rfloor = 6$.

When $128 = 2^7 \le n < 2^8 = 256$, or $n = 128, 129, 130, \ldots, 255$, $k = \lfloor \log_2 n \rfloor = 7$.

When $256 = 2^8 \le n < 2^9 = 512$, or $n = 256, 257, 258, \ldots, 511$, $k = \lfloor \log_2 n \rfloor = 8$.

When $512 = 2^9 \le n < 2^{10} = 1024$, or $n = 512, 513, 514, \ldots, 1023$, $k = \lfloor \log_2 n \rfloor = 9$.

So the answer is $2 + 8 + 32 + 128 + (999 - 512 + 1) = 658$.

5. Applications of Gaussian Function

5.1. Calculations involving Gaussian function

Example 7. Find the integer and decimal parts of $\sqrt{5} - 3$.

Solution: -1, $\sqrt{5} - 2$.

Since $2 < \sqrt{5} < 3$, subtracting 3 from the inequalities yields $-1 < \sqrt{5} - 3 < 0$.

Thus, the integer part of $\sqrt{5} - 3$ is $[\sqrt{5} - 3] = -1$ and the decimal part is $\{\sqrt{5} - 3\} = \sqrt{5} - 3 - (-1) = \sqrt{5} - 2$.

Example 8. Compute $\left\lfloor \dfrac{1}{\sqrt{16 - 6\sqrt{7}}} \right\rfloor$.

Solution: 2.

$16 - 6\sqrt{7} = 9 - 2\sqrt{7} \cdot \sqrt{9} + 7 = (\sqrt{9})^2 - 2 \cdot 3 \cdot \sqrt{7} + (\sqrt{7})^2 = (\sqrt{9} - \sqrt{7})^2$.

$$\frac{1}{\sqrt{16 - 6\sqrt{7}}} = \frac{1}{\sqrt{9} - \sqrt{7}} = \frac{3 + \sqrt{7}}{2}.$$

Since $2 < \sqrt{7} < 3$, $\dfrac{5}{2} < \dfrac{3 + \sqrt{7}}{2} < 3$.

Thus $\left\lfloor \frac{1}{\sqrt{16-6\sqrt{7}}} \right\rfloor = 2.$

Example 9. Compute $\lfloor\sqrt{1}\rfloor+\lfloor\sqrt{2}\rfloor+\lfloor\sqrt{3}\rfloor+\cdots+\lfloor\sqrt{2016}\rfloor$.

Solution: 59378.
The square numbers are 1, 4, 9, …, $(n-1)^2$. There are $(k+1)^2-k^2=2k+1$ positive integers (x_i with $\lfloor\sqrt{x_i}\rfloor=k$) in the region $[k^2, (k+1)^2)$.

For example, there are $2\times1+1=3$ integers with the value of 1.
$\lfloor\sqrt{1}\rfloor=1$, $\lfloor\sqrt{2}\rfloor\approx\lfloor1.414\rfloor=1$, $\lfloor\sqrt{3}\rfloor\approx\lfloor1.732\rfloor=1$,
There are $2\times2+1=5$ integers with the value of 2.
$\lfloor\sqrt{4}\rfloor=2$, $\lfloor\sqrt{5}\rfloor\approx\lfloor2.236\rfloor=2$, $\lfloor\sqrt{6}\rfloor\approx\lfloor2.449\rfloor=2$, $\lfloor\sqrt{7}\rfloor=2$, $\lfloor\sqrt{8}\rfloor=2$.

$2016>1936=44^2$.
$2016-1936+1=81$.
So the sum will be $1\times3+2\times5+\cdots+43\times87+44\times81$

$$=\sum_{n=1}^{43}n(2n+1)+44\times81$$

$$=\frac{2}{6}\times43\times44\times87+\frac{1}{2}\times43\times44+44\times81$$

$= 59378$.

Example 10. Find the value of $\sum_{a=1}^{100}\left\lceil\frac{n+2}{n}\right\rceil$ for natural number n.

Solution: 103.
Expanding $\sum_{a=1}^{100}\left\lceil\frac{n+2}{n}\right\rceil$, we get

$$\sum_{a=1}^{100}\left\lceil\frac{n+2}{n}\right\rceil=\left\lceil1+\frac{2}{1}\right\rceil+\left\lceil1+\frac{2}{2}\right\rceil+\left\lceil1+\frac{2}{3}\right\rceil+\cdots+\left\lceil1+\frac{2}{100}\right\rceil.$$

Therefore $\sum_{a=1}^{100}\left[\dfrac{n+2}{n}\right]=(1+2)+(1+1)+(1+0)+\cdots+(1+0)=103$.

Example 11. Calculate $\sum_{N=1}^{1024}\lfloor\log_2 N\rfloor$.

Solution: 8204.
Method 1:

$$\lfloor\log_2 N\rfloor=\begin{cases}0 & \text{for } 1\le N<2^1\\ 1 & \text{for } 2\le N<2^2\\ 2 & \text{for } 2^2\le N<2^3\\ \vdots & \quad\vdots\\ 9 & \text{for } 2^9\le N<2^{10}\\ 10 & N=2^{10}\end{cases}$$

The sum is

$$0+1(2^2-2)+2(2^3-2^2)+3(2^4-2^3)+\cdots+9(2^{10}-2^9)+10$$
$$=9\cdot 2^{10}-(2^9+2^8+2^7+\cdots+2)+10$$
$$=9\cdot 2^{10}-1022+10=8204.$$

Method 2:
For $m\in[2^k, 2^{k+1})$, $\lfloor\log_2 m\rfloor=k$. For example, if $4=2^2\le m<2^3=8$, $\lfloor\log_2 4\rfloor=2$, $\lfloor\log_2 5\rfloor=2$, $\lfloor\log_2 6\rfloor=2$, $\lfloor\log_2 7\rfloor=2$.
1024 = 1 + 2 + 4 + 8 + 16 + 32 + 64 + 128 + 256 + 512 + 1.

$$\lfloor\log_2 1\rfloor+\lfloor\log_2 2\rfloor+\lfloor\log_2 3\rfloor+\cdots+\lfloor\log_2 1024\rfloor$$
$$=0\times1+1\times2+2\times4+3\times8+4\times16+5\times32+6\times64.$$
$$+7\times128+8\times256+9\times512+10\times1=8204$$

Example 12. Calculate $\sum_{N=1}^{2016}\lceil\log_2 N\rceil$.

Solution: 20140.

$\lceil \log_2 1 \rceil = 0$,

$\lceil \log_2 2 \rceil = 1$,

$\lceil \log_2 3 \rceil = 2$, $\lceil \log_2 4 \rceil = 2$,

$\lceil \log_2 5 \rceil = 3$, $\lceil \log_2 6 \rceil = 3$, $\lceil \log_2 7 \rceil = 3$, $\lceil \log_2 8 \rceil = 3$,

....

$\lceil \log_2 513 \rceil = \lceil \log_2 514 \rceil = \cdots = \lceil \log_2 1024 \rceil = 10$,

$\lceil \log_2 1025 \rceil = \lceil \log_2 1026 \rceil = \cdots = \lceil \log_2 2016 \rceil = 11$.

$2016 = 2^0 + 2^1 + 2^2 + 2^3 + 2^4 + 2^5 + \cdots + 2^9 + 993$

$= 1 + 2 + 4 + 8 + 16 + 32 + 64 + 128 + 256 + 512 + 993$.

So $\lceil \log_2 1 \rceil + \lceil \log_2 2 \rceil + \lceil \log_2 3 \rceil + \cdots + \lceil \log_2 2016 \rceil$

$= 2^0 \times 1 + 2^1 \times 2 + 2^2 \times 3 + 2^3 \times 4 + 2^4 \times 5 + 2^5 \times 6 + \cdots + 2^9 \times 10 + 993 \times 11$.

$= 20140$.

5.2. Function involving Gaussian function

Example 13. 1990 ARML (Note: In this problem, the brackets represent the Greatest Integer Function.) Compute the number of values of n, with $1 < n < 165$, for which $\left[\frac{n}{2}\right] + \left[\frac{n}{3}\right] = \frac{n}{2} + \frac{n}{3}$.

Solution: 27.

Since $\left[\frac{n}{2}\right] \le \frac{n}{2}$ and $\left[\frac{n}{3}\right] \le \frac{n}{3}$, equality occurs if and only if each fraction is an integer. Therefore n is an integer multiple of 6. For $1 < n < 165$, the answer would be $\left[\frac{165}{6}\right]$; for the strict inequality, the answer is $\left[\frac{165-1}{6}\right] = \left[\frac{164}{6}\right] = 27$.

Example 14. (AIME) Suppose r is a real number for which

$$\left[r+\frac{19}{100}\right]+\left[r+\frac{20}{100}\right]+\left[r+\frac{21}{100}\right]+\cdots+\left[r+\frac{91}{100}\right]=546$$

Find $[100r]$. (For real x, $[x]$ is the greatest integer less than or equal to x.)

Solution: 743.

Method 1 (official solution):

The given sum has 73 terms, each of which equals either $[r]$ or $[r]+1$. This is because 19/100, 20/100, ... ,91/100 are all less than 1. In order for the sum to be 546, it is necessary that $[r]$ be 7, because $73 \cdot 7 < 546 < 73 \cdot 8$. Now suppose that $[r + k/100] = 7$ for $19 \le k \le m$ and $[r + k/100] = 8$ for $m + 1 \le k \le 91$. Then $7(m - 18) + 8(91 - m) = 546$, giving $m = 56$. Thus $[r + 56/100] = 7$ but $[r + 57/100] = 8$. It follows that $7.43 \le r \le 7.44$, and hence that $[100r] = 743$.

Method 2 (our solution):

The given sum has $91 - 19 + 1 = 73$ terms. each of which equals either $[r]$ or $[r]+1$. This is because 19/100, 20/100, ... ,91/100 are all less than 1. In order for the sum to be 546, it is necessary that $[r]$ be 7, because $73 \cdot 7 < 546 < 73 \cdot 8$. $546 = 73 \times 7 + 35$. So each of the last 35 terms is 8, and each of the rest of terms is 7. Then $100r + (91 - 35 + 1) \ge 800$ and $100r + (91 - 35 + 1) < 800$.

So $[100r] = 800 - 91 + 35 - 1 = 743$.

5.3. Equations involving Gaussian function

Example 15. Solve $\left[3x-4\frac{5}{6}\right]-2x-1=0$. $[x]$ is the greatest integer not exceeding x. For examples: $[0.9] = 0$, $[\pi] = 3$, $[5] = 5$.

Solution: $x = 6$ or $x = 6\ 1/2$.

The original equation can be rewritten as: $\left[3x-4\frac{5}{6}\right]=2x+1$.

Let $2x + 1 = t$ $(t \in z)$.

Solving for x, we get $x=\dfrac{t-1}{2}$.

Substituting $\dfrac{t-1}{2}$ for x into the rewritten original equation, we get

$3x - 4\frac{5}{6} = \frac{3}{2}t - 6\frac{1}{3}$.

The original equation is now in the form of $\left[\frac{3}{2}t - 6\frac{1}{3}\right] = t$.

Based on the property of [x], we have $t \le \frac{3}{2}t - 6\frac{1}{3} < t + 1 \Rightarrow 12\frac{2}{3} \le t < 14\frac{2}{3}$.

Since t is integer, $t = 13$ or 14. Therefore, $x = 6$ or $x = 6\ 1/2$.

Example 16. (AMC) Let $\lfloor x \rfloor$ be the greatest integer less than or equal to x. Then the number of real solutions to $4x^2 - 40\lfloor x \rfloor + 51 = 0$ is

(A) 0 (B) 1 (C) 2 (D) 3 (E) 4

Solution: $x = \frac{\sqrt{29}}{2}, \frac{\sqrt{189}}{2}, \frac{\sqrt{229}}{2}, \frac{\sqrt{269}}{2}$.

Method 1 (official solution):

Since $40\lfloor x \rfloor$ is even, $40\lfloor x \rfloor - 51$ is odd, implying that $4x^2$ must also be an odd integer, say $2k + 1$, and $x = \frac{\sqrt{2k+1}}{2}$. Substituting in the original equation, it follows that $\left\lfloor \frac{\sqrt{2k+1}}{2} \right\rfloor = \frac{k+26}{20}$, hence one must have $k \equiv 14 \bmod 20$.

Furthermore, $\frac{k+26}{20} \le \frac{\sqrt{2k+1}}{2} < \frac{k+26}{20} + 1$.

Treating the two inequalities separately, multiplying by 20, squaring and completing the square, one obtains $(k - 74)^2 \le 70^2$ and $(k - 54)^2 > 30^2$. Since x^2 must be positive, k is nonnegative, and it follows from the first inequality that $4 \le k \le 144$, and from the second one that either $k < 24$ or $k > 84$. Putting these together, one finds that either $4 \le k < 24$ or $84 < k \le 144$. In these intervals the only values of k for which $k \equiv 14 \bmod 20$ are $k = 14, 94, 114, 134$, yielding the four solutions

$$x = \frac{\sqrt{29}}{2}, \frac{\sqrt{189}}{2}, \frac{\sqrt{229}}{2}, \frac{\sqrt{269}}{2}.$$

Method 2:

We observe that $x > 0$.

Let $[x] = t$ ($t \in N$).
Substituting t for $[x]$ into the original equation we get $4x^2 - 40t + 51 = 0$.

Solving the quadratic for x, we have: $x = \sqrt{\dfrac{40t-51}{4}}$.

Since $0 \le x - [x] < 1$, $0 \le \sqrt{\dfrac{40t-51}{4}} - t < 1$.

Simplifying, we get $\dfrac{3}{2} \le t < \dfrac{5}{2}$ or $\dfrac{11}{2} \le t < \dfrac{17}{2}$.
We know that t is an integer, so the values for t are $t = 2, 6, 7, 8$.

When $[x] = 2, 6, 7, 8$,

$x_1 = \pm\dfrac{1}{2}\sqrt{29}$, $\quad x_2 = \pm\dfrac{1}{2}\sqrt{189}$

$x_3 = \pm\dfrac{1}{2}\sqrt{229}$, $\quad x_4 = \pm\dfrac{1}{2}\sqrt{269}$.

Since $x > 0$, the solutions are $x = \dfrac{1}{2}\sqrt{29}$, $\dfrac{1}{2}\sqrt{189}$, $\dfrac{1}{2}\sqrt{229}$, and $\dfrac{1}{2}\sqrt{269}$.

Example 17. Solve $[\dfrac{5+6x}{8}] = \dfrac{15x-7}{5}$.

Solution: $x = \dfrac{7}{15}$ or $\dfrac{4}{5}$.

Let $t = \dfrac{15x-7}{5}$, where t is integer. Solving for x, we get $x = \dfrac{5t+7}{15}$.

Substituting this into the given equation, we get $[\dfrac{10t+39}{40}] = t$.

So $0 \le \dfrac{10t+39}{40} - t < 1$.

Solving for t, we get $-\frac{1}{30} < t \le \frac{13}{10}$. Since t is an integer, t equals 0 or 1.

Substituting these values into the equation $t = \frac{15x-7}{5}$ and solving for x, we obtain $x = \frac{7}{15}$ or $\frac{4}{5}$.

Example 18. (2013 ARML) Compute the sum of all real numbers x such that $\left\lfloor \frac{x}{2} \right\rfloor - \left\lfloor \frac{x}{3} \right\rfloor = \frac{x}{7}$

Solution: −21.

Because the quantity on the left side is the difference of two integers, x/7 must be an integer, hence x is an integer (in fact a multiple of 7). Because the denominators on the left side are 2 and 3, it is convenient to write $x = 6q + r$, where $0 \le r \le 5$, so that $\left\lfloor \frac{x}{2} \right\rfloor = 3q + \left\lfloor \frac{r}{2} \right\rfloor$ and $\left\lfloor \frac{x}{3} \right\rfloor = 2q + \left\lfloor \frac{r}{3} \right\rfloor$.

Then for r = 0; 1,…,5, these expressions can be simplified as shown in the table below.

r	0	1	2	3	4	5
$\lfloor \frac{x}{2} \rfloor$	$3q$	$3q$	$3q+1$	$3q+1$	$3q+2$	$3q+2$
$\lfloor \frac{x}{3} \rfloor$	$2q$	$2q$	$2q$	$2q+1$	$2q+1$	$2q+1$
$\lfloor \frac{x}{2} \rfloor - \lfloor \frac{x}{3} \rfloor$	q	q	$q+1$	q	$q+1$	$q+1$

Now proceed by cases:

$r = 0$: Then $q = x/6$. But from the statement of the problem, $q = x/7$, so $x = 0$.

$r = 1$: Then $q = (x-1)/6 = x/7 \Rightarrow x = 7$.

$r = 2$: Then $q = (x-2)/6$ and $q + 1 = x/7$, so $(x+4)/6 = x/7$, and $x = -28$.

$r = 3$: Then $q = (x-3)/6$ and $q = x/7$, so $x = 21$.

$r = 4$: Then $q = (x-4)/6$ and $q + 1 = x/7$, so $(x+2)/6 = x/7$, and $x = -14$.

$r = 5$: Then $q = (x-5)/6$ and $q + 1 = x/7$, so $(x+1)/6 = x/7$, and $x = -7$.

The sum of these values is $0 + 7 - 28 + 21 - 14 - 7 = -21$.

Example 19. (2010 ARML) Compute the smallest positive real number x such that $\frac{\lfloor x \rfloor}{x - \lfloor x \rfloor} = 35$.

Solution: $\frac{36}{35}$.

Method 1 (official solution):

The equation can be rewritten as follows: $\frac{x - \lfloor x \rfloor}{\lfloor x \rfloor} = \frac{1}{35} \Rightarrow \frac{x}{\lfloor x \rfloor} - 1 = \frac{1}{35} \Rightarrow$

$$\frac{x}{\lfloor x \rfloor} = \frac{36}{35}$$

Now $0 < x < 1$ is impossible because it makes the numerator of the original expression 0. To make x as small as possible, place it in the interval $1 < x < 2$, so that $[\,x\,] = 1$. Then $x = \frac{36}{35} \cdot \lfloor x \rfloor = \frac{36}{35}$.

Method 2 (our solution):

$$\frac{x - \lfloor x \rfloor}{\lfloor x \rfloor} = \frac{1}{35} \quad \Rightarrow \quad x - \lfloor x \rfloor = \frac{1}{35}\lfloor x \rfloor \quad \Rightarrow \quad 35x - 35\lfloor x \rfloor = \lfloor x \rfloor \quad \Rightarrow$$

$$35x = 36\lfloor x \rfloor.$$

Since we want the smallest positive value for x, we let $[\,x\,] = 1$. Then $x = \frac{36}{35} \cdot \lfloor x \rfloor = \frac{36}{35}$.

Example 20. Solve $x^3 - [x] = 3$.

Solution: $x = \sqrt[3]{4}$.

Since $x = [x] + a$, $(0 \le a < 1)$, $[x] = x - a$.

The original equation becomes $x^3 - x + a = 3$, so $a = -x^3 + x + 3$.

We know that $0 \le a < 1$, so we have

$0 \le -x^3 + x + 3 < 1$.

or $2 < x(x^2 - 1) \le 3$. (1)

We split up the values of x into the two following cases:

Case I: $x < 0$
Since $x(x^2 - 1) > 2$, $x^2 - 1 < 0$. Solving for x, we get
$-1 < x \le 0$, so $-1 \le x^2 - 1 < 0$.
Then $x(x^2 - 1) < 1$, which contradicts (1).
Case II: $x > 0$
Since $x(x^2 - 1) > 2$, $x^2 - 1 > 0$. Solving for x, we get $x > 1$.
Since $x(x^2 - 1) \le 3$, $1 < x < 2$, and $[x] = 1$.
When $[x] = 1$, $x^3 = 4$.
The solution is $x = \sqrt[3]{4}$.

Method 2:
The given equation can be written as $[x] = x^3 - 3$. So
$0 \le x - (x^3 - 3) < 1$
$\Rightarrow 2 < x(x^2 - 1) \le 3$
When $x \le 1$, by observation we can easily see that the above inequality is not true.
Similarly, $x \ge 2$ is also not true.
So $1 < x < 2$ or $[x] = 1$, and the original equation can be written as $x^3 - 1 = 3$.
Solving for x, we get the only solution: $x = \sqrt[3]{4}$.

Example 21. $\lfloor x \rfloor$ is the greatest integer value not greater than x. How many pairs of positive integer solutions are there for the equation $[1.9x] + [8.8y] = 36$?

Solution: 3.
Since y is a positive integers, we know that $y \ge 1$.
We also know that $[8.8y] < 36$. So $y \le 4$.
So we let $y = 1, 2, 3, 4$ and substitute these values into the original equation. The solutions are (15, 1), (10, 2), (1, 4). The answer is 3.

Example 22. Which of the following are the solutions to the system of equations

$$\begin{cases} 3\lfloor x \rfloor + 2\lceil y \rceil = 18 \\ 3\lceil x \rceil - \lceil y \rceil = 4 \end{cases} ?$$

(A) $\begin{cases} 2 < x \le 3, \\ 5 \le y < 6. \end{cases}$ (B) $\begin{cases} 2 \le x < 3, \\ 5 < y \le 6. \end{cases}$ (C) $\begin{cases} 2 \le x < 3, \\ 5 \le y < 6. \end{cases}$ (D) $\begin{cases} 2 < x \le 3, \\ 5 < y \le 6. \end{cases}$

Solution: (C).
We know that $\{x\} = [x] + 1$, and $\{y\} = [y] + 1$.
The given equations become:

$$\begin{cases} 3\{x\} + 2\{y\} = 16 \\ 3\{x\} - \{y\} = 1 \end{cases}$$

Solving the system of equations, we get $\{x\} = 2$, $\{y\} = 5$.
Therefore $2 \le x < 3$ and $5 \le y < 6$.

Example 23. 2001 (ARML) Let $[\, x\,]$ represent the greatest integer less than or equal to x. Compute the number of first quadrant ordered pair (x, y) solutions to the following system:
$x + [\, y\,] = 5.3$
$y + [\, x\,] = 5.7$

Solution: 6.
Let $x = n + 0.3$ and $y = m + 0.7$ for non-negative integers m and n. Then $m + n = 5$ and there are 6 pairs of integers from (0, 5) to (5, 0) for which this is true. The solutions are (0.3, 5.7), (1.3, 4.7), (2.3, 3.7), (3.3, 2.7), (4.3, 1.7), and (5.3, 0.7).

5.4. Inequalities involving Gaussian function

Example 24. Solve $2[x]^2 - 11[x] - 6 \le 0$. $[x]$ is the greatest integer not exceeding x.
(A) [0, 6]. (B) [–1, 6] (C) [0, 7). (D) [– 1, 7)

Solution: (C).
The original inequality can be written as $(2[x] + 1)([x] - 6) \le 0$.
Solving for x, we get: $-\dfrac{1}{2} \le [x] \le 6 \quad \Rightarrow \quad 0 \le x < 7$.

Example 25. Find the smallest positive integer n for which
$\lfloor \log_2 1 \rfloor + \lfloor \log_2 2 \rfloor + \lfloor \log_2 3 \rfloor + \cdots + \lfloor \log_2 n \rfloor > 2016$
(For real x, $\lfloor x \rfloor$ is the greatest integer $\le x$.)

Solution: 315.

Method 1:
For $m \in [2^k, 2^{k+1})$, $\lfloor \log_2 m \rfloor = k$. For example, if $4 = 2^2 \le m < 2^3 = 8$, $\lfloor \log_2 4 \rfloor = 2$, $\lfloor \log_2 5 \rfloor = 2$, $\lfloor \log_2 6 \rfloor = 2$, $\lfloor \log_2 7 \rfloor = 2$.

For $\lfloor \log_2 1 \rfloor + \lfloor \log_2 2 \rfloor + \lfloor \log_2 3 \rfloor + \cdots + \lfloor \log_2 n \rfloor$
$= 0\times1 + 1\times2 + 2\times4 + 3\times8 + 4\times16 + 5\times32 + 6\times64 + 7\times128 = 1538$.

$n = 1 + 2 + 4 + 8 + 16 + 32 + 64 + 128 = 255$.

For $\lfloor \log_2 1 \rfloor + \lfloor \log_2 2 \rfloor + \lfloor \log_2 3 \rfloor + \cdots + \lfloor \log_2 n \rfloor$
$= 0\times1 + 1\times2 + 2\times4 + 3\times8 + 4\times16 + 5\times32 + 6\times64 + 7\times128 + 8\times256 = 3586$.

$n = 1 + 2 + 4 + 8 + 16 + 32 + 64 + 128 + 256 = 511$.
Since $1538 < 2016 < 3586$, the desired solution n is between 255 and 511.

We see that when $256 = 2^8 \le m \le 2^9 = 512$, $\lfloor \log_2 m \rfloor = 8$.

$2016 - 1538 = 478 = 8 \times 59 + 6$.

The solution is $n = 255 + 59 + 1 = 315$. When $n \ge 315$,
$\lfloor \log_2 1 \rfloor + \lfloor \log_2 2 \rfloor + \lfloor \log_2 3 \rfloor + \cdots + \lfloor \log_2 n \rfloor > 2016$.

Method 2:
For $m \in [2^k, 2^{k+1})$, $\lfloor \log_2 m \rfloor = k$. Let $2^k \le n < 2^{k+1}$
So $f(n) = \lfloor \log_2 1 \rfloor + \lfloor \log_2 2 \rfloor + \lfloor \log_2 3 \rfloor + \cdots + \lfloor \log_2 n \rfloor$
$= 0 + 1 + 1 + 2 + \cdots + k$
$= 1\times0 + (2^2 - 2)\times1 + (2^3 - 2^2)\times2 + \cdots + (2^k - 2^{k-1})\times(k-1) + (n - 2^k + 1)k$.
Let $S_{k-1} = 1\times0 + (2^2 - 2)\times1 + (2^3 - 2^2)\times2 + \cdots + (2^k - 2^{k-1})\times(k-1)$.
Then $S_0 = 0$.
$S_k = 2\times1 + 2^2\times2 + \cdots + 2^k\times k = (k-1)\times2^{k+1} + 2$.
Since $S_7 = 1538 < 2016$, and $S_8 = 3586 > 2016$, we let $k - 1 = 7$, or $k = 8$. Then
$f(n) = S_{k-1} + (n - 2^k + 1)k = S_7 + (n - 2^8 + 1)\times8$
$= 1538 + 8n - 2040 = 8n - 502$.

Let $f(n) \ge 2017$ $\Rightarrow$ $n \ge 314\frac{7}{8}$.

The smallest value of n is 315.

5.5. Integers and digits

Example 26. Find the units digit of $\left\lfloor \dfrac{10^{2001}}{10^{29}-2} \right\rfloor$.

Solution: 6.

Let $\dfrac{10^{2001}}{10^{29}-2} = \dfrac{(10^{29})^{69}-2^{69}}{10^{29}-2} + \dfrac{2^{69}}{10^{29}-2} = A + B$, where $B = \dfrac{2^{69}}{10^{29}-2} = \dfrac{8^{23}}{10^{29}-2} < 1$

.

$A = (10^{29})^{68} + (10^{29})^{67}\cdot 2 + (10^{29})^{66}\cdot 2^2 + \cdots + 10^{29}\cdot 2^{67} + 2^{68}$

$2^{68} \equiv 2^4 \equiv 6 \pmod{10}$.

$\left\lfloor \dfrac{10^{2001}}{10^{29}-2} \right\rfloor = \lfloor A + B \rfloor = A$.

The units digit is 6.

Example 27. (1991 ARML) (Note: In this problem, the brackets represent the Greatest Integer Function.) Compute $\left[\dfrac{3^{31}+2^{31}}{3^{29}+2^{29}} \right]$.

Solution: 8.

Method 1: The fraction is equal to

$$\frac{9\cdot 3^{29}+4\cdot 2^{29}}{3^{29}+2^{29}} = \frac{8(3^{29}+2^{29})-4\cdot 2^{29}}{3^{29}+2^{29}} = 8 + \frac{3^{29}-2^{31}}{3^{29}+2^{29}}.$$

Since that last fraction is clearly positive, but less than 1, the answer is 8.

Method 2: By long division,

$$\begin{array}{r|l} & 9 \\ 3^{31}+9\cdot 2^{29} & 3^{31} \qquad\qquad +2^{31} \\ & 3^{31}+9\cdot 2^{29} \\ \hline & \quad -9\cdot 2^{29}+2^{31}=-5\cdot 2^{29} \end{array}$$

The quotient is $9-\dfrac{5\cdot 2^{29}}{3^{29}+2^{29}}$.

Clearly the last fraction is less than 1, so the answer is 8.

Example 28. (2012 ARML) Let $N=\lfloor(3+\sqrt{5})^{34}\rfloor$. Compute the remainder when N is divided by 100.

Solution: 47.

Method 1 (official solution):

Let $\alpha=3+\sqrt{5}$ and $\beta=3-\sqrt{5}$, so that $N=\lfloor\alpha^{34}\rfloor$, and let $M=\alpha^{34}+\beta^{34}$.

When the binomials in M are expanded, terms in which $\sqrt{5}$ is raised to an odd power have opposite signs, and so cancel each other out.

Therefore M is an integer. Because $0<\beta<1$, $0<\beta^{34}<1$, and so $M-1<\alpha^{34}<M$. Therefore $M-1=N$.

Note that α and β are the roots of $x^2=6x-4$. Therefore $\alpha^{n+2}=6\alpha^{n+1}-4\alpha^{n}$ and $\beta^{n+2}=6\beta^{n+1}-4\beta^{n}$. Hence $\alpha^{n+2}+\beta^{n+2}=6(\alpha^{n+1}+\beta^{n+1})-4(\alpha^{n}+\beta^{n})$. Thus the sequence of numbers $\{\alpha^{n}+\beta^{n}\}$ satisfies the recurrence relation $c_{n+2}=6c_{n+1}-4c_n$. All members of the sequence are determined by the initial values c_0 and c_1, which can be computed by substituting 0 and 1 for n in the expression $\alpha^{n}+\beta^{n}$, yielding $c_0=(3+\sqrt{5})^0+(3-\sqrt{5})^0=2$, and $c_1=(3+\sqrt{5})^1+(3-\sqrt{5})^1=6$. Then

$$\begin{aligned} c_2 &= (3+\sqrt{5})^2+(3-\sqrt{5})^2=6c_1-4c_0=36-8=28, \\ c_3 &= (3+\sqrt{5})^3+(3-\sqrt{5})^3=6c_2-4c_1=168-24=144, \end{aligned}$$

n	1	2	3	4	5	6	7	8	9	10	11	12	13	14	15	16	17
c_n	6	28	44	52	36	8	4	92	36	48	44	72	56	48	64	92	96

n	18	19	20	21	22	23	24	25	26	27	28	29	30	31	32	33	34
c_n	8	64	52	56	28	44	52	36	8	4	92	36	48	44	72	56	48

Thus N leaves a remainder of 48 − 1 = 47 when divided by 100.

Method 2 (our solution):

Theorem:

The recursion relation of $a_n = Ax^n + By^n$ is $a_{n+2} = (x+y)a_{n+1} - xya_n$.

Let $a_n = (3+\sqrt{5})^{2n} + (3-\sqrt{5})^{2n}$ $(n = 1, 2,\ldots)$

$a_n = (14+6\sqrt{5})^n + (14-6\sqrt{5})^n$.

The following recursion relationship is true:

$a_{n+2} = [(14+6\sqrt{5})+(14-6\sqrt{5})]a_{n+1} - [(14+6\sqrt{5})\times(14-6\sqrt{5})]a_n = 28a_{n+1} - 16a_n$.

$a_1 = (14+6\sqrt{5})^1 + (14-6\sqrt{5})^1 = 28$,

$a_2 = (14+6\sqrt{5})^2 + (14-6\sqrt{5})^2 \equiv 52 \pmod{100}$.

$a_3 = 28a_2 - 16a_1 = 28\times 52 - 16\times 28 \equiv 08$.

$a_4 = 28a_3 - 16a_2 = 28\times 8 - 16\times 52 \equiv 92$

$a_5 = 28a_4 - 16a_3 = 28\times 92 - 16\times 8 \equiv 48$

$a_6 = 28a_5 - 16a_4 = 28\times 48 - 16\times 92 \equiv 72$

$a_7 = 28a_6 - 16a_5 = 28\times 72 - 16\times 48 \equiv 48$

$a_8 = 28a_7 - 16a_6 = 28\times 48 - 16\times 72 \equiv 92$

$a_9 = 28a_8 - 16a_7 = 28\times 92 - 16\times 48 \equiv 08$

$a_{10} = 28a_9 - 16a_8 = 28\times 8 - 16\times 92 \equiv 52$

$a_{11} = 28a_{10} - 16a_9 = 28\times 52 - 16\times 8 \equiv 28$

$a_{12} = 28a_{11} - 16a_{10} = 28\times 28 - 16\times 52 \equiv 52$

…..

We see the pattern $a_n = a_{n+10}$

So $a_{17} = (3+\sqrt{5})^{2\times 17} + (3-\sqrt{5})^{2\times 17} \equiv a_7 \equiv 48$. Since $0 < (3-\sqrt{5})^{34} < 1$

$\lfloor (3+\sqrt{5})^{34} \rfloor$ leaves a remainder of 48 − 1 = 47 when divided by 100.

PROBLEMS

Problem 1. Find the values of the following expressions:

(a) $\lfloor \pi \rfloor$. (b) $\lfloor e \rfloor$. (c) $\lfloor -\sqrt{2} \rfloor$.

Problem 2. Find the values of the following expressions:

(a) $\lceil 3.14 \rceil$. (b) $\lceil e \rceil$. (c) $\lceil -\sqrt{2} \rceil$.

Problem 3: Find the integer part of $\sqrt[3]{n^3+n^2+n+1}$. n is any integer.

Problem 4. (1986 China Middle School Math Contest) For natural number *n*, if $I=(n+1)^2+n-\left\lfloor \sqrt{(n+1)^2+n+1} \right\rfloor^2$, then

(A) $I>0$ (B) $I<0$ (C) $I=0$ (D) All three cases are possible for different values of *n*.

Problem 5. What is the value of $\left[\frac{1}{2^2}+\frac{1}{3^2}+\cdots+\frac{1}{n^2}\right]$ if $n\geq 2$?

A. 0 B. 1 C. 2 D. Undecided.

Problem 6. (AIME) For each real number *x*, let $\lfloor x \rfloor$ denote the greatest integer that does not exceed x . For how many positive integers n is it true that $n < 1000$ and that $\lfloor \log_2 n \rfloor$ is a positive even integer?

Problem 7. Find the integer and decimal parts of $\frac{\sqrt{5}+\sqrt{2}}{\sqrt{5}-\sqrt{2}}$.

Problem 8. Find $\left[\frac{2+\sqrt{2}}{2}\right]+\left[\frac{3+\sqrt{3}}{3}\right]+\cdots+\left[\frac{1989+\sqrt{1989}}{1989}\right]+\left[\frac{1990+\sqrt{1990}}{1990}\right]$.

$[x]$ is the greatest integer not exceeding *x*. For example: $[0.9] = 0$, $[\pi] = 3$, $[5] = 5$.

Problem 9. Compute $\lfloor\sqrt{S}\rfloor$ if $S=\lfloor\sqrt{1}\rfloor+\lfloor\sqrt{2}\rfloor+\lfloor\sqrt{3}\rfloor+\cdots+\lfloor\sqrt{1988}\rfloor$.

Problem 10. Calculate $\sum_{n=1}^{100}\left\lceil\frac{23n}{101}\right\rceil$.

Problem 11. Calculate $\sum_{N=1}^{2048}\lfloor\log_2 N\rfloor$.

Problem 12. Calculate $\sum_{N=1}^{1991}\lceil\log_2 N\rceil$.

Problem 13. (2000 China Middle School Math Contest) How many positive integer values are there less than 100 such that $[\frac{n}{2}]+[\frac{n}{3}]+[\frac{n}{6}]=n$?

Problem 14. (ARML) Let $[x]$ denote the greatest integer function. For all $x \geq 1$, let f be the function defined as follows:

$$f(x)=\begin{cases}\lfloor x\rfloor\cdot\left|x-\lfloor x\rfloor-\dfrac{1}{2\lfloor x\rfloor}\right| & \text{if } x<\lfloor x\rfloor+\dfrac{1}{\lfloor x\rfloor}\\ f\left(x-\dfrac{1}{\lfloor x\rfloor}\right) & \text{otherwise}\end{cases}$$

Let $g(x) = 2x - 2007$. Compute the number of points in which the graphs of f and g intersect.

Problem 15. Solve $2[x] = x + 2\{x\}$.

Problem 16. (1992 ARML) (Note: In this problem, the brackets represent the Greatest Integer Function.) Compute the number of intersection points of the graphs of $(x-\lfloor x\rfloor)^2+y^2=x-\lfloor x\rfloor$ and $y=\frac{1}{5}x$.

Problem 17. Solve $[x]+[\frac{1}{x}]=3$.

Problem 18. (1989 ARML) (Note: In this problem, the brackets represent the Greatest Integer Function.) Compute the smallest positive integer x greater than 9 such that $[x]-19\cdot\left[\frac{x}{19}\right]=[x]-89\cdot\left[\frac{x}{89}\right]$.

Problem 19. (1987 China Middle School Math Contest) $\lfloor x \rfloor$ is the greatest integer not exceeding x. Find the sum of all the solutions to the equation $\lfloor 3x+1 \rfloor = 2x-\frac{1}{2}$.

Problem 20. $\{x\}$ is the decimal part of x. $[x]$ is the greatest integer not exceeding x. The solutions to the equation $\{x\}^2 + 4([x] + 1) + 4 = 0$ are

(A) $x = -2$. (B) $x < -2$ (B) $x > -3$. (D) $-3 < x < -2$.

Problem 21. $\lfloor x \rfloor$ is the greatest integer value not greater than x. Find the number of integer solutions to the equation $[-77.66x] = [-77.66]x + 1$.

(A) 1. (B) 2. (C) 3. (D) 4.

Problem 22. Find the sum of a and b if $a < x + y < b$ satisfying the system of equations:

$$\begin{cases} y = 2[x] + 5 \\ y = 3[x-4] + 13. \end{cases}$$

Problem 23. Find $[x + y]$ if $\begin{cases} 2[x]-y=-2, \\ 3[x-2]+y=16 \end{cases}$.

Problem 24. (2000 ARML) Let [x] denote the greatest integer less than or equal to x. Compute the largest integer n such that $\lfloor \sqrt[n]{2000} \rfloor > 1$.

Problem 25. Find the smallest positive integer n for which $\lfloor \log_2 1 \rfloor + \lfloor \log_2 2 \rfloor + \lfloor \log_2 3 \rfloor + \cdots + \lfloor \log_2 n \rfloor \ge 2001$. (For real x, $\lfloor x \rfloor$ is the greatest integer $\le x$.)

Problem 26. Compute the last two digits of $\left[\dfrac{10^{93}}{10^{31}+3} \right]$.

Problem 27. Compute $\lfloor (\sqrt{3}+\sqrt{2})^{16} \rfloor$.

SOLUTIONS:

Problem 1. Solutions:

(a) $\lfloor \pi \rfloor = 3$. (b) $\lfloor e \rfloor = 2$ (b) $\lfloor -\sqrt{2} \rfloor = -2$ (not -1).

Problem 2. Solutions:

(a) $\lceil 3.14 \rceil = 4$. (b) $\lceil e \rceil = 3$. (b) $\lceil -\sqrt{2} \rceil = -1$.

Problem 3: Solution: n.

$n^3 < n^3 + n^2 + n + 1 < n^3 + 3n^2 + 3n + 1 = (n+1)^3$.

So $n < \sqrt[3]{n^3 + n^2 + n + 1} < n + 1 \qquad \Rightarrow \qquad n \le \lfloor \sqrt[3]{n^3 + n^2 + n + 1} \rfloor$.

Therefore $[\sqrt[3]{n^3 + n^2 + n + 1}] = n$.

Problem 4. Solution: (A).

By property (8), since n is a positive integer, we have

$\lfloor \sqrt{(n+1)^2 + n + 1} \rfloor^2 = \lfloor \sqrt{(n+1)(n+2)} \rfloor^2 = (n+1)^2$.

Therefore $I = (n+1)^2 + n - \lfloor \sqrt{(n+1)^2 + n + 1} \rfloor^2 = (n+1)^2 + n - (n+1)^2 = n > 0$.

The answer is (A).

Problem 5. Solution: A.

We know that $0 < \frac{1}{2^2} + \frac{1}{3^2} + \cdots + \frac{1}{n^2} < \frac{1}{1\times 2} + \frac{1}{2\times 3} + \cdots + \frac{1}{(n-1)\times n} = 1 - \frac{1}{n} < 1$.

Thus, $0 \le \left[\frac{1}{2^2} + \frac{1}{3^2} + \cdots + \frac{1}{n^2} \right] < 1$.

Because there lies no integer between 0 and 1, $\left[\frac{1}{2^2} + \frac{1}{3^2} + \cdots + \frac{1}{n^2} \right] = 0$.

Problem 6. Solution: 340.

Method 1 (our solution):

We see that $\lfloor \log_2 n \rfloor = k \qquad \Leftrightarrow \qquad 2^k \le n < 2^{k+1}$,

When $2 = 2^1 \le n < 2^2 = 4$, or $n = 2, 3$, $\lfloor \log_2 2 \rfloor = 1$, $\lfloor \log_2 3 \rfloor = 1$.

When $4 = 2^2 \le n < 2^3 = 8$, or $n = 4, 5, 6, 7$, $k = \lfloor \log_2 n \rfloor = 2$.
When $8 = 2^3 \le n < 2^4 = 16$, or $n = 8, 9, 10, 11, 12, 13, 14, 15$, $k = \lfloor \log_2 n \rfloor = 3$.
When $16 = 2^4 \le n < 2^5 = 32$, or $n = 16, 17, \ldots, 31$, $k = \lfloor \log_2 n \rfloor = 4$.
When $32 = 2^5 \le n < 2^6 = 64$, or $n = 32, 33, 34, \ldots, 61$, $k = \lfloor \log_2 n \rfloor = 5$.
When $64 = 2^6 \le n < 2^7 = 128$, or $n = 64, 65, 66, \ldots, 127$, $k = \lfloor \log_2 n \rfloor = 6$.
When $128 = 2^7 \le n < 2^8 = 256$, or $n = 128, 129, 130, \ldots, 255$, $k = \lfloor \log_2 n \rfloor = 7$.
When $256 = 2^8 \le n < 2^9 = 512$, or $n = 256, 257, 258, \ldots, 511$, $k = \lfloor \log_2 n \rfloor = 8$.
When $512 = 2^9 \le n < 2^{10} = 1024$, or $n = 512, 513, 514, \ldots, 1023$, $k = \lfloor \log_2 n \rfloor = 9$.

So there are 4 + 16 + 64 + 256 = 340 possible choices for n.

Method 2:
When $2^{2k} \le n < 2^{2k+1}$, $\lfloor \log_2 n \rfloor = 2k$.
$n = (2^3 - 2^2) + (2^5 - 2^4) + (2^7 - 2^6) + (2^9 - 2^8) = 340$.

Problem 7. Solution: $\dfrac{2\sqrt{10}-5}{3}$.

$$\frac{\sqrt{5}+\sqrt{2}}{\sqrt{5}-\sqrt{2}} = \frac{(\sqrt{5}+\sqrt{2})^2}{3} = \frac{7+2\sqrt{10}}{3}.$$

Since $3 < \sqrt{10} < 4$, $4.5 < \dfrac{7+2\sqrt{10}}{3} < 5$.

The integer part of $\dfrac{\sqrt{5}+\sqrt{2}}{\sqrt{5}-\sqrt{2}}$ is $[\dfrac{\sqrt{5}+\sqrt{2}}{\sqrt{5}-\sqrt{2}}] = 4$, and the decimal part is $\{\dfrac{\sqrt{5}+\sqrt{2}}{\sqrt{5}-\sqrt{2}}\} = \dfrac{\sqrt{5}+\sqrt{2}}{\sqrt{5}-\sqrt{2}} - 4 = \dfrac{2\sqrt{10}-5}{3}$.

Problem 8. Solution: 1989.

When $n \ge 2$, $1 = \dfrac{n}{n} < \dfrac{n+\sqrt{n}}{n} < \dfrac{n+n}{n} = 2$.

Because there lies no integer between 1 and 2, $\left\lfloor \dfrac{n+\sqrt{n}}{n} \right\rfloor = 1$.

There are 1989 values for n ($n = 2, 3, \ldots, 1990$), and so the sum of the given expression is 1989.

Problem 9. Solution: 241.
The square numbers are $1, 4, 9, \ldots, (n-1)^2$. There are $(k+1)^2 - k^2 = 2k + 1$ positive integers (x_i with $\lfloor\sqrt{x_i}\rfloor = k$) in the region $[k^2, (k+1)^2)$.

For example, there are $2 \times 1 + 1 = 3$ integers with the value of 1.
$\lfloor\sqrt{1}\rfloor = 1$, $\lfloor\sqrt{2}\rfloor \approx \lfloor 1.414\rfloor = 1$, $\lfloor\sqrt{3}\rfloor \approx \lfloor 1.732\rfloor = 1$,

There are $2 \times 2 + 1 = 5$ integers with the value of 2.
$\lfloor\sqrt{4}\rfloor = 2$, $\lfloor\sqrt{5}\rfloor \approx \lfloor 2.236\rfloor = 2$, $\lfloor\sqrt{6}\rfloor \approx \lfloor 2.449\rfloor = 2$, $\lfloor\sqrt{7}\rfloor = 2$, $\lfloor\sqrt{8}\rfloor = 2$.

$1988 > 1936 = 44^2$.
$1988 - 1936 + 1 = 53$.
So the sum will be $1 \times 3 + 2 \times 5 + \cdots + 43 \times 87 + 44 \times 53$

$$= \sum_{n=1}^{43} n(2n+1) + 44 \times 53$$

$$= \frac{2}{6} \times 43 \times 44 \times 87 + \frac{1}{2} \times 43 \times 44 + 44 \times 53$$

$= 58146$.

$\lfloor\sqrt{S}\rfloor = \lfloor\sqrt{58146}\rfloor = 241$.

Problem 10. Solution: 1100.
When $n = 1, 2, \cdots, 100$, the value $\frac{23n}{101}$ is not integer.

$$\frac{23n}{101} + \frac{23(101-n)}{101} = 23.$$

Then $\{\frac{23n}{101}\} + \{\frac{23(101-n)}{101}\} = 1$.

$$[\frac{23n}{101}] + [\frac{23(101-n)}{101}] = 22.$$

Therefore $\sum_{n=1}^{100}\left[\frac{23n}{101}\right]=\sum_{n=1}^{100}\left[\frac{23(101-n)}{101}\right]$.

So $\sum_{n=1}^{100}\left[\frac{23n}{101}\right]=\frac{1}{2}\sum_{n=1}^{100}\left([\frac{23n}{101}]+[\frac{23(101-n)}{101}]\right)=\frac{1}{2}\times 22\times 100=1100$.

Problem 11. Solution: 18445.

Method 1:

$$\lfloor \log_2 N\rfloor=\begin{cases}1 & \text{for } 2\le N<2^2\\ 2 & \text{for } 2^2\le N<2^3\\ \vdots & \quad\vdots\\ 9 & \text{for } 2^9\le N<2^{10}\\ 10 & \text{for } 2^{10}\le N<2^{11}\\ 11 & \text{for } N=2^{11}\end{cases}$$

The sum is

$$\begin{aligned}&1(2^2-2)+2(2^3-2^2)+3(2^4-2^3)+\cdots+10(2^{11}-2^{10})+11\\ &=10\cdot 2^{11}-(2^{10}+2^9+2^8+\cdots+2)+11\\ &=10\cdot 2^{11}-(2^{10}+2^9+2^8+\cdots+2+1)+12\\ &=10\cdot 2^{11}-(2^{11}-1)+12\\ &=9\cdot 2^{11}+13=9(2048)+13=18445\end{aligned}$$

Method 2:

For $m\in[2^k, 2^{k+1})$, $\lfloor \log_2 m\rfloor=k$. For example, if $4=2^2\le m<2^3=8$, $\lfloor \log_2 4\rfloor=2$, $\lfloor \log_2 5\rfloor=2$, $\lfloor \log_2 6\rfloor=2$, $\lfloor \log_2 7\rfloor=2$.

2014 = 1 + 2 + 4 + 8 + 16 + 32 + 64 + 128 + 256 + 512 + 1024 + 1.

$\lfloor \log_2 1\rfloor+\lfloor \log_2 2\rfloor+\lfloor \log_2 3\rfloor+\cdots+\lfloor \log_2 2048\rfloor$

$=0\times 1+1\times 2+2\times 4+3\times 8+4\times 16+5\times 32+6\times 64$.

$+7\times 128+8\times 256+9\times 512+10\times 1024+11\times 1=18445$.

Problem 12. Solution: 19854.

$\lceil \log_2 1 \rceil = 0$,

$\lceil \log_2 2 \rceil = 1$,

$\lceil \log_2 3 \rceil = 2$, $\lceil \log_2 4 \rceil = 2$,

$\lceil \log_2 5 \rceil = 3$, $\lceil \log_2 6 \rceil = 3$, $\lceil \log_2 7 \rceil = 3$, $\lceil \log_2 8 \rceil = 3$,

....

$\lceil \log_2 513 \rceil = \lceil \log_2 514 \rceil = \cdots = \lceil \log_2 1024 \rceil = 10$,

$\lceil \log_2 1025 \rceil = \lceil \log_2 1026 \rceil = \cdots = \lceil \log_2 1991 \rceil = 11$.

$1991 = 2^0 + 2^1 + 2^2 + 2^3 + 2^4 + 2^5 + \cdots + 2^9 + 967$

$= 1 + 2 + 4 + 8 + 16 + 32 + 64 + 128 + 256 + 512 + 967$.

So $\lceil \log_2 1 \rceil + \lceil \log_2 2 \rceil + \lceil \log_2 3 \rceil + \cdots + \lceil \log_2 1991 \rceil$

$= 2^0 \times 1 + 2^1 \times 2 + 2^2 \times 3 + 2^3 \times 4 + 2^4 \times 5 + 2^5 \times 6 + \cdots + 2^9 \times 10 + 967 \times 11$.

$= 19854$.

Problem 13. Solution: 16.

Without the Gaussian notation, $\frac{n}{2} + \frac{n}{3} + \frac{n}{6} = n$. We also know that $[\frac{n}{2}] \le \frac{n}{2}$, $[\frac{n}{3}] \le \frac{n}{3}$, and $[\frac{n}{6}] \le \frac{n}{6}$, so $[\frac{n}{2}] + [\frac{n}{3}] + [\frac{n}{6}] \le n$.

The equality occurs if and only if n is a multiple of 6, and so among the first 100 numbers, there are $\left[\frac{100}{6}\right] = 16$ such numbers.

Problem 14. Solution: 4,022,030.

For a fixed positive integer n we first find a formula for f over the range $[n, n + 1/n]$, obtaining $f(x) = n\left|x - n - \frac{1}{2n}\right| = \left|xn - n^2 - \frac{1}{2}\right|$. For example, when $n = 4$, we obtain $f(x) = \left|4x - 16 - \frac{1}{2}\right|$ for $4 \le x \le 4\frac{1}{4}$. In this example, $f(4) = f(4\frac{1}{4}) = \frac{1}{2}$

and $f(4\frac{1}{8})=0$. Similarly, in the general case, $f(n)=f(n+\frac{1}{n})=\frac{1}{2}$ and $f(n+\frac{1}{2n})=0$. Thus, the graph of f on $[n, n+1/n]$ is the absolute value of a line and it forms a V with equal values at the ends as shown in the graph below:

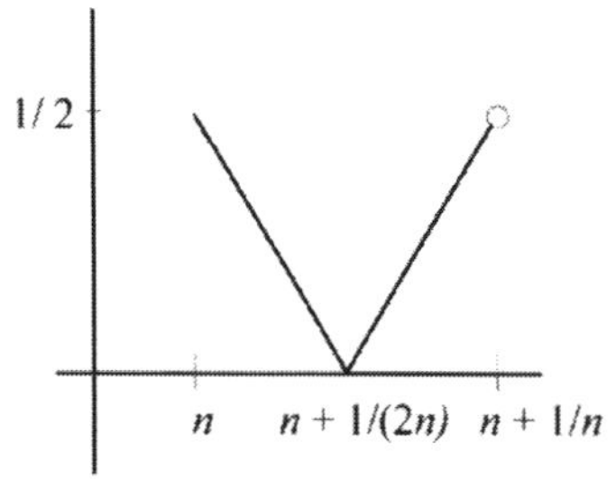

For the arbitrary range $n+\frac{k}{n}\le x<n+\frac{k+1}{n}$ where $0\le k<n$, successive iterations of f give $f(x)=f(x-\frac{k}{n})$. Hence, from n to $n+1$, the graph of f consists of n copies of V as shown below.

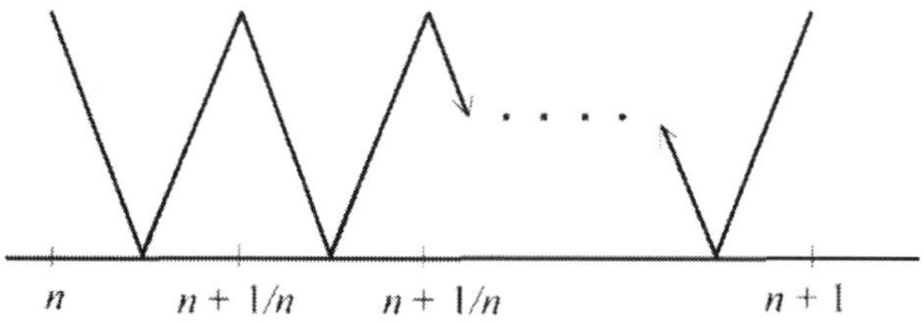

Since $g(x) = 2^{x-2007}$ is a positive increasing function and $g(2006) = 1/2$, then g intersects each V of the graph of f twice in the domain $1\le x\le 2006$. The total number of intersection points is
$2(1 + 2 + 3 + ... + 2005) = 2\cdot(2005 + 1)\cdot 2005/2 = 2005\cdot 2006 = 4{,}022{,}030$.

Problem 15. Solution: $x = 0, \frac{4}{3}$, or $\frac{8}{3}$.

The original equation can be written as: $2[x] = [x] + \{x\} + 2\{x\}$, or $3\{x\} = [x]$.
Since $0\le \{x\} < 1$, $0\le [x] < 3$.

$[x]$ can only be 0, 1, or 2 and $x = [x] + \{x\} = \frac{4[x]}{3}$.

When $[x] = 0$, $x = 0$.

When $[x] = 1$, $x = \frac{4}{3}$.

When $[x] = 2$, $x = \frac{8}{3}$.

Problem 16. Solution: 11.

"Completing the square" in $(x - [x])^2 - (x - [x]) + y^2 == 0$ produces $(x - [x] - \frac{1}{2})^2 + y^2 = \frac{1}{4}$, which is $(x - ([x] + \frac{1}{2})^2 + y^2 = \frac{1}{4}$.

Now examine what happens in the intervals $0 \le x < 1$, $1 \le x < 2$, $2 \le x < 3$, etc. (and also $-1 \le x < 0$, $-2 \le x < -1$, etc.). For each interval, we get a circle of radius 1/2 with center at $([x] + \frac{1}{2}, 0)$. Thus the graph consists of a set of tangent congruent circles whose centers lie on the x – axis! The line $y = (1/5)x$ goes through both the origin and the point $(5/2, 1/2)$, which is the highest point of one of the circles; it intersects the first graph in 11 points [remember to count points to the left of the y-axis also!].

Problem 17. Solution: $\frac{1}{4} < x \le \frac{1}{3}$ or $3 \le x < 4$.

Since the sum is positive, $x > 0$.

Let $[x] = m$, $[\frac{1}{x}] = n$.

The original equation becomes $m + n = 3$, where both m and n are nonnegative integers.

When $\begin{cases} m = 0, \\ n = 3. \end{cases}$, $\begin{cases} 0 < x < 1, \\ 3 \le \frac{1}{x} < 4 \end{cases}$. Solving for x, we get $\frac{1}{4} < x \le \frac{1}{3}$.

When $\begin{cases} m = 1 \\ n = 2 \end{cases}$, $\begin{cases} 1 \le x < 2, \\ 2 \le \frac{1}{x} < 3 \end{cases}$ These two equations contradict each other, however.

When $\begin{cases} m=2 \\ n=1 \end{cases}$, $\begin{cases} 2 \le x < 3, \\ 1 \le \dfrac{1}{x} < 2 \end{cases}$ These two equations contradict each other, however.

When $\begin{cases} m=3 \\ n=0 \end{cases}$, $\begin{cases} 3 \le x < 4, \\ 0 \le \dfrac{1}{x} < 1. \end{cases}$. Solving for x, we get $3 \le x < 4$.

Combining the results, we get the solutions $\frac{1}{4} < x \le \frac{1}{3}$ or $3 \le x < 4$.

Problem 18. Solution: 1700.

Note that for integer $k > 0$, $k \cdot \left[\frac{x}{k}\right]$ is the greatest multiple of k that does not exceed x. Now for integer x, $[x] - 19 \cdot \left[\frac{x}{19}\right]$ is the difference between x and the greatest multiple of 19 that does not exceed x. Therefore, x is 9 more than a multiple of 19. Also, x is 9 more than a multiple of 89. Therefore x must be 9 more than a multiple of $19 \cdot 89$. The smallest such positive x is $(19)(89) + 9 = 1700$.

Problem 19. Solution: –2.

Let $[3x + 1] = t$.

$0 \le (3x + 1) - t < 1$.

$t = 2x - \frac{1}{2}$

$0 \le (\frac{3}{2}t + \frac{7}{4}) - t < 1$.

$-\frac{7}{2} \le t < -\frac{3}{2}$.

Thus $t = -2$ or -3

When $t = -2$, $x_1 = -\frac{3}{4}$,

$t = -3$, $x_2 = -\frac{5}{4}$.

So $x_1 + x_2 = -\frac{3}{4} + (-\frac{5}{4}) = -2$.

Problem 20. Solution: (D).
We know that $\{x\} = [x] + 1$. The given equation can be written as $\{x\}^2 + 4\{x\} + 4 = 0$ or $(\{x\} + 2)^2 = 0$.
Solving gives us $\{x\} = -2$. Therefore the values for x are $-3 < x < -2$.

Problem 21. Solution: $x = 3, 4, 5$.
The given equation can be written as

$$[-77.66x] = -78x + 1, \text{ or } [(-78 + 0.34)x] = -78x + 1.$$

Since x is integer, $-78x + [0.34x] = -78x + 1$.

This can be simplified into:
$[0.34x] = 1$.
Therefore
$1 \le 0.34x \le 2 \quad \Rightarrow \quad 3 \le x \le 5$.
The values for x are $x = 3, 4, 5$.

Problem 22. Solution: 35.
We have
$2[x] + 5 = 3[x - 4] + 13$,
$2[x] + 5 = 3([x] - 4) + 13$,
$[x] = 4$.
Thus, $4 < x < 5$, and $y = 2[x] + 5 = 13$. Therefore $17 < x + y < 18$. $a + b = 35$.

Problem 23. Solution: 14.
We are given that $\begin{cases} 2[x] - y = -2, \\ 3[x-2] + y = 16 \end{cases}$
Adding the two equations together, we have $2[x] + 3[x - 2] = 14$. Using the property: $[n + x] = n + [x]$, $2[x] + 3[x - 2] = 14$ becomes $5[x] - 6 = 14$.
Solving for $[x]$ gives us $[x] = 4$.
Substituting this value into the original equations, gives us the value for y: $y = 10$.
Therefore $[x + y] = [x + 10] = 14$.

Problem 24. Solution: 10.
Since we want $\sqrt[n]{2000} \ge 2$ 2, then $2000 \ge 2^n$. Sine $2^{10} < 2000 < 211$, $n = 10$.

Problem 25. Solution: 313.
Method 1:
For $m \in [2^k, 2^{k+1})$, $\lfloor \log_2 m \rfloor = k$. For example, if $4 = 2^2 \le m < 2^3 = 8$,
$\lfloor \log_2 4 \rfloor = 2$, $\lfloor \log_2 5 \rfloor = 2$, $\lfloor \log_2 6 \rfloor = 2$, $\lfloor \log_2 7 \rfloor = 2$.

For $\lfloor \log_2 1 \rfloor + \lfloor \log_2 2 \rfloor + \lfloor \log_2 3 \rfloor + \cdots + \lfloor \log_2 n \rfloor$
$= 0\times1 + 1\times2 + 2\times4 + 3\times8 + 4\times16 + 5\times32 + 6\times64 + 7\times128 = 1538$.
$n = 1 + 2 + 4 + 8 + 16 + 32 + 64 + 128 = 255$.

For $\lfloor \log_2 1 \rfloor + \lfloor \log_2 2 \rfloor + \lfloor \log_2 3 \rfloor + \cdots + \lfloor \log_2 n \rfloor$
$= 0\times1 + 1\times2 + 2\times4 + 3\times8 + 4\times16 + 5\times32 + 6\times64 + 7\times128 + 8\times256 = 3586$.
$n = 1 + 2 + 4 + 8 + 16 + 32 + 64 + 128 + 256 = 511$.

Since $1538 < 2001 < 3586$, the desired solution n is between 255 and 511.
We see that when $256 = 2^8 \le m \le 2^9 = 512$, $\lfloor \log_2 m \rfloor = 8$.

$2001 - 1538 = 463 = 8 \times 57 + 7$.
When $n = 255 + 57 = 312$.
$\lfloor \log_2 1 \rfloor + \lfloor \log_2 2 \rfloor + \lfloor \log_2 3 \rfloor + \cdots + \lfloor \log_2 312 \rfloor < 2001$

However, $2002 - 1538 = 464 = 8 \times 58$.
When $n = 255 + 58 = 313$, $\lfloor \log_2 1 \rfloor + \lfloor \log_2 2 \rfloor + \lfloor \log_2 3 \rfloor + \cdots + \lfloor \log_2 313 \rfloor = 2002$
When $n \ge 313$, $\lfloor \log_2 1 \rfloor + \lfloor \log_2 2 \rfloor + \lfloor \log_2 3 \rfloor + \cdots + \lfloor \log_2 n \rfloor > 2001$.

Method 2:
For $m \in [2^k, 2^{k+1})$, $\lfloor \log_2 m \rfloor = k$. Let $2^k \le n < 2^{k+1}$
So $f(n) = \lfloor \log_2 1 \rfloor + \lfloor \log_2 2 \rfloor + \lfloor \log_2 3 \rfloor + \cdots + \lfloor \log_2 n \rfloor$
$= 0 + 1 + 1 + 2 + \cdots + k$
$= 1\times0 + (2^2 - 2)\times1 + (2^3 - 2^2)\times2 + \cdots + (2^k - 2^{k-1})\times(k-1) + (n - 2^k + 1)k$.
Let $S_{k-1} = 1\times0 + (2^2 - 2)\times1 + (2^3 - 2^2)\times2 + \cdots + (2^k - 2^{k-1})\times(k-1)$.

Then $S_0 = 0$.
$S_k = 2\times1+2^2\times2+\cdots+2^k\times k = (k-1)\times2^{k+1}+2$.
Since $S_7 = 1538 < 2001$, and $S_8 = 3586 > 2001$, we let $k - 1 = 7$, or $k = 8$. Then
$f(n) = S_{k-1} + (n-2^k+1)k = S_7 + (n-2^8+1)\times8$
$= 1538 + 8n - 2040 = 8n - 502$.

Let $f(n) \ge 2001 \quad\Rightarrow\quad n \ge 312\frac{7}{8}$.

The smallest value of n is 313.

Problem 26. Solution: 08.

We have $\dfrac{10^{93}}{10^{31}+3} = \dfrac{(10^{31})^3+3^3}{10^{31}+3} - \dfrac{3^3}{10^{31}+3} = (10^{62}-3\times10^{31}+9) - \dfrac{3^3}{10^{31}+3}$.

So $10^{62}-3\times10^{31}+8 < \dfrac{10^{93}}{10^{31}+3} < 10^{62}-3\times10^{31}+9$.

$$\left[\frac{10^{93}}{10^{31}+3}\right] = 10^{62}-3\times10^{31}+8.$$

The last two digits are 08.

Problem 27. Solution: 970.

Let $a_n = (\sqrt{3}+\sqrt{2})^{2n} + (\sqrt{3}-\sqrt{2})^{2n}$ $(n = 1, 2,\ldots)$

$a_n = (5+2\sqrt{6})^n + (5-2\sqrt{6})^n$.

The following recursion relationship is true:

$a_{n+2} = [(5+2\sqrt{6})+(5-2\sqrt{6})]a_{n+1} - [(5+2\sqrt{6})\times(5-2\sqrt{6})]a_n = 10a_{n+1} - a_n$.

$a_1 = (5+2\sqrt{6})+(5-2\sqrt{6}) = 10$,

$a_2 = (5+2\sqrt{6})^2+(5-2\sqrt{6})^2 = 98$.

Since $0 < (5-2\sqrt{6})^n < 1$, $(5+2\sqrt{6})^n + 1 = \lfloor a_n - (5-2\sqrt{6})^n \rfloor + 1 = a_n$.

That is, a_n is the smallest integer greater than $(\sqrt{3}+\sqrt{2})^{2n}$.

$a_3 = 10a_2 - a_1 = 10\times98 - 10 \equiv 970$.

L

M

N

O

P

Q

R

S

T

V

X

Y

Z

30895915R00130

Made in the USA
Middletown, DE
11 April 2016